WRITING AS RESISTANCE

FOUR WOMEN CONFRONTING THE HOLOCAUST

RACHEL FELDHAY BRENNER

Writing as

Resistance

FOUR WOMEN
CONFRONTING
THE
HOLOCAUST

EDITH STEIN ∞ SIMONE WEIL
ANNE FRANK ∞ ETTY HILLESUM

THE PENNSYLVANIA STATE UNIVERSITY PRESS
UNIVERSITY PARK, PENNSYLVANIA

Library of Congress Cataloging-in-Publication Data

Brenner, Rachel Feldhay
    Writing as resistance : four women confronting the Holocaust : Edith Stein, Simone Weil, Anne Frank, Etty Hillesum / Rachel Feldhay Brenner.

        p.   cm.
    Includes bibliographical references and index.
    ISBN 0-271-01623-X (alk. paper)
    1. Holocaust, Jewish (1939–1945) – Sources.   2. Stein, Edith, 1891–1942.
3. Weil, Simone, 1909–1943.   4. Frank, Anne, 1929–45.   5. Hillesum, Etty,
1914–1943.   6. Autobiography – Women authors.   7. Autobiography – Jewish
authors.   8. Jewish women – biography – History and criticism.   9. Holocaust,
Jewish (1939–1945) – Moral and ethical aspects.   10. World War, 1939–1945 –
Women.   I. Title.
D804.19.B74   1997
940.53'18 – dc20   96-20613
                                                                   CIP

It is the policy of The Pennsylvania State University Press to use acid-free paper for the first printing of all clothbound books. Publications on uncoated stock satisfy the minimum requirements of American National Standard for Information Sciences – Permanence of Paper for Printed Library Materials, ANSI Z39.48–1992.

CONTENTS

PART FOUR
RESISTANCE AND WOMANHOOD

ACKNOWLEDGMENTS

Writing this book was a long, lonely, and often painful process. My gratitude to those who helped is therefore heartfelt and sincere.

First, I would like to thank Mr. Philip Winsor, Senior Editor at Penn State Press, whose encouragement and trust in this project were invaluable to me. Without his steadfast dedication this book could not have been written. I remain deeply grateful to Mr. Winsor for his exceptional support. I am particularly thankful to Professor Judith Van Herik, who read the manuscript twice and whose illuminating comments and suggestions shaped this book into its final form. Professor Van Herik demonstrated the rare quality of a true mentor and influenced my scholarly thinking in a most significant way. I thank my good friend, John Hobbins, whose intellectual involvement in my project helped me face the challenges that this work presented. John's close reading of the manuscript was a labor of love for which I will always be grateful.

I would also like to express my appreciation to Ms. Peggy Hoover, Senior Manuscript Editor at Penn State Press, for her exceptional editorial work on the manuscript. I thank Professor Herbert Richardson for having introduced me to some of the ideas out of which this book developed.

My loving gratitude goes to my children, Shelly and Guy. I admire their patience with their at times not-easy-to-understand mother. I know that their being made this book possible.

In Memory of My Grandparents,
Nehama and Moshe,
who died in the Warsaw Ghetto,
and
Rachel and Nathan,
who perished in Treblinka

WRITING AS RESISTANCE

FOUR WOMEN CONFRONTING THE HOLOCAUST

EDITH STEIN

SIMONE WEIL

ANNE FRANK

ETTY HILLESUM

Introduction:
Meanings
of Resistance

I was struggling to find the reason for my sufferings, my slow dying. I sensed my spirit piercing through the enveloping gloom. I felt it transcend that hopeless, meaningless world, and from somewhere I heard a victorious "Yes" in answer to my question of the existence of ultimate purpose.

—*Viktor Frankl, about his experience in Auschwitz*

The insuperable Nazi scheme to annihilate European Jewry elicited responses that compel us to reconsider the meaning of resistance. "We left the camp singing," wrote Etty Hillesum on a card thrown out of the train from Westerbork to Auschwitz on September 7, 1943.[1] The meaning of this resistance is the main focus of this study, which is based on the legacy of resistance of Edith Stein (b. 1891), who was gassed in Auschwitz in 1942; Simone Weil (b. 1909), who starved herself in London in 1943; Anne Frank (b. 1929), who died of starvation and typhus in Bergen-Belsen in 1945; and Etty Hillesum (b. 1914), who died in Auschwitz in 1943.

Emil Fackenheim claims that while the Holocaust is a *novum,* so is "the astounding fact" that "the Nazi logic [of destruction] was irresistible, yet was being resisted.[2] A philosopher-theologian, Fackenheim sees spiritual resistance in the victim's determination to survive the dehumanization and destruction of the Holocaust. Fackenheim admits to being "radically, permanently astonished" by testimonies such as that of an Auschwitz survivor, Pelagia Lewinska, who recalls that the moment she "grasped the motivating principle" of the Nazi plan, which condemned her and the other inmates "to die in our own filth, to drown in mud, in our own excrement," she "felt under orders to live . . . as a human being."[3]

Lewinska's example of survival as resistance is by no means unique. Another survivor remembers the moment her brother died in her arms in the transport wagon as the beginning of her determined struggle against the forces of annihilation, " 'I am going to live.' I made up my mind to defy Hitler. I am not going to give in. Because he wants me to die, I am going to live. This was our way of fighting back."[4]

These testimonies were given by victims-resisters who lived to tell the tale, and their narratives attest to their triumph over the tyranny of destruction. As one survivor admits, "The world condemned me to die. I write because, through my books, I bear witness to my existence."[5] These victims survived despite the implacability of the Final Solution. Their postwar stories tell about the heroism of survival.

But what about the Holocaust diarists, chroniclers, and writers who did not survive and whose writings therefore do not reflect after-the-fact retrospection? Geoffrey Hartman tells us that the decision to resist the Nazi terror was made in a situation of complete lack of foresight, when "few could hope to make sense of the events . . . [or] link what they had learned in the past to what now befell them."[6] Dori Laub corroborates Hartman's observation, claiming that, paradoxical as it may seem, the act of witnessing the Holocaust took place after the event. Witnessing during the Holocaust could not occur because "the degree to which bearing witness was required entailed such an outstanding measure of awareness and comprehension of the event, . . . of its radical *otherness* to all known frames of reference . . . , that it was beyond the limits of human ability (and willingness) to grasp, to transmit, or to imagine." Therefore, according to Laub, the attempts to bear witness "*during the actual occurrence*" through chronicles, diaries, pictures, and other documentation "were doomed to fail."[7]

These contentions of lack of foresight, awareness, and comprehension *at the time of* the Holocaust do not seem to do justice to the literary remains of Stein, Weil, Frank, and Hillesum. Their legacies demonstrate conclusively that they correctly assessed the "radical otherness" of the catastrophe and consciously defied terror. The foresight, awareness, and comprehension of these four women thinker-writers *at the time of* their resistance is compelling.

The four resisted Hitlerian tyranny through the act of writing. As testimonies of the unfolding terror and destruction, their writings challenge the argument that the witnessing victim is unable to understand the signification of the Final Solution. These writings present fascinating documentation of the authors' clear view of the situation and its impact on their sense of identity and moral outlook.

The growing awareness of these women prompted them to bear witness to the evolving catastrophe; the "radical otherness" of the situation made them conscious of their identity as the victims and of their connectedness to the other sufferers. Their resistance through humanistic responses to the world in crisis attests to the women's penetrating "awareness and comprehension of the event."

It is especially the autobiographical works of the four women that call our attention to self-introspection as a mode of resistance. Life narratives affirm individuality and personhood under the rule of terror that sought their dehumanization. The autobiographical works of these women constitute the center of this discussion of responses to the Nazi persecution.

The autobiographical texts were published long after their authors had died: Stein's autobiographical *Life in a Jewish Family* in 1965, Weil's "Spiritual Autobiography" and letters in the 1950s, Anne Frank's *Diary* in 1953, and Etty Hillesum's *Diary and Letters from Westerbork* in the 1980s. These life stories speak with the voices of the dead. In contrast to writer-survivors whose testimonies attest to their victorious emergence from the *extremis* of the death camps, the tragic fate of the four authors brings us face-to-face with the effectiveness of the Nazi system of destruction.

To listen to the voices of the Holocaust dead is disturbing. They bring forth the atrocity of the Final Solution and compel us to consider unspeakably painful realities. Indeed, the posthumous, hagiographical treatments of the four women signal the postwar tendency to mitigate the horror. Stein, the Carmelite, was beatified as a Christian martyr; Frank became the universal icon of victimized children; Weil and Hillesum entered the pantheon of saintly altruists.

Such representations of the victims of the Final Solution (Weil too, despite her denial, was the victim of the Nazi policy of exclusion and banishment) tend to universalize the particularity of Jewish persecution in the Holocaust. Furthermore, they intimate that, after all, justice has prevailed.

The idolization of testimonies of the women's final moments is symptomatic of the post-Holocaust proclivity to make Holocaust suffering more manageable. Eyewitnesses remember Stein showing quiet courage when she and her sister, Rosa, were delivered to the Gestapo from the convent in Echt; fellow inmates recall Frank weeping over the children on their way to the gas; friends tell how Hillesum was offering comfort to other inmates at the moment of her deportation;

biographers glorify Weil's self-inflicted starvation as a sign of solidarity with the French people under the German occupation. Reverence enshrines these individuals, separating them from masses of other victims. Such attitudes attenuate the victim's experience of pain, suffering, and despair.

The realization that each death interrupted an intellectual work in progress brings home the tragedy of interrupted lives. At the time of her deportation, Stein, who had finished her autobiography in 1940, was working on a book about the mysticism of Saint John of the Cross, later published as *Science of the Cross*. Just before her death in 1943, Weil finished *The Need for Roots,* in which she outlined the sociopolitical future of France. Almost from her deathbed she continued to share her ideas with family and friends in her letters. Frank was literally taken away from her diary and her stories. And the deportation interrupted both Hillesum's diary and her correspondence with non-Jewish friends in Amsterdam.

This book examines the four women's literary, especially autobiographical, activity as resistance. Such a form of intellectual resistance at the time of Hitlerian atrocity makes us ponder the questions of its motivating forces, intentions, and significance. To answer these questions, we need to explore the historical, cultural, and philosophical attitudes that promoted the response of writing—and introspective self-writing in particular. Autobiographical writing records the process of inner development, and I examine the extent to which the authors' self-representations reflect maturation processes, changing self-perceptions, and mutating *Weltanschauungen.*

We can attain a preliminary understanding of the specific nature of these four women's autobiographical responses to terror by considering their work in the context of other self-representational writings at the time of the Holocaust. The most prominent examples are the Warsaw ghetto diaries of Chaim Kaplan and Emmanuel Ringelblum. In contrast to Hartman's and Laub's contention that the victims lacked the foresight to comprehend the Holocaust at the time it was occurring, these diarists demonstrate a full awareness and comprehension of the situation.

Convinced that they were witnessing the spiritual and the physical annihilation of Polish Jewry, both men felt compelled to document the unfolding history of the destruction. Kaplan, who saw himself as "the grandson of Isaiah the prophet," felt driven to write. In his diary he proclaimed, time and again, the imperative of his "historical mission" to record. Ringelblum saw his vocation to be a historian of the destruction. His writing was intended to document the facts, to give a concise, factual, and objective record of the events.[8]

As narratives of the destruction of the ghetto, the Warsaw diaries in fact present bills of indictment both of Nazi barbarism and of the betrayal of Polish population.

As acts of resistance composed under most terrible circumstances, the diaries are, in Alvin Rosenfeld's words, "nothing less than a form of heroism, an assertion of dignity and even nobility in the face of death."[9]

Viktor Frankl, who survived Auschwitz, asserts that "life remains potentially meaningful under any conditions, even those which are most miserable," and that even in the most terrible circumstances, we can discover the meaning of life "by the attitude we take toward unavoidable suffering."[10] The diaries of Kaplan and Ringelblum present a remarkable example of Frankl's assertion of the meaning of life even in suffering. The two men's determination to function as historians of the destruction infused meaning into their hopeless situation. The sense of responsibility to bear witness to the history of Jewish annihilation became their raison d'être. As Jews, they felt an obligation toward their people—a mission—that empowered them to carry on their intellectual effort despite depression, constant hunger, and deprivation. Kaplan's "spirit of dedication"[11] to the history of his people underlined his identification with the fate of Israel. The overriding concern about the survival of his nation superseded the pain of individual suffering. As the ghetto diaries demonstrate, the totality of the diarists' involvement with Jewish destiny shaped their resistance to the Nazi terror.

In his discussion of Holocaust testimonies, James Young argues that "each victim 'saw'—i.e., understood *and* witnessed—his predicament differently, depending on his own historical past, religious paradigms, and ideological explanations."[12] To follow Young's postulation, each Holocaust testimony must be read with its author's ideological, cultural, and religious background in mind. A testimony is not merely a narration of facts and events, but also a personal interpretation of history. As an expression of a personal perspective, the intentionality of the testimony needs to be discussed in the context of its author's particular situation and orientation. As much as they were conscious of the "radical otherness" of the situation, the victims' responses to the catastrophe emerged from the historical, ethical, and cultural context that shaped their world views.

The formative influences that motivated the Warsaw ghetto diarists to write against the catastrophe helps to define *by contrast* the realities and attitudes that affected the writings of Stein, Weil, Frank, and Hillesum. It is clear that the determination of the Warsaw diarists to bear witness was informed by an unequivocal sense of Jewish identity and of solidarity with the Jewish community. As self-aware Jews, they were impelled to produce historical records of the atrocity committed against their people.

In the case of the Western Jews—the German Stein and Frank, the French Weil, and the Dutch Hillesum—the determination to respond to the Nazi terror did not imply as clear-cut a distinction between the Jewish and the non-Jewish worlds as it did for the Polish-born yet deeply Jewish Kaplan and Ringelblum. In contrast to the ghetto diarists who adhered to Jewish enlightenment, these Western European women were the daughters of Jewish parents who were deeply integrated in the general society and who had no true sense of Jewishness. Coming from well-off, well-educated families that identified wholeheartedly with Western liberalism, these Jewish women knew little if anything about their Jewish heritage.

Exceptionally intelligent, they were educated in the best schools of Europe. Stein, who did her doctorate on phenomenology with Edmund Husserl, studied at the Universities of Göttingen and Freiburg; Weil had an education with special emphasis on philosophy in the prestigious Parisian schools Lycée Henri IV and École Normale Supérieure; Hillesum studied law and Slavonic languages at the University of Amsterdam; Frank attended non-Jewish schools before the war and, as the list of the books she read in hiding demonstrates, her intellectual interests focused on European literature and history.

None of the women felt the need or desire to establish close ties with Judaism. On the contrary, all four saw Gentile society as their natural environment. The faith in the brotherhood of all human beings and in their inalienable rights to liberty and equality informed their world view. And while they had neither knowledge of nor interest in the Jewish religious tradition, each demonstrated a strong attraction to Christianity, which they saw as the religion of universalism and progress.

In view of their cultural background and religious predilection, the reality of the Nazi anti-Jewish terror signified for the four women not merely the menace of physical persecution, degradation, and annihilation, but also a profound predicament of an ideological and spiritual nature. The Final Solution represented the total collapse of the ideals of humanism. At the same time, it confronted the victims with their ethnoreligious origins, with which they felt no identification. The Final Solution divested the cosmopolitan Western Jews of the post-Enlightenment era of their ideological fulcrum and sentenced them to death for an identity that they had effectively repressed or simply ignored.

The intellectual creativity of the four women thus presents a complex case of resistance. Chaim Kaplan and other ghetto diarists insisted that they had a responsibility to bear witness to the destruction of the Jews. It was solidarity that turned them into voices demanding justice and revenge for the crimes committed against their people. By contrast, none of the four women claimed a similar sense of affinity with the Jewish people. Their determination to resist through writing presents a different historical self-perception.

The main purpose of the writings of these four women was not to indict or accuse, and they were not motivated by a desire to avenge through a documented indictment. Rather, their writing was guided, to a remarkable extent, by their persistent faith in the ethics of the humanistic ideal. The ideological and cultural legacy of the Enlightenment seems to have played a considerable role in their self-assertion against the Nazi politics of dehumanization. Cosmopolites brought up in the cultural milieu of the Enlightenment, they believed in the humanist and humane future of the world predicated on the individual's moral obligation to humanity. Intellectuals raised in the spirit of universalist humanism, they focused their work on reaffirming the ideal of human fellowship in the situation of global war and mass murder. As paradoxical as it may seem, the autobiographical writings of these Jewish women doomed to death reflect a staunch yet not blindly naive belief in the humanistic creed as a guideline to the moral redemption of the world.

The women's preoccupation with the moral condition of a world bent on their destruction demonstrates a remarkable sense of responsibility for the destiny of humanity at large. Yet their altruistic concern for the world cannot be considered in isolation from the problem of identity that each woman was bound to face. All four knew (though Weil never openly admitted) that their ethnic origins turned them into the primary victims of the Nazi terror. Declared Jewish, these assimilated women contended with an identity they did not know, as well as with the terrible and inescapable implications of this identity. Their unexpected, brutal social exclusion was inextricably related to their Jewishness, which condemned them to death.

The adherence to the humanist ideal, which posited the liberty and equality of all human beings, needed somehow to be reconciled with the imposed identification as the outlawed Jew. This difficulty was compounded by the women's obvious affinity with Christianity, which rendered their identity crisis even more complex. As mentioned before, their ideological outlook was deeply influenced by the notion of Christianity as the religion of universal humanistic rebirth. Stein converted to Catholicism and eventually took the vows of the Carmelite Order, while Weil became an ardent Christian mystic and a zealous advocate of ancient and Far Eastern theologies. Hillesum read the Gospels and endorsed Saint Augustine's teachings. And in her prayers, Frank, the least "Christian" of the four, turned to a pantheistic God of peace and mercy.

The context of the resistance of these women, therefore, discloses strong theological underpinnings. In the reality of the Final Solution, they contended not only with the problem of a humanistic response to Nazi inhumanity, but also with the religious orientation of such a response. Should they defy the Final Solution as Christian humanists or as Jewish victims? Is it the Christian God or the Jewish God whom they should seek in their suffering and pain? Is it possible to reconcile

Christian orientation with Jewish origins? These questions demonstrate the ethnoreligious identity crisis of these four Jews raised on the premises of Christian
humanism.

To comprehend the multiple sociohistorical components that shaped each
woman's writing as a mode of resistance, we need to investigate the philosophical,
theological, and cultural background that determined, to use Young's terms, how
they "saw, understood, and witnessed" history. At the same time, we should be
aware that the moral collapse of the world they knew perforce induced the need to
reassess these orientations.

In a very real sense, their writings signified an intellectual and spiritual quest
for the moral redemption of the world. The act of writing thus gave these women a
measure of control in a situation where what had seemed immutable ideals and
beliefs were in a state of total collapse. As we shall see, the intellectual resistance
of the dehumanizing terror both shaped and reflected an inner struggle to maintain
spiritual and ethical values in a human world devoid of humaneness.

Following Frankl's notion of search for meaning under the most terrible
conditions, I propose that it was the struggle to preserve faith in the reality of a
faithless world, to continue to love the world despite its lovelessness, that infused
meaning into the lives of these women. The degree of intellectual freedom
attained in the defiant act of writing afforded a sense of direction in this unprecedented situation. The artistic activity of literary self-portrayal communicates a
measure of control over destiny and a sense of uniqueness intended to offset, to
some extent at least, the specter of despair.

It is important to note that the consciousness of womanhood underlay and
reinforced the four women's defiance of the Hitlerian terror. The affirmations of
humanistic values under most inhuman circumstances conflated (even, as we shall
see, in the problematic case of Weil) with the sense of a woman's singular
capabilities and particular destiny. All four writers' views on women are indelibly
connected to their hopes and plans for the world's moral redemption. While, as
Jews, they were condemned to isolation, suffering, and death, they continued to
see themselves as women with obligations toward the world.

The historico-philosophical, theological, artistic, and feminist aspects in the
writings guide us in exploring the roots and the nature of these women's resistance. At the same time, their reassessments of religious, ethical, and spiritual
values at the time the catastrophe was unfolding are important in terms of the post-
Holocaust future. The problem of human intercourse and of humane conduct in
a world that had seen the ultimate evil in humankind materialize has preoccupied postwar ethical thinkers, theologians, and feminist philosophers. In
many respects, the resistance of Stein, Weil, Frank, and Hillesum anticipates the

post-Holocaust views of Arendt, Levinas, Fackenheim, Tillich, Gilligan, Noddins, and others. The struggle of the four women to preserve the humanist ideal demonstrates remarkable foresight into the ethical predicament of postwar society. Their resistance leaves us with a complex legacy of searching for the meaning of life in a reality of senseless brutality, unimaginable hatred, and atrocious death.

PART ONE

RESISTANCE AND HUMANISTIC ETHICS

1

THE DIS/CONTINUED DIALOGUE
WITH THE ENLIGHTENMENT

To what extent do we remain obligated to the world even when we have been expelled from it or have withdrawn from it?

—Hannah Arendt

The literary acts of Edith Stein, Simone Weil, Anne Frank, and Etty Hillesum offer a complex but unequivocal answer to Hannah Arendt's poignant question "To what extent do we remain obligated to the world even when we have been expelled from it or have withdrawn from it?"[1] As transmitted in their work, their sense of obligation to the world did not cease under the most trying circumstances. Stein's escape from Germany to Holland after *Kristallnacht,* Weil's flight from France to Casablanca and then to New York in 1942, Frank's entrapment in the Annex, and Hillesum's stay in Westerbork highlight the extent of their banishment and condemnation to death. Nevertheless, all four continued to voice their dismay about humanity's moral condition and to express their anxious hope for spiritual rehabilitation in the future. The following expressions of concern for the world in moments of displacement and danger provide a glimpse into the four women's ethical steadfastness.

On the brink of the war in 1939, Stein, already in exile, pronounced her readiness to sacrifice herself for the necessary spiritual renewal of the world. From her hiding in the convent in Echt, Holland, she wrote to the Mother Superior begging "permission to offer [herself] to the Heart of Jesus as a sacrificial expiation for the sake of true peace, . . . if possible without another world war, . . . that a new order may be established, . . . because it is already the twelfth hour."[2]

Weil, writing to Father Joseph-Marie Perrin, her Catholic mentor, from her Casablanca exile in 1942, talked about the moral sickness of the world that needed to be cured. "We are living in times that have no precedent," she wrote. "To-day . . . we must have the saintliness demanded by the present moment, a new saintliness, itself also without precedent." As if in anticipation of Camus' *The Plague*, Weil argued: "The world needs saints who have genius, just as a plague-stricken town needs doctors."[3]

Hillesum too was determined to seek remedy for the sick world. In her *Diary*, she declared her intention to begin preparing for the "new order," which, as she well knew, she would not live long enough to see. Despite the awareness that "they [the Gestapo] are after . . . our total destruction," Hillesum promised to "devote [her] life to curing the bad," so that "those who come after me do not have to start all over again, need not face the same difficulties."[4]

Frank, in her *Diary*, confessed her desperation over "the ideals, dreams and cherished hopes [that] rise within us, only to meet the horrible truth and be shattered."[5] However, in the stories she was writing at the same time, like Stein, Weil, and Hillesum, she sought ways to cure the world. "How lovely," Frank wrote, "to think that no one need to wait a moment, we can start now . . . changing the world" by treating everybody with kindness. This moment will come when "Europe and finally the whole world would realize that people were really kindly disposed towards one another, that they are all equal and everything else is just transitory."[6]

As these sample excerpts demonstrate, the four women were aware of the extreme degree of the world's moral collapse, yet none of them gave up the expectation of moral restoration. In fact, we can see their continuing struggle to maintain hope despite increasing hopelessness. Their lucid appreciation of the crisis, combined with a steadfast search for a solution, communicates their strong involvement with the moral welfare of the world.

Evident correspondences with Albert Camus' *The Plague* elucidate the degree to which the women subscribed to the ethics of responsibility. Hillesum's voluntary service at Westerbork probably best translates *The Plague*'s metaphor of the sick world into the reality of the Jewish genocide. Hillesum's selfless devotion to the victims of the Nazi "plague" actualizes the novel's theme of caring for the other as the only safeguard against deathly terror. Unlike Camus' protagonists, Hillesum did not survive; her choice to stay with the victims exacted the ultimate price of extermination in Auschwitz. Another correspondence with the Camus novel emerges in Frank's seemingly naive hope for redemption even at the time all moral values were collapsing. In effect, Frank's belief in human kindness as a redemptive feature is harmonious with the ethics of the Camus protagonists' sense of solidarity with stricken humanity. Camus' Rambert, for instance, realizes that his place is with the victims of the plague because, as he says with reference to the disease, "this business is everybody's business"[7] — the bonds of responsibility tie human beings to each other. Rambert's self-identification as a responsible and caring member of humanity reflects Frank's affirmation that caring relationships among people are a prerequisite for the world's moral restitution.

In a situation that is infinitely more threatening and more constricting than that of the non-Jewish Camus, these four Jewish victims of the Nazi "plague" experienced directly the failure of the humanistic ideal of empathy and solidarity. Yet, like Camus, the four women continued to believe in humanism as the healing force of the sick world. Such a hopeful attitude, maintained in an atmosphere of racial hatred and life-threatening conditions, is most astonishing. It raises the question of the Weltanschauung that enabled the victims to maintain their vision of a better future for the world despite the danger of imminent death.

A partial answer can be found in the historical-cultural *Zeitgeist* of post-Emancipation Western Jews. Since the Emancipation, the acculturated Western Jews have sought to establish their social position through friendly, well-meaning relationships of cooperation with their Gentile fellow citizens. Having enthusiastically espoused the French Revolution ideals of liberty, equality, and brotherhood, these Jews perceived themselves as proponents of the universal humanistic values set forth by liberalism.

Referring specifically to Jewish-German relationships, George Mosse argues that the desire to establish close ties with the Gentile world reflected "the search for a personal identity beyond religion and nationality," an identity to which the German Jews "clung until the bitter end."[8] It is important to mention that the intention to define identity through relationships with Gentiles was not typical only of Jews in Germany. Zygmunt Bauman notes: "The story of the [assimilation of the] German Jews occupies the central, and in many senses a prototypical, place" in the history of Western Jewry.[9]

The situation of the Jews in Germany was therefore representative of the process of assimilation in the rest of Western Europe. Hence, the assimilationist background of the German-Jewish Stein and Frank did not differ considerably from the atmosphere of assimilation that Weil and Hillesum experienced in France and in Holland.

In general, Jews enjoyed a deceptively secure social position in all the countries of post-Emancipation Western Europe. In the Netherlands, Jews were granted equal rights in 1796. In the nineteenth and twentieth centuries, they gained effective entry into most sectors of the economic and political life in that country.[10] In France, Jews were granted equality in 1846 and quickly reached highly visible positions as intellectuals and middle-class professionals. As Paula Hyman observes, French Jews "selectively adopted the liberal principles of the Revolution," while ignoring the "growing visibility of anti-Semitism."[11] Even the Dreyfus trial was interpreted, somehow paradoxically, as further proof of the emancipatory progress.

In Germany too the situation was similar. Although officially they attained emancipation only in the Weimar Republic era, the Jews in pre–World War I Germany felt that they had been fully accepted in German society despite persisting political anti-Semitism.[12]

Legal equality and social acceptance in the post-Emancipation world required, first and foremost, that Jews relinquish their communal religious and national ties and join the mainstream culture. The well-known declaration of French statesman Clermont-Tonnerre—"To the Jews as individuals, everything; to the Jews as a nation, nothing"[13]—indicates the identity transformation that was expected of the post-Emancipation Jew. The enfranchisement of the Jews was predicated on their full integration into the general society when they became willing to abandon their ethnic identification. Thus, the Jews, "and particularly the richest and the most educated among them," happily subscribed to the assumption that once "the cultural idiosyncrasies had been effaced and diversity dissolved in a uniform national culture, the indiscriminately *human* face [of the Jew] would emerge and be recognized as such."[14]

With the eruption of the Nazi terror, therefore, the four women unexpectedly found themselves in a critical situation: the world they had trusted and considered secure was discriminating against their Jewishness, dehumanizing them, and sentencing them to annihilation. Yet their responses to this traumatic upheaval did not focus on vindictive condemnation, and they did not repudiate the world or express a desire to withdraw from it. Rather, as noted earlier, their responses articulated a desire to initiate the process of moral restitution.

The responses of the four women communicate that they felt an obligation to salvage a world that proved unable to act on the enlightened view of humanity. This perception conveys the conviction that, while the promise of humanistic progress failed abominably, the conceptual fulcrum of this promise—that all human beings are free and equal—remains valid. Therefore, the "new order" of friendly interaction—to recall Frank and Hillesum—needs to be reaffirmed in view of despotism and terror. Or, as Weil and Stein see it, a selfless, "saintly" approach is required to heal the world's moral aberration. The four victims of the failed Enlightenment did not profess resignation; they foresaw the moral recuperation of the enlightened world in the reinstitution of the humanistic idea.

To gain a better perspective on the four women's seemingly absurd and apparently quite incongruous pledge of loyalty to the vanquished legacy of humanism, we can resort to the speech Hannah Arendt delivered in Hamburg in 1959. Herself an escapee from the Nazi regime, Arendt spoke in tribute to Gotthold Lessing, one of the principal proponents of the Enlightenment, and reconfirmed his humanist position. She presented Lessing's notion of friendly discourse as the only way in which liberty and tolerance can be actualized. Lessing, Arendt claimed, "was concerned solely with humanizing the world by incessant and continual discourse. . . . He insisted that truth can exist only where it is humanized by discourse. . . . Every truth outside this area . . . is inhuman in the literal sense of the word."[15] Despite the failure of the Enlightenment in the Holocaust, Arendt reasserts Lessing's position and remains convinced that, even in the post-Holocaust era, relationships based on an open dialogue among equals are the only thing that will guarantee a humane future for humankind.

The example of Lessing is historically relevant to our investigation of humanistic thinking in the reality of the Holocaust. Lessing not only preached but also actualized his idea of enlightened friendship. For Western Jewry, his plays about friendly relationships with Jews, and his celebrated friendship with Moses Mendelssohn, became symbolic representations of emancipation, tolerance, and brotherhood. As George Mosse argues, the ideal of friendship indicated the possibility of Christian-Jewish dialogue and of "a solid and durable chain linking Christians and Jews."[16]

From the emancipatory perspective, the interest of the four women in mending the collapsing ideal sought to keep alive the tradition of the dialogue. Despite the impending death sentence, they followed the vision of humanizing the world through discourse. Their attempts to continue the discourse therefore imply continuing trust in liberating dialogue—an ideal that, as Arendt demonstrated, continued to shape the humanist world view in the postwar world. Furthermore, their insistence on a dialogue that would address humanity's moral needs communicates the four women's enduring sense of obligation to the world.

In the reality of the Final Solution, however, these efforts to rescue the world through dialogic reconnection manifest a perplexing lack of congruity, which invites further investigation. As Jews, the four women were banished and ostracized; they were targeted as the enemies of humankind and sentenced to persecution and annihilation. Hence, they were addressing a world that had cut off all communication with them and, in effect, had condemned them to silence even before the death sentence was carried out.

It follows that the four women remained committed to the world of Enlightenment that reneged on its commitment to its Jewish citizens. This blatantly asymmetrical relationship indicates that, at best, the emancipatory process in Western Europe created a dialogue that was unidirectional and as such cannot be termed enlightened at all. To gain a better understanding of this dialogue, which de facto turned into a monologue, we need to shift our attention from the aspect of social ethics to the aspect of what we might call "the ethics of relationship to one's self."

So far my discussion of the four women's defiance of the Nazi terror has focused on their feeling that the enlightened citizen had an obligation to the world and that every citizen was accountable to the world. This self-image as a responsible member of society was grounded in a view of the responsible self—that is, in a particular sense of the obligations an individual owes to society. Our vision will now turn to the strong belief that Stein, Weil, Frank, and Hillesum had in self-improvement as an individual's social responsibility.

2

THE ONGOING EDIFICATION OF THE SELF

Even if condemned by the group—by all groups, as a matter of fact—individual conduct may still be moral.

—Zygmunt Bauman

The concern the four women had for the world that presented a direct threat to their lives reveals personalities of particularly strong ethical conviction. Rather than the naive trust of the Western Jews in the slogans of the Enlightenment, the steadfastness of their concern points to a Weltanschauung that reflects principled determination not to yield to dehumanizing terror. As long as possible, the four women were striving not to permit the horror of the Final Solution to reduce their existence to a struggle for mere physical survival. Their writing consistently attests to their insistence on remaining in control in face of the overwhelming terror. As acts of spiritual and intellectual freedom, their writing manifested an overriding desire to maintain dignity and self-respect.

This determination to remain enlightened human beings in face of the world's barbaric inhumanity and moral darkness assumed the form of ethical self-development. Their autobiographical writings show that all four women considered the anguish to which history had submitted them an opportunity for inner growth—that is, they saw the effort to maintain dignity and self-respect in the increasingly threatening situation as a test of their ethical and spiritual mettle. Through courageous confrontation with the hardships of anxiety, alienation, displacement, confinement, and, worst of all, despair, they expected to meet their ideals of spiritual fortitude.

This attitude communicates that they perceived a meaningful life as one in which the highest ethical values are practiced. Paradoxical as it may sound, their attempts to fend off the terror of physical destruction found a shape in their persistent endeavors to become better human beings. The autobiographical writings of Anne Frank, Etty Hillesum, and Simone Weil demonstrate the extent to which they were alert to their self-education as independent, morally accountable individuals.

In an entry written just before her deportation on July 15, 1944, Anne Frank considers her self-improvement, a process that has preoccupied her all along. She feels that she has reached the stage of total responsibility for her emotional and intellectual development. "Parents," Frank claims, "can only give good advice or put [their children] on the right paths, but the final forming of a person's character lies in their own hands." And while she asserts her independence and accountability, she also acknowledges how difficult and demanding the process of growth can be. She confesses to have tried to overcome her weaknesses "by seeing for myself what was wrong in my behavior and keeping it before my eyes."[1] It was then the process of unsparing self-search that allowed Frank to become a mature, accountable person.

Like Frank, Etty Hillesum is preoccupied with her inner development and finds the process of maturation a rigorous, solitary endeavor. Writing in her diary at the close of 1941, Hillesum claims that nobody can relieve the individual of personal responsibility to become an independent, self-reliant person: "It is a slow and painful process, this striving after true inner freedom. Growing more and more certain that there is no help or assurance or refuge in others. . . . I have confidence in myself and shall manage by myself. The only measure you have is yourself."[2] In Hillesum's reckoning, the satisfaction of one's own standards is most difficult to attain; the individual must be confident enough not to rely on others, but rather determine her own ethical standards and strive to live up to them. Only the awareness of having become an independent, mature person will grant a sense of inner liberation from emotional dependency on others.

Weil's striving for emotional independence emerges in a somewhat different context. In her "Spiritual Autobiography," which she sent Father Perrin on her departure for Casablanca in May 1942, Weil relates a traumatic experience that outlined the trajectory of her lifelong inner struggle for meaningful existence. She writes that at the age of fourteen she "fell into one of those fits of bottomless despair" that made her want to die. When she realized her mediocrity compared with her mathematical-genius brother, she felt "excluded from that transcendent kingdom to which only the truly great have access and wherein truth abides." She reports that the illumination came when she realized that "any human being . . . can penetrate to the kingdom of truth . . . if only he longs for truth and perpetually concentrates all his attention upon its attainment." The "kingdom of truth" consists of the values of "beauty, virtue, and every kind of goodness," as well as in "the conviction . . . that when one hungers for bread one does not receive stones."[3] Thus, at about the same age as Frank, Weil consciously outlined the pattern of her self-education. Her decision to actualize her own "genius" reflected her understanding of life as a single-minded pursuit of truth in beauty, goodness, and justice. It is also interesting to note that, like Frank, Weil felt the need to assert herself as an independent individual in relation to her family. It was not just a whimsical need to liberate herself from sibling rivalry. The decision to write her "Spiritual Autobiography" at the particularly traumatic moment of exile demonstrates that she was determined to attain her goal. Even at the painful moment of her enforced uprooting from her beloved France—the motherland that had turned into a death trap—Weil was unsparingly searching her soul and reaffirming the path on which she had embarked at the age of fourteen.

As these autobiographical confessions demonstrate, Frank, Hillesum, and Weil saw the meaning of life in ethical self-actualization. Each spoke about her independent and lonely progression toward reaching the goal to become a better and more independent person. Invariably, the women remained self-critical, each of them constantly trying to measure up to her own vision of the ideal self. Each honestly confronted her inadequacies. Frank struggled to overcome her impatience and irritability toward her companions in hiding. She wanted to develop more self-control and to maintain her principles. Hillesum strove to free herself from both her possessiveness of and her dependency on her lover, Julius Spier. She wished for maturity and self-sufficiency to open herself to the beauty of the world and of humanity despite suffering and terror. Weil strove for integrity, afraid of "failing in [intellectual honesty]," of compromising her principles and thus straying from the values of truth, love, and virtue.[4]

The historical situation of these critical self-characterizations draws attention to how strict the self-judgments of these women were. The writings show their constant dissatisfaction with their self-development. Their discontent by no means indicates the end of their endeavors, but on the contrary prompted further, tireless attempts at self-improvement. At the same time, the historical circumstances infused these pursuits of ethical self-actualization with a sense of urgency. The growing premonitions of the forthcoming end generated pressure to hasten the process of moral and spiritual maturation.

In view of the haunting reality of the Final Solution, such an ethical orientation is truly perplexing. What were the roots of the preoccupation with emotional maturity, moral accountability, and intellectual honesty that persisted even in circumstances of inexorably approaching violence and death? How can we account for such self-directed, demanding moral standards of women condemned to death by a world that had lost its moral countenance?

These questions elicit an investigation of the conceptual framework of such a steadfast ethical orientation. Edith Stein's phenomenological concept of the person, as developed in her doctoral dissertation "On the Problem of Empathy" (completed in 1916), facilitates our understanding of the philosophical basis of the four women's preoccupation with moral self-actualization even at that particular historical time. It is significant that Stein's philosophical work addresses itself to the issue of the phenomenology of the ethical self.

Stein was working on her dissertation at the time of World War I. In light of our previous discussion of the assimilationist tendencies of German Jews, it is of interest here to mention Stein's loyalty to Germany. She volunteered to serve as a nurse's aide in a lazaretto in Weisskirchen, Austria, for purely patriotic reasons, out of her sense of solidarity with the German cause. As she explains in her autobiography, *Life in a Jewish Family*, "All my fellow students were in the service and I could not see why I should be better off than they were."[5]

Despite the period of almost twenty years that had elapsed since the war, Stein's autobiography, which she began writing in 1933, presents a vivid, detailed description of the lazaretto, of the medical staff, and particularly of the sick and the wounded. The traumatic war experience had considerable impact on Stein's choice of her study subject. The experience of her several-month-long voluntary service seems to have shaped her scholarly interest in the phenomenology of human personality and its social implications. Indeed, when describing her doctoral work in her autobiography, Stein admits that, after having "examined the act of 'empathy' as a particular act of cognition," she "went on to something which was personally close to my heart and which continually occupied me anew in all later work: the constitution of the human person."[6] It is therefore of interest to note that Stein's preoccupation with human personality was not purely theoretical. Rather, her philosophical-phenomenological thought stemmed from personal observation of human behavior in the traumatic situation of war.

In her phenomenological analysis of human personality, Stein focuses on the notion of the "kernel," which, she claims, is the unchangeable "true content of personality" representing the "value world" of the person. The spiritual values, or physical attributes, such as "goodness, readiness to make sacrifices, the energy I experience in my activities, . . . reveal their special position by standing outside of the causal order." According to Stein, the core—or particular potential of a person—is an invariable given. Its potential cannot be affected by external factors, such as historical circumstances, but the development of the potential may be either enhanced or curtailed by external circumstances. The potential therefore does not always unfold completely, and adverse circumstances might prevent complete actualization of the potential.

According to Stein—and this is essential within the framework of this discussion—the unfolding of the person is "the meaning of life."[7] In other words, progression toward the actualization of the individual's "true content of personality," or of her "value world," defines the purpose of human existence. To a remarkable extent, Frank's evolving self-awareness seems to corroborate Stein's theory of the unfolding "kernel" as the meaning of life. Frank was aware of her developing personality, but she also noted the hitherto unsuspected qualities of her personality as they developed. When she reread the harsh criticism she used to pass on her parents, she reproached herself for her "moods which kept my head under water . . . and only allowed me to see things subjectively." With a truly remarkable self-insight she realizes, "I hid myself within myself."[8]

Frank's unsparing self-evaluation is significant on more than one level. In terms of her maturation process, she was capable of a new understanding of her relations with her parents and could openly admit her error of judgment. On the conceptual level, she was capable of assessing the weaknesses of undeveloped self-awareness. Frank's comment thus indicates her appreciation of the emerging "hidden" self— her true "kernel"—as it allows a more objective understanding of self and others.

Developing self-consciousness enabled Frank to confront her failings, and consequently to become a better and more tolerant person. She traced the painful process of her growth with great insight. In her diary, she relates that as the younger daughter she was an imaginative, talented, and popular girl indulged by parents and relatives—"the darling of . . . the teachers, spoiled from top to toe by Mummy and Daddy." With the move into hiding, however, the atmosphere of love and care changed drastically. Confronted with the "setbacks, the quarrels," she was "taken completely by surprise." With the happy modus vivendi shattered, what followed was a stressful relationship with her parents—"fits of crying and an acute sense of loneliness."[9] Frank also recounts her escalating struggle for emotional fortitude and moral self-improvement. Her initial distress over the disappearance of the world of gentleness and protection was followed, she notes, by successive stages of ethical and spiritual development. Looking back, she observes "how I began to see all my faults and shortcomings. . . . Alone I had to face the difficult task of changing myself. . . . In due time I quieted down and discovered my boundless desire for all that is beautiful and good."[10]

Frank's awakening passion for the good and the beautiful in life reminds us of Weil's overriding desire to focus her attention uniquely on the truth of beauty and goodness. Equally significant is the striking affinity between Stein's theory and Frank's praxis. Frank's *Diary*'s increasing emphasis on the process of inner growth provides an apt illustration of Stein's theory of the unfolding personality.

The commonality of Stein's and Frank's emphasis on self-actualization draws attention to the biographical resemblance of both women's formative years. In her *Life in a Jewish Family,* Stein tells of a childhood very much like Frank's. As a child, she was "mercurially lively," precocious, and stubborn. She was a brilliant student, an imaginative young girl, inclined to fantasizing and daydreaming. The youngest child in a large family, Stein was adored and pampered by her relatives and had a special bond with her mother.[11]

The normalcy of Stein's childhood—which was followed by an excellent academic education, conversion to Christianity, and a career as a Catholic feminist educator until the rise of the Nazis in 1933—brings forth the extent of the freedom Frank would also have enjoyed had the historical circumstances not changed. The course of Frank's young life had been disrupted even before the hiding period. Threatened by the Nazi rise to power, the Frank family had emigrated from Germany to the Netherlands. Under the Nazi occupation of the Netherlands, the decrees of separate schools for Jewish children, and other restrictions and prohibitions, spelled gradual suppression of all freedoms.

The similarity of Stein's and Frank's childhood narratives allows a better understanding of the deprivations Frank had to endure. At the same time, this contextualization of Frank's singular conditions illuminates the remarkable potential of her "kernel." We have seen Frank's astute observation of her own development. The intensity and sincerity of her narration highlights the importance she attached to her ethical self-fulfillment. And the scrutiny of the progression toward self-realization as a responsible, mature person seems to underlie Frank's self-representations as well as those of the other women. This emphasis reaffirms Stein's view of the unfolding "content of personality" as "the meaning of life."

The significance of the process of self-improvement as the meaning of life elucidates each woman's determination to confront the exacerbating adversity with dignity and rectitude. Such determination signifies resistance. The Weltanschauung that sees the meaning of life in striving for goodness, spiritual beauty, and virtue *becomes* resistance to terror. The women attempted, often with considerable success, to overcome debilitating fear and despair by approaching the situation as a challenge to their inner strength.

Thus, Frank hints at her fear of future trials when she says, "I was glad when I first realized [that I was courageous and strong], because I don't think I shall easily bow down before the blows that inevitably come to everyone."[12] It does not seem too far-fetched to conjecture that the "blows" Frank has in mind were a euphemism for deportation.

Hillesum is even more explicit about the impact of the situation on her emotional and ethical development. Threatened by the constantly worsening life conditions and the prospect of exile, she nevertheless maintains: "Instead of living an accidental life, you feel deep down, that you have grown mature enough to accept your 'destiny.' " When confronted with the possibility of her lover's expulsion from Amsterdam, Hillesum writes about her developing strength to deal with the inevitable suffering: "I suddenly felt oddly serious and grown-up and sure. . . . Something has matured in me during the past few months, . . . something fresh has appeared and all I have to do is . . . to take it upon myself, to bear it forward and to let it flourish."[13]

For Weil, the decision to escape the danger signifies a flaw that is unacceptable. The suspicion that her flight to Casablanca might be considered an act of cowardice causes her to suffer throes of despair. In a letter to Father Perrin written on her departure to Casablanca, Weil declares: "For me there is no question in this departure of an escape from suffering and danger. My anguish comes precisely from the fear that in spite of myself, and unwittingly, by going I shall be doing what I want above everything else not to do—that is to say, running away."[14] Soon after, desperately searching for a way to return from New York to Europe, Weil writes: "I have the feeling that I committed an act of desertion. This thought is unbearable."[15] Weil's place is with those who suffer; to be elsewhere is to betray the victims as well as her moral self. Indeed, unable to stay away, Weil returned from New York to London to work with the Free French Front.

These modes of resistance demonstrate that—to recall the epigraph to this chapter—the obligation to maintain individual moral conduct, even if condemned by a group, outweighed the four women's other considerations, even those of physical safety. The roots of this overriding sense of ethical obligation seem to lie, in large measure, in the cultural climate of their formative years, a climate that posited self-actualization as a person's most pertinent obligation to oneself and to society.

The ethics of self-education to which the women subscribed were closely related to the concept of *Bildung,* a prominent aspect of the Enlightenment. Supported by the liberal ideology, the Enlightenment, and particularly its emancipatory thrust, the women perceived the future of egalitarian society in terms of progression toward the fellowship of all human beings. The concept of *Bildung* focused on the construct of the enlightened person in an enlightened society. It addressed the individual's position and obligation vis-à-vis human progress.

Grounded in the premise of the equality of all human beings, *Bildung* promoted the perception that every human personality contains the potential for self-improvement. Following Kant and his emphasis on critical mind informed by reason, *Bildung* claimed that this potential can be actualized through rationality, self-discipline, and self-education. As George Mosse tells us, *Bildung* postulated that "all those who were willing to use and develop their reason could attain [the] ideal" combination of the intellectual, the moral, and the aesthetic.[16] Having evolved in the reality of the emancipatory progress, the concept of *Bildung* was espoused wholeheartedly by the Western Jews. According to Mosse, the emancipated Jews saw *Bildung*'s emphasis on equality and self-improvement as the way to actualize their liberal ideal and embraced it "as a new faith."[17]

The "new faith" of *Bildung* promised to transcend the barriers of religion and nationality, and also communicated confidence in human reasoning and responsible behavior. Directed by reason, the individual is able to control emotions, irrational drives, and instinctual tendencies and thus fulfill her responsibility of rational self-education.

The importance of cultivating reason in order to overcome the power of instinct finds a parallel in Freud's concept of the Ego and the Id.[18] Even though, as we shall see, Freud himself later doubted the efficacy of reason as a controlling dimension, his early psychoanalytical theory both reflects and strengthens the concept of *Bildung* by arguing that the instinctual forces of the psyche can be subdued through knowledge gained in the process of rational self-examination.

The conflict between powerful instincts and the forces of reason is indicative of an evolving moral potential, but this evolution cannot take place in the confined recesses of a solitary mind. The evolution of the moral self is imprinted with the consciousness of the outer world. "Moral behaviour," Bauman reminds us, "is conceivable only in the context of coexistence."[19] The growth of the moral self can be measured only through the individual's interaction with others, and only through acts performed in relation to other human beings will the individual's moral potential continue to grow.

The ideal of *Bildung*—of individual moral self-education—therefore cannot be actualized in separation from its social environment. On the contrary, interaction among individuals committed to self-improvement will bring into being the liberal ideal of human fellowship. From the point of view of the Jewish minority, *Bildung* promised to promote close interrelationships between Jews and Gentiles. The historical reality of post-Emancipation Europe, or at least the hope it excited, made it possible for Jews to subscribe to *Bildung*. It was a partly idealistic, partly utilitarian outlook that thoroughly believed in the promise of the desired goal of equal partnership in general society.

It is not difficult to understand the impact of *Bildung* on the world views of the four women. They were raised to have a sense of obligation as individuals, particularly Jewish individuals, to integrate into the enlightened world. However, in the reality of the Final Solution, which reduced European Jews to helplessness and decreed their genocide, the cultivation of *Bildung* as an entrance ticket to Gentile society no longer made any sense. The total fiasco of the liberal ideal exposed the failure of *Bildung* and cut off all possibility of ethical self-development in a social context. Thus, the intense preoccupation with the moral world and the moral self that we observe in the self-representations of the four women raises questions about the rationality of their assiduous sense of obligation.

Why would the women continue to embrace values and practice ideals that certainly did not serve their interests at that time? A much more realistic approach would have had them concentrate on their own welfare. Instead, Stein refused a British certificate that would have allowed her to go to Palestine because her sister was refused one. Weil returned from New York to besieged London to promote her plan to fight in France. Hillesum refused to go into hiding, but instead chose to be a volunteer as a social worker in Westerbork. And in a different but no less poignant context, Frank's realization of Peter's moral weakness made her end the relationship rather than compromise her ideals and principles.

These refusals to compromise point to extremely self-demanding moral outlooks that transcend all utilitarian considerations. In fact, the selfless nature of these decisions indicates that these individuals were inclined to dissociate from egocentric considerations. Although emancipation, which promised equality, and *Bildung,* which promised to create a morally better human being, had proven to be totally ineffectual, the moral outlook of these women did not waver. On the contrary, the increasingly threatening situation intensified their steadfast belief that the meaning of life lies in the unfolding of moral values that need to be communicated and shared. In fact, it seems as if the deepening crisis compelled them against all logic to insist on faith in moral values.

Viktor Frankl postulates: "It is the spiritual freedom—which cannot be taken away—that makes life meaningful and purposeful."[20] Undoubtedly, the choice the four women made to stay with the world instead of to withdraw from it constituted an act of freedom. As we have seen, their insistence on responsible behavior toward their relatives (Stein), toward their country (Weil), toward their community (Hillesum), and toward oneself (Frank), at a time when there was a breakdown of all ethical social intercourse, determined the meaning and purpose of their lives. At the same time, let us not forget that they were fully aware of the terrible consequences that such a choice of freedom entailed. And it was precisely that awareness of the risk that highlights the ethical imperative that compelled them to exercise freedom.

What, then, was the compelling motivation of this "illogical" resistance to—in Fackenheim's terms—the "irresistible logic of destruction"? In what way did the gratification it promised supersede the interest in survival? I suggest the centrality of interpersonal relationships as a decisive motive in the four women's resistance. As represented in the thought and practice of the four women, the function they attributed to the other in their life narratives offers an important insight into their assertion of spiritual freedom in face of the reality of destruction. Our attention now shifts to this aspect of their ethical thinking.

3

THE TRANSCENDING
CONSCIOUSNESS OF THE OTHER

*The positive and pure fellow-feeling . . . is a true grasping beyond
oneself and entrance into the Other person and the Other's individual
condition, a true and actual transcendence of one's own self.*

—Max Scheler

It is appropriate to open this discussion with Edith Stein's and Simone Weil's views
of human interrelations as they relate to Max Scheler's consideration of the nature
of social interaction. Edmund Husserl's associate and Stein's colleague, Scheler
was preoccupied with the phenomenology of the value structure of the person, as
well as with the role that values play in the position of the person in relation to
society. In other words, Scheler studied the essential components in human
personality that make social interaction possible. The evolution of his thought
from symmetrical (reciprocal) relations between self and other, to the concept of
the asymmetrical (receptive) relationship with the other—offers a helpful framework for looking at Stein's and Weil's concepts of human interaction.

"I" and "You" in Reciprocity

As Max Scheler sees it, "the other" is a priori present in one's personal sphere. The existence of the other would be evident even in the other's absence. To recall Scheler's well-known example, a Robinson Crusoe would experience the absence—*the missing presence*—of the other, because lack of companionship would be communicated through feelings of isolation and loneliness.[1] According to Scheler, therefore, the other is (1) an indubitable aspect of human personality and (2) indispensable to the person's sense of well-being.

Building on these premises, Scheler argues that besides the individual person there is in each human being also the collective person. These aspects of the person are "necessary and essential sides of a concrete whole which comprises person and world." Scheler postulates that "the *essential* character of human consciousness is such that the community is in some such sense implicit in every individual, and that man is not only part of society, but that society and the social bond are an essential part of himself." This construct, which presupposes the existence of the "social nexus" in every individual, is, according to Scheler, the source of "all morally relevant acts."[2]

In light of this theory, the four women's continuing involvement with the world exemplifies Scheler's notion of the inherence of the "collective person" in the individual personality. The "morally relevant acts" of these women—their constant self-education, and their moral stance regarding the world—corroborate the fundamental component of the "social nexus" of human personality.

But how, in Scheler's view, do "morally relevant acts"—acts that arise in the context of involvement and relationship with the other—actually come into being? Here Scheler establishes the "founding laws" of his theory of sympathy. Our *Verstehen,* or intersubjective understanding, he claims, is given in intuition. We are capable of interacting with the other because we are capable of "fellow feeling." This capability allows a person to respond to the other vicariously—that is, with the full comprehension "of the independence of the Other person with whom one fellow-feels."[3] In other words, the person recognizes her distinction from the other person, and at the same time she can participate in the experience of the other person sympathetically, through her intuitive *Verstehen.*

Scheler's concept of "fellow feeling" displays important correspondences with Stein's theory of empathy. Like Scheler, Stein considers the ability of the individual to interact with others to be a fundamental component of personality. Stein, however, does not claim, like Scheler, the a priori existence of the other in one's personal sphere, communicated through the sense of unfulfillment, or loneliness.

This discrepancy between the two theories is important because Stein's proof of the existence of the other as an indubitable evidence of the self's "social nexus" foregrounds her ethics of self-development and responsibility.

Stein's proof of the existing other evolves logically from her phenomenological premise of the "I" as a living body. The living body "senses, thinks and wills"; it relates itself to the external world, and it also relates the "I" and the external world to each other. The living body "faces this world and communicates with me."[4] The living body enables the "I" to experience, and therefore the "I" and the living body are inseparable.

To experience is to be capable of imagining, remembering, and fantasizing. As the experiencing subject, the "I" remembers itself experiencing and thereby casts the remembered "I" as object. The act of remembering constitutes the link between the present "I" and the past "I." The "I" that I remember and the remembering "I" are not identical. The ability of the "I" to experience itself as same and distinct simultaneously makes it possible for the "I" to sense its living body "from the inside," and also to imagine that it is watching itself "from the outside."[5]

The "I" is therefore able to watch its living body acting independently, as if it were another "I." This ability of the "I" to split itself into the observer and the observed provides an insight into the essence of empathy, a value that relates the "I" and the other. Because I can imagine myself from "the outside" as a "living body," I can also see the other, who is outside me, as a living body. The other is not me, but she is like me; her experience can never be mine, but it can be like mine. This recognition of the typologically familiar experience of another "I" generates the sense of empathy.

The paradigm of concurrent distinction and sameness is central to Stein's view of personal relationships, and indeed constitutes a cornerstone in her concept of social interaction as an essential factor in one's self-development. The distinction between "I" and "you" eliminates the notion of identity fusion. The other is other than " 'I' because it is given to me in another way than 'I.' Therefore, it is 'you.' But because it experiences itself as I experience myself, the 'you' is another 'I.' "[6]

The response of empathy is predicated on intersubjective experience, whereby human beings recognize both their sameness and their distinctness. Stein's philosophical exposition proves the inherent value of the equality of all human beings: because I am able to see another living body experiencing itself as I experience myself, I must admit that, as living bodies, we are all bound by the same responses and faculties. At the same time, my empathic experience of the other enriches my world image;[7] it extends my perspective and teaches me about myself and others. My ability to retain my "I" enables me to evaluate the other against myself, to contrast the other person's moral constitution with my own. "As Scheler has shown us," Stein concedes, "inner perception contains within it the possibility of deception." But she argues that "empathy . . . offers itself as a corrective for such deceptions."[8]

The corrective lies in the capability of self-evaluation through empathy. The notion of self-evaluation invokes the previously discussed concept of the "kernel." Indeed, in Stein's view, the unfolding of "the true content of personality" is predicated on empathic interaction with other human beings. On the one hand, empathy helps me to evaluate the "kernel" of the other. On the other hand, my ability to empathize with the foreign experience enables me to grasp the other's empathic experience and to "get the 'image' the other has of me, . . . the appearances in which I present myself to him."[9] Such an experience of "reflexive sympathy"[10] enables me to obtain a better understanding of myself. This new self-knowledge offers a corrective to self-deception and allows me to develop my ethical potential.

Stein's philosophical theory of the self in interaction complements her theory of the "kernel." It expands our understanding of the women's response to the historical crisis. Her consideration of intersubjectivity as an empathic phenomenon elucidates the four women's defiance of terror, which threatened them directly. As Stein sees it, connections among people are the function of intrinsic properties of human nature. In this sense, the notion that all human beings are equal is engendered by the ability of the person, as a living "I," to identify the other as a comparable "you." This perception of the other as equal both precedes and transcends the circumstantial, variable factors—that is, the political, ideological, or historical shifting conditions that incessantly affect and transform human relationships.

Stein's phenomenology of interpersonal relationships emphasizes the interdependence of self and other in terms of ethical self-education. This interdependence is indispensable to the self's autoperception as an unfolding personality. Only through the empathic encounter with the other can I see myself as I am from a detached point of view and thus make progress in the actualization of my "kernel."

In her *Diary*, Anne Frank provides a particularly apt demonstration of Stein's concept of self-development through the intersubjectivity of empathic interaction. In one of her final entries, she embarks on serious self-analysis, a self-search triggered by a discussion with her boyfriend, Peter, and her sister, Margaret. The two excuse their weaknesses while commenting enviously on Frank's strength. "Yes," Frank quotes them telling her, "if I was as strong and plucky as you are, . . . if I had such persistent energy. . . ."

In her self-reckoning, which follows the discussion, Frank rejects the "easy" choices, which in her view signify moral defeat. She decides to follow her "own conscience," which encourages her to actively overcome her weaknesses. "I can't imagine," she marvels, "how anyone can say: 'I'm weak,' and then remain so. After all, if you know it, why not fight against it, why not try to train your character?" And she confesses to have been "searching for days, searching for a good argument against the terrible word 'easy,' something to settle it once and for all."[11]

This episode demonstrates Stein's theory of empathic interaction in praxis. Frank realizes how others see her, and this realization motivates her self-reevaluation. But the element of reflexivity makes her also reevaluate others, because their perception of her personality has exposed their way of thinking. As a result, Frank gains a comparative perspective that allows her to have a better understanding of her own personality and of her interlocutors, and consequently she re-views her opinions, reassesses the way she will pursue the unfolding of her "kernel," and articulates her thinking process in writing.

It is also important to note that Frank's decisions do not indicate the end of her social intercourse with her peers. We may recall Arendt's view of Lessing's humanizing "incessant and continual discourse" in which each person says "what he 'deems truth.' "[12] Frank's intense search for "a good argument" is harmonious with Lessing's concept of a continuing debate. The seriousness of her quest for arguments demonstrates the importance she attaches to the ideas of her interlocutors, even though she does not accept them. This empathic encounter and its intellectual aftermath signal a stage in Frank's ethical growth.

The ethical content of Frank's personality unfolds clearly, thanks to a dialogic connection. The exchange of ideas among equal parties (herself, Peter, and Margaret) clarifies her perception of a meaningful way of life, which she intends to follow. Frank's self-development is therefore grounded in the notion of intersubjectivity. As Stein deduced through philosophical reasoning, and as Frank actually experienced, self-improvement takes place in the symmetrical situation of reciprocal relations.

Stein's view of dialogic, reciprocal interrelationships among empathic selves corresponds, in large measure, to Scheler's notion of "fellow feeling." Each of the philosophers postulates the inseparability of human physical existence and of interaction with others. This connectedness exists because of, in Scheler's lexis, the value of sympathy and, in Stein's lexis, the value of empathy that make meaningful communication among people possible. At the same time, the channels of communication—Scheler's intuitive "fellow feelings" and Stein's typological recognition of "sameness"—position the communicating agents as equal, independent individuals in a symmetrical, reciprocal exchange.

"I" and "You" in Receptivity

Scheler's evolving view of individual and society suggests the existence of relationships based on a principle other than reciprocity. Such relationships are dominated by the value of love. According to Scheler, love transcends the dialogic, reciprocal relationships grounded in the construct of intuitive "fellow feelings." Love means giving up the need to change, educate, or dominate the other. The desire to impose one's will on the other, even with the best of intentions, signifies not love but self-imprisonment, "the inability to become free from one's inclinations on behalf of one's *own* ideas, feelings and interests."[13] In the experience of "an authentic, pure act of love for a person," according to Scheler, we detach ourselves "from all simultaneously existing, feeling-given value layers of our personal value-world, especially those layers which are still bound to our senses and our life feelings."[14]

In Scheler's view, love is the absolute value and ultimately transcends all other values. True love for another signifies an unconditional acceptance of the other. Love therefore designates a relationship that originates in receptiveness rather than in reciprocity. Such a relationship is asymmetrical, because it implies that my concern for the other becomes the primary interest and supersedes my interest in myself.

In a sense, Scheler sees love as liberation from the instincts of the will to power and domination, instincts often concealed under the guise of reciprocal relations. His discrimination between selfish and selfless interrelations with the other offers a useful introduction to Weil's concept of human interaction. Weil's notion of interpersonal relationships focuses on total receptivity, which requires total obliteration of the egotistical, possessive self.

Like Stein, Weil ponders the essence of human personality. For her, the values of good and justice are the fundamental elements in human existence. We shall recall her autobiographical recollection of the formative truth that "when one hungers for bread one does not receive stones." In her important essay "Human Personality," Weil reasserts this truth, claiming that "at the bottom of the heart of every human being there is something that goes on indomitably expecting, . . . in the teeth of all experience of crimes committed, suffered and witnessed, that good and not evil will be done to him." That is why, Weil argues, "every time that there arises from the depths of the human heart the childish cry . . . 'Why am I being hurt?' then there is certainly injustice."[15]

The pain of suffering is injustice that as moral persons we are not allowed to ignore. Yet, because of the nature of human personality, we are unable to face suffering and pain. We are aware that, at any moment, "what I am might be abolished and replaced by anything whatsoever of the filthiest and most contempt-ible sort."[16] Like the afflicted, we may also lose everything we have and become dispossessed. Yet, instead of identifying with the afflicted we are repulsed by their misfortune; the denigration of destitution is something we cannot bear even to imagine happening to us. But precisely because we know that it may happen to us too, we choose to ignore it.

Let us recall that Stein sees the empathic meeting with the other as a catalyst of "reflexive sympathy." Weil also sees the meeting with the other — in Weil's case it is always the meeting with the afflicted other — as an experience that reveals the kernel of one's being. In contrast to Stein — who stresses the ethical aspects of sameness — Weil's view is that the sense of sameness brings forth immorality and injustice. According to Weil, the inability to accept sameness points to the fear of affliction. The fear precludes openness to the afflicted and manifests itself in immoral behavior.

Weil feels that the notion of sameness evokes the possibility of similar fate. If the other is my equal, affliction similar to hers may be inflicted on me too. An acknowledgment of the universality of suffering and pain would amount to an admission of affinity with the afflicted. Our inability to contemplate such an affinity because of our fear of affliction causes us to dissociate from the afflicted or, worse, to exploit or dominate the victim. Such an attitude is immoral, because it constitutes a transgression of the fundamental trust in the good and justice in every human being.

As Weil sees it, the way to respond to injustice meaningfully is to face the inconceivable and actually take on the other's suffering, pain, and loss. With a sense of love and affinity, we must renege on our individuality and receive the affliction of the other into our souls. Recall Scheler, who sees love as uncondi-tional, detached from the value-world reception of the other. Weil sees love expressed in the acceptance of the afflicted as the ultimate manifestation of human responsibility. In this respect, both Scheler and Weil see love as concern for the other, concern that supersedes all personal, self-centered considerations.

Weil's radical position, however, exceeds Scheler's position on selfless love. In her view, the notion of responsibility for the other amounts to total self-renunciation. She claims that love for the afflicted requires absolute abolition of the self, a process that amounts to no less than a miracle because it stands in diametrical opposition to natural human inclinations. "Only by the supernatural working of grace," Weil argues, "can a soul pass through its own annihilation to the place where alone it can get the sort of attention which can attend to truth and to affliction. . . . The name of this intense, pure, disinterested, gratuitous, generous attention is love."[17]

Weil's view of the egotistical "I," which needs the miracle of grace to identify with the other, differs considerably, therefore, from Stein's concept of the empathic "I." According to Stein, empathy helps us to actualize the potential of our kernel and at the same time affirm the typological sameness of the other. The equality engendered in the recognition that "you" is another "I" allows for an empathic comprehension of the other's experience.

In contrast to Stein, who sees the developing "I" strengthened through the recognition of its sameness with the "you," Weil sees in the recognition of sameness with the afflicted other an experience that entails the destruction of the "I." Stein grounds the ability to empathize in the distinct identity of every human being. Weil predicates the ability to feel for another in the dissolution of identity. Only obliteration of identity enables total acceptance of the other. Only elimination of the dominant and the domineering autonomous self makes it possible to hear the voice of those who are hurt. The feelings of pity and sympathy are possible when one abolishes one's own ego. Weil claims: "Compassion and humility are connected. . . . Compassion is natural to man if the obstacle of the feeling of the 'I' is removed"[18] because "our personality is the part of us which belongs to error and sin."[19]

Weil's exhortation of self-renunciation therefore polarizes Stein's advocacy for self-fulfillment. Stein suggests that ethical self-actualization takes place in growing self-consciousness, a process contingent on one's participation in society and on the empathic perception of the other. For Weil, however, ethical self-actualization is achieved in the anonymity of total attention to the afflicted.

From Loving-kindness to Attentive Love

The issues of injustice, attention to the other, and the moral situation of the world preoccupy all four women. The writings of Anne Frank and Etty Hillesum express concerns about individual responsibility and reflect an evolution of ethical thought remarkably similar to that of Stein and Weil. Both Frank and Hillesum were increasingly preoccupied with suffering and, more significant, with proper ethical attitudes toward suffering. Despite her youth and the constricting situation of hiding, Frank was extremely sensitive to the misery of others. Her empathic recognition of the needy, her consciousness of social injustice, and her suggestions as to how to redress iniquity all demonstrate the symmetrical paradigm of reciprocal interpersonal relationships.

While Frank's response to the needy illustrates Stein's view of reciprocity, Hillesum's relations with the afflicted seem to illustrate Weil's thought of receptivity in love. In a remarkable way, Hillesum put Weil's concept of attentive love into practice. Hillesum's attitude toward the afflicted presents us with an extraordinary example of unconditional acceptance of the other through selfless love. The distinctness of Frank's and Hillesum's notions of "giving" outlines compassionate yet diverging positions vis-à-vis the suffering other.

In a short essay entitled "Give," which she wrote in March 1944, Frank addresses the problem of the destitute. She turns to the reader with a plea for material support of the needy and for supportive generosity of spirit. Frank starts with a query that evokes both Stein's notion of empathy and Weil's concept of attention, "I wonder if any of the people sitting in warm, comfortable houses have any idea what it must be like to be a beggar?" and continues by asserting equality: "We are all born alike." Then she goes on to reaffirm everyone's right to good and justice. Everyone, she says, "has the right to a friendly word." It is not only money that poor people necessarily need; even more important is kindness and "the feeling that they are human beings too."[20]

Generosity, according to Frank, is the key element in a world of justice. "Give of yourself . . . as much as you can," she asks, "then there would be much more justice in the world." It is important to note that, in Frank's world picture, generosity will be amply rewarded: "Give and you shall receive, much more than you would have ever thought possible."[21]

Generosity, therefore, is not selfless, because the giver can be sure of being rewarded. The prize is incorporated in the charitable act itself, as each instance of giving contributes to humanity's, and hence to the giving individual's, better future. Frank's argument is grounded in the view of harmonious and mutually rewarding personal and common interests.

Indeed, Frank emphasizes her unshaken faith in the inherent goodness of character. "Everyone," she claims, "is born with a great deal of good in him." At the same time, she asserts the logic of giving in reciprocity. "No one," she maintains, "has ever become poor from giving."[22] An empathic response to the needy redresses the world's immorality and injustice. But empathy also helps the individual to actualize her inherent potential of goodness. Through the act of giving, the individual recognizes the poor as her equal, because in the act of giving—that is, sharing—the giver implies that "if a poor beggar's child were to receive [what I have], then there wouldn't be any difference at all."[23] Frank also touches on the reluctance to acknowledge misery, when she observes that "the generous donor usually shudders at having to touch a dirty hand."[24] In this respect, she approaches Weil's position on human repulsion from affliction. In contrast to Weil, however, she assumes that those who are in the position to give understand that it is in their interest to overcome their reluctance and to acknowledge the equality of the afflicted.

In a remarkable way, Frank attempted to assume the responsibility of giving. Despite the nerve-racking precariousness of her constricted existence, Frank did not deplore her fate, but gave her attention to those she considered most in need. In the entry of January 13, 1943, Frank writes about the destitution of homeless Dutch children: "The children run about in just a thin blouse and clogs . . . and no one helps them. . . . I could go on for hours about the suffering the war has brought." Instead of focusing on her undeniably worse destiny as a Jewish child, Frank berates herself for selfishness: "We are even so egotistic as to talk about 'after the war,' brighten up over the thought of having new clothes and new shoes, whereas we really ought to save every penny, to help other people, and save what is left of the wreckage after the war."[25]

In Frank, therefore, we detect the desire to maintain the prewar, Enlightenment-bred Weltanschauung. In her still somewhat childish manner, Frank accurately expresses the liberal humanist assumption whereby the individual's interests and common good complement each other. Taking care of the needy will bring equal happiness and justice to all and thus benefit the giver.

Hillesum, by contrast, shows a growing understanding that the old notions of liberal humanism need to be replaced with a new vision of responsibility toward the world. Like Frank, Hillesum emphasizes the act of "giving" to the world. However, her way of giving reveals a proclivity for absolute and unconditional "self-givenness" to the afflicted.

Hillesum refused to listen to her friends, who pleaded with her to go into hiding. Rejecting their claim that she should save herself because she has "so much to give," Hillesum argues: "Whatever I may have to give to others, I can give no matter where I am, here in the circle of my friends or over there, in a concentration camp." Therefore, she argues, she has no right to a different treatment than others.[26]

"Giving," as Hillesum sees it, signifies serving suffering humanity with total disregard of the self. While, like Frank, Hillesum's friends still believed that they had a moral responsibility to share with those who suffer unjustly, Hillesum defined moral responsibility as a unilateral act of giving oneself unconditionally to the afflicted. Hillesum's concept of "giving" thus resembles and at the same time transcends Frank's notion of "giving." Like Frank, Hillesum insisted on the absolute responsibility to help the unfortunate. In Hillesum's view, however, giving does not entail the reward of the emotional satisfaction of sharing, nor does it imply the consciousness of contributing to a better world.

To be sure, both Frank and Hillesum expressed the hope that acts of goodness and love will contribute to a better future, that, as Hillesum predicts, "one day we shall be building a whole new world."[27] In Hillesum's case, however, it was not the hopeful outlook for the future that shaped her sense of solidarity with the inmates of Westerbork, nor was it a promise of reciprocity and reward that motivated her voluntary service in Westerbork. On the contrary, the longer Hillesum stayed in Westerbork, the more she became aware that her deportation was inevitable. Despite opportunities to escape, she was adamant about remaining in the camp. Her determination reflected a compulsive need to help the suffering victims.

The position on suffering humanity that Hillesum developed in her diary and in her letters reechoes Weil's philosophy of attention. Furthermore, in her readiness to assume the fate of the inmates of Westerbork, Hillesum in effect put into practice Weil's idea of loving attention to the afflicted.

Hillesum therefore presents us with an extraordinary example of resistance in "self-giving" to the needy. What is the rationale of such a mode of resistance? What world view does this resistance communicate?

An examination of these issues in conjunction with Weil's position toward suffering can help us understand the conceptual framework of Hillesum's response to the situation of the Final Solution. Especially, the connection that Weil establishes between attention and anonymity illuminates Hillesum's self-effacement with regard to the victims as progression toward the freedom of self-empowerment in the reality of total powerlessness.

The two women's similar attitudes toward evil establish common ground for their perceptions of suffering. Unlike the world of the liberal, enlightened Weltanschauung, which aimed at the eradication of evil, injustice, and suffering, the two women see "bad"—that is, hurtful—things that people inflict on people, as an integral part of human existence. "Pleasure and pain are inseparable companions," Weil argues. "Thus the better we are able to conceive of the fullness of joy, the purer and more intense will be our suffering in affliction and our compassion for others."[28]

Watching the horror of Westerbork, Hillesum seems to echo Weil when she claims that "everywhere things are both very good and very bad at the same time. The two are in balance, everywhere and always."[29] Rather than an aberration, which will disappear in a world that will actualize the ideals of enlightened humanism, the existence of human evil must be accepted as a given. If the existence of evil is unobliterable, then suffering inflicted by human beings is inseparable from life experience. We must act in the world with the full knowledge that suffering is unavoidable. If suffering is essential to human condition, then its function cannot be ignored. Both the consciousness and the experience of suffering affect our understanding of the world, shape our characters, and structure our relations with others.

The concept of the inevitability of suffering affirmed in the situation of the Holocaust evokes Viktor Frankl's perception of suffering. Frankl, let us recall, had been an inmate in Auschwitz. He claimed in his postwar psychoanalytical study of the concentration camp experience that "if there is a meaning in life at all, then there must be a meaning in suffering. Suffering is an ineradicable part of life, even as [is] fate and death."[30] In situations when suffering is unavoidable — and such was the suffering that the Final Solution inflicted on Jews — then, Frankl argues, "meaning is possible even in spite of suffering."[31] In other words, even in a world that seems suffused in suffering, in which there is nothing else but suffering, it is still possible to find meaning.

Frankl suggests therefore that the search for meaning in situations of unavoidable suffering is the only way in which we can resist the desire to give in to despair. The attitude that there are things worthy of living even in a situation of overwhelming pain and anguish, even in a time of unspeakable degradation and destitution, makes such suffering meaningful. Frankl teaches that we must find meaning in the experience of suffering in order not to allow the force of despair inherent in suffering to destroy us. His sense that even or precisely the suffering of the Holocaust must be given meaning evokes the question of the meaning that Hillesum found in her ordeal.

What made Hillesum proclaim the existence of good in a world that exhibited unspeakable evil? What made her argue that "life is good after all, . . . and that's what stays with me, even now, even when I'm about to be packed off to Poland [Auschwitz] with my whole family"?[32] And why — despite the worsening situation that she describes as "the mounting human suffering, . . . the persecution and oppression and despotism and the impotent fury and the terrible sadism" — does she find that she can nevertheless "lie against the naked breast of life and [feel] her arms round me . . . so gentle and so protective"?[33]

What seems to have enabled Hillesum to celebrate life in the midst of the misery of Westerbork was the sense of her own growth. She found meaning in her self-development against the reality of suffering and death. She rejoiced in her new-born maturity, which spelled liberation from egotism and possessiveness. As mentioned before, Hillesum was waging a struggle against her tendency to "possess" others, especially her lovers.[34] The emerging sense of inner freedom allowed her to assert her independence, and that sense of inner freedom allowed her to develop the capacity to give herself to others out of unconditional love for humankind.

As she saw correctly, her need to control others reflected her immaturity and dependency. Her ability to put the needs of the inmates of Westerbork before her own marks a transformation from a personality inwardly torn and tormented by the ambition to dominate others to a whole, altruistic, and generous personality, free to give of herself to others. The center of meaning shifted from the desire to satisfy egotistical possessiveness to the desire to satisfy the needs of suffering humanity.

Weil's concept of anonymity illuminates the meaning of Hillesum's development toward altruistic selflessness. Weil claims, "Perfection is impersonal. . . . Truth and beauty dwell on [the] level of the impersonal and the anonymous."[35] She argues that in order to attain truth and beauty our egotistic tendencies need to be eliminated. Hillesum corroborates Weil's notion of the "annihilation" of the egotistic "I" when she claims that her desire to possess the other must be "eradicated" and "that hunger for the absolute must be crushed inside me." She feels she must accept that life is precarious, uncertain, and ambivalent. "The absolute," she declares, "does not exist, [because] life and human relations are full of subtleties."[36] Once Hillesum manages to overcome her narcissistic desire to "own" the other, she feels free to let herself be "owned" by the all-encompassing, ever-present flow of life.

The measure of independence that Hillesum gains in relation to her lovers allows her to reach the "beauty and the truth" of the impersonal "cosmic space,"[37] a space beyond all egotistical concerns. With the ability to accept pain and pleasure, suffering and joy, beauty and ugliness, comes the sense of oneness with the universal truth of life. Only as a self-sufficient individual in control of her self can she disentangle herself from the trappings of the personal, "all preconceptions, all slogans [and] find courage to let go of everything."[38]

Thus Hillesum attains what Weil calls the perfection of anonymity. The sense of impersonality frees her from egotistic ambitions and aspirations that shaped the "old" personality motivated by self-love and self-absorption.

The anonymity of the impersonal allows the acceptance of life in its totality, with its uncertainties and ambiguities. This ability to accept life as it is causes her to abandon her own interests and to proclaim the other as her main interest. Thus, the other actually becomes the center of her life. As she notes in the following remarkable passage in her diary, Hillesum reaches a state of mind of complete identification with suffering in attentive love:

"It still comes down to the same thing: life is beautiful. And I believe in God. And I want to be right in the thick and still be able to say: life is beautiful." . . . Sometimes I might sit down beside someone, put an arm round a shoulder, say very little and just look into their eyes. Nothing was alien to me, not one single expression of human sorrow. . . . I am not afraid to look suffering straight in the eyes. And at the end of each day, there [is] always the feeling: I love people so much. Never any bitterness about what was done to them, but always love for those who knew how to bear so much although nothing had prepared them for such burdens.[39]

This response to the suffering inmates of Westerbork exemplifies, to a remarkable extent, Weil's theory of attention. "The capacity to give one's attention to a sufferer," Weil argues, happens when "the soul empties itself of all its own contents in order to receive into itself the being it is looking at, just as he is, in all his truth."[40]

Hillesum acts out Weil's theory in her description of looking into the victim's eyes with fearless acceptance of the suffering she discovers there. The selfish fear that this suffering may become hers disappears; self-love is replaced by the love of selfless, compassionate assimilation of the other's experience of affliction.

Hillesum's complete disregard of her own interests puts into practice Weil's idea of attention, especially when she defines her purpose of life in rendering services, however small, to the suffering: "You must learn to forgo all personal desires and to surrender completely. And to surrender does not mean . . . fading away with grief, but offering what little assistance I can wherever it has pleased God to place me."[41]

Weil's construct of attention as the process of "emptying" oneself for the other marks the distinction between the ethics of equality and reciprocity in Stein and Frank and the ethics of receptivity and acceptance in Hillesum.

Hillesum's resistance to the Nazis' irresistible logic of destruction represents what would normally be considered an illogical response of selfless sympathy with the afflicted other. She reasons: "Why am I in such a hurry to share the deprivations of those behind barbed wire? There is an iron band round my skull and the debris of a whole city weighs down on my head. I really do not want to be a sick, dry leaf dropping from the stem of the community."[42] She refuses exemption from Westerbork because she cannot and will not stay away from those who suffer. Affection and responsibility, as she sees them, are the forces that allow her to generate the strength needed "to bear real suffering, your own and the world's."[43]

The feeling of complete devotion enabled Hillesum to endure the hopelessness of the situation. Paradoxically, she found hope and strength in the ability to accept and to endure hopelessness. Her metaphorical self-representation, "My heart is the floodgate for a never-ending tide of misery,"[44] seems to embody Frankl's postulation of meaning in suffering. She found the meaning of life in shifting her attention from herself to the other.

The freedom that Hillesum found in her "self-givenness" to the other's needs turned into a source of empowerment at the time of terror. The sense of control in giving up control enabled her to attain a sense of potency that erected a protective shield against despair. As the exclusive focus of Hillesum's attention and devotion, the suffering inmates of Westerbork became the liberating raison d'être of her own existence.

Between "Self-Givenness" and Self-Offering

We have observed in Hillesum's response to suffering a representation of Weil's ethical theory, but we must not remain under the impression that Weil was not willing to practice what she believed to be the meaningful attitude toward suffering. In fact, time and again Weil requested permission to perform sacrificial acts for the afflicted. In contrast to Hillesum, however, who went to serve the inmates of Westerbork, Weil never experienced the situation of the victims of the Nazi persecution.

While Hillesum found meaning in concrete ways of alleviating the physical and mental hardship of her fellow inmates, Weil sought meaning in a spectacular act of self-offering. In her striving for total self-sacrifice, Weil, in a way, surpassed her own teachings. The concept of annihilation of the ego in total acceptance of the afflicted transformed into the passion for physical annihilation as both an emblem of ultimate suffering and a symbol of redemption.

Weil was not allowed to sacrifice herself for the suffering world, despite her struggle with the authorities to enable her to implement her plans. Her lonely death of starvation, allegedly out of solidarity with the suffering French people under Nazi occupation, demonstrates the intensity of her self-sacrificial passion. Its suicidal undertones confront us with the problematic of self-offering as a mode of resistance.

Weil left France with her parents in 1942, fleeing the Nazi anti-Jewish persecution. She agreed to go in exile very reluctantly, and soon after her arrival in New York she began a desperate campaign to return to Europe. Writing to her old friend Maurice Schumann, she asked for his assistance in securing a permit to go to London. "I imagine," Weil wrote, "you are in a position to help me, and I urgently beg for your support. I really believe I can be useful; and I appeal to you as comrade to get me out of the too painful moral situation in which I find myself."[45]

Weil provides a twofold rationale for her return: the morally painful situation of exile from France, and her useful service to the Free French Front in London. As discussed before, Weil was mortified by her departure from France, which she considered a despicable betrayal. We should recall that Weil was raised in an assimilated family, imbued with patriotic love for France. In World War I, her father, Dr. Bernard Weil, served as an army physician, taking along his family to the towns in which he was stationed.[46] In a sense, Weil's desire to serve France under German occupation can be seen as following her father's model.

But it was not only the family tradition of patriotic service that motivated Weil's return. An urgent emotional need superseded all other considerations. As she perceived it, the abandonment of her country under duress contradicted the very essence of her Weltanschauung, or meaning of life, which she defined in her "Spiritual Autobiography." Her departure from the suffering country seemed an inglorious ending of her lifelong struggle to attain the state of mind of total attention to the afflicted.

Thus Weil's argument that she could be of use to the Free French Committee was not empty rhetoric. In fact, Weil was returning to Europe with a plan for the world's moral rescue. The project, entitled "Plan for an Organization of Front-Line Nurses," suggested a humanitarian mission. A group of nurses were to be sent to the most dangerous battlefields of Europe to care for the wounded soldiers.

Weil realized that an unarmed group of women could offer hardly any practical aid under fire, but the merit of the plan, she claimed, lay in its moral value. First, the "moral support to all those [soldiers that the nurses] assisted would be . . . inestimable."[47] Second, the mission would be an adequate response to the S.S. "heroism [which] originates from an extreme brutality."[48] The services "performed by women and with maternal solicitude" will deliver "a signal of defiance of the inhumanity which the enemy has chosen for himself and which he compels us also to practise."[49]

Weil's plan of front-line nurses was dismissed by the Free French Committee as yet another impractical thought of a brilliant thinker. Nevertheless, quite a few scholarly works on Weil have related sympathetically to the nurses' corps plan. They tend to present it as evidence of Weil's somewhat naive yet noble and benevolent humanism. Robert Coles and others compare this plan to Weil's other rather eccentric and unsuccessful, but well-meant, ideas to experience the life of the oppressed. These critics remind us that Weil previously went to work in a factory assembly line, that she was a menial worker on farms and in the fields, and that, although she had neither military training nor experience, she went to fight in the Spanish War.[50]

These explanations seem to brush aside the nurses' project as an eccentricity, in order to enhance Weil's image of a "saintly" altruist. However, the nurses' plan represents *more than* a problematic mode of resistance to terror; it also allows an insight into the complexity of Weil's response to have been excluded, as a Jew, from her social setting.

On one level, the plan seems to conform with the humanistic ideal of the Enlightenment. Acts of mercy on the battlefield will demonstrate an unflinching faith in the eventual victory of humaneness over barbarism. These exemplary deeds will restore the world's humanistic value-system based on kindness and compassion. The humanitarian aspect of the operation responds to the need to help the suffering victims of the war.

From this point of view, the plan demonstrates the importance that Weil attached to humanistic values and ethics. She was aware of the moral downfall not only of the enemy soldier but of the Resistance fighter as well. War, she implies, destroys moral fiber and engenders despair, cruelty, and oppression. In this respect, her plan clearly communicates her concern for the world. The sight of the nurses under fire, Weil argues, "would be a spectacle so new, so significant, and charged with such obvious meaning, that it would strike the imagination more than any of Hitler's conceptions have done."[51]

To oppose Hitler's barbarism, Weil asserts, we must demonstrate creativity and imagination. And she maintains that to fight against oppression "we ought to create something new. This gift of creation is in itself a sign of moral vitality which will encourage the hopes of those who count upon us."[52]

At another level, however, it is impossible to ignore the fact that Weil's plan to mend the world at war meant sending to death a group of defenseless and untrained women. In fact, Weil acknowledged that the women would undoubtedly be killed—she knew that the mission she proposed was suicidal. Obviously, Weil attached importance to the symbolism of the act itself, not its tragic ramifications. She claimed that the death of the nurses was necessary "to impress the general public."[53] Weil conceded that most of the women would die on the battlefield, but she claimed, with what might be considered unconscionable calculation, that "these losses would be infinitesimal in number, on the scale of the war."[54]

As a "remedy" for the world's moral sickness, the plan reveals, on the one hand, caring and concern for humanity, and on the other hand, a certain insensitivity about fellow humans that verges on callous irresponsibility. In terms of Weil's philosophy of ethics, however, the plan reveals a deep, even if controversial, ethical dimension. In the framework of the asymmetrical relationship between self and other, the sacrifice for the dying soldiers is not intended to restore the liberal-humanistic order of reciprocity, but rather to introduce a new order grounded in the receptivity of selfless love and sacrificial attention to the afflicted. In this sense, the inevitable death of the nurses is symbolic of the new order in which the other's need precedes mine. The quixotic nature of Weil's plan draws attention to her vision of saving the world through interpersonal-sacrificial relations.

In this sense, the plan is not just one of Weil's impractical but well-meant ideas, as some of Weil's supporters would have it. On the contrary, because she intended, of course, to be the leader of the nurses' corps, the subtext of the plan reveals its author's personal plea for the opportunity to offer herself for the oppressed.

This intention of self-offering emerges clearly in the alternative plan that Weil devised in response to the rejection of the nurses' plan. Once she had realized that the nurses' squad would not be allowed to materialize, she offered herself to be parachuted behind the enemy lines on a mission of sabotage.

Weil's readiness to undertake a solo suicidal mission raises the possibility that her previous plan of the nurses articulated, in fact, an unconscious, or perhaps conscious, wish to die in an act of self-sacrifice. As both plans clearly show, her aim was not to work for the Resistance, but rather to die for it. In her final letter to Maurice Schumann, written shortly before her death, Weil unequivocally reveals her true intentions:

> The proposition [to be parachuted in France] I put to you—the proposition of the scapegoat—is an easy one for me. It implies nothing more than was incumbent on me in any case. . . . There is no possible half-way house for me between total sacrifice and cowardice. And I really cannot make the second choice. . . . There is something stronger in me that forbids it.[55]

Weil's "proposition of the scapegoat" spells her true intention. The paradigm of "total sacrifice" and "cowardice" demonstrates the unmitigated, radical way in which Weil determined her life's goals. The options she established were either death or irredeemable disgrace.

Weil's position of "total sacrifice" suggests an inner preoccupation that transcends the ethical concern for the moral state of the world at war. The biblical reference of the sacrificial "scapegoat" signals the component of religious faith in this inquiry of resistance. Ostensibly, Weil offers to fight the German occupier as any Resistance fighter, but her sense of mission—of this, as she calls it, "something stronger" that commands her to the absolute obedience of a self-sacrificial scapegoat—implies a religious component that transcends both the reciprocal and the receptive parameters of resistance.

There is no doubt that for Weil the act of resistance amounts to self-sacrificial death. In fact, death was something she ardently desired. "I always believed," she confesses in her "Spiritual Autobiography," "that the instant of death is the center and object of life. . . . It is the instant when . . . pure truth, naked, certain, and eternal, enters the soul."[56] This statement raises the question as to the nature of this truth that Weil wished so passionately to attain in the agony of a violent, self-sacrificial death.

In the same letter in which she presented "the proposition of the scapegoat," Weil shares her devastation at being unable "to think with truth at the same time about the affliction of men, the perfection of God, and the link between the two," and she admits to "have the inner certainty that this truth . . . will be revealed only when I myself am physically in affliction, and in one of the extreme forms in which it exists at present."[57]

Weil knows that the truth of the ultimate meaning of life lies in the reconciliation of the extremes of the divine goodness—"the perfection of God," with human suffering—"the affliction of men." She also knows that the connection between these two apparently mutually exclusive components of existence becomes evident in the moment of physical agony.

Weil's desire to become a self-sacrificial scapegoat is significant to this discussion of the four women's perception of the suffering other. Weil's desire to offer herself for the other opens a new direction in our discussion of resistance. The focus seems to shift from the search for ways to connect with the other to the search for ways to understand God's connection with the afflicted humanity. Would it be possible to argue that the reality of the war atrocities and of the Final Solution motivated, or at least intensified, the quest for an understanding of the contradictory coexistence of apocalyptic affliction and the divine?

Weil suggests that self-sacrificial death is both an expression of faith in providential justice and a path to understanding God's ways. It is interesting that she detects the manner of suffering that will lead her to truth in "the extreme forms in which [affliction] exists at the present." Could it be that Weil was unconsciously relating her dismay at the affliction of the Jews in death camps? This is, of course, merely a conjecture, because Weil specifies neither the forms of affliction nor their extremity, nor does she mention the victims. Yet she must have been aware, as the three other women were, that as a Jew she was the victim of not only a global war but also an unprecedented plan of genocide.

The traumatic confrontation of the four assimilated women with their official identification as Jews resulted in searing identity crises. Yet none of the women made their Jewishness the starting point or center of their self-reflection, at least not on the conscious level. Rather, they emphasized their humanity in the world ruled by dehumanizing terror. And so the issue of the meaning of suffering in a reality that condemned them to suffering became extremely pertinent. At the same time, the enormity of the world's suffering and of their own suffering effected a quest for an understanding of the interrelationships between the notion of the divine and affliction. Such a quest reveals the four women's resistance to terror in valiant yet extremely complex efforts to affirm their spiritual selves.

PART TWO

RESISTANCE AND
RELIGIOUS IDENTIFICATION

4

BETWEEN ECUMENISM
AND ANTI-JUDAISM

Before God, then, Jew and Christian both labor at the same task. To us [Jews] he gave eternal life by kindling the fire of the Star of his truth in our hearts. Them [the Christians] he set on the eternal way by causing them to pursue the rays of that Star of his truth for all time unto the eternal end.

—Franz Rosenzweig

Did you ever think
that you were not one of the chosen people
that it was undoubtedly difficult
to be Jewish,

. . . .

Who would have thought, Anne Frank,
that being Jewish
was like being under death's sinister,
swift heels?

—Marjorie Agosín

The issue of human suffering in God's world is not new. The need to understand the mutually exclusive truths of the divine, perfect justice and of the injustice of human pain and misery has preoccupied thinkers, theologians, and believers throughout the history of humankind. However, Weil's notion that she can reach the divine truth of affliction only at the moment of her ultimate sacrifice for France is puzzling on some accounts. Most conspicuous is that it raises the painful problem of Weil's total silence about the Holocaust. We note that Weil wanted to die for France and starved herself to death for the French people under occupation at the time when her own people were suffering the incomparably more horrific decree of the Final Solution. I discuss the complex issue of Weil's silence and her anti-Semitic sentiments in later chapters.

A related problem emerges in the enigmatic connection that Weil makes between the rationale for her desire to die and the manner in which she wanted to die. The suffering that she wanted to endure in order to discover the truth about God's justice was at the same time meant to be a spectacular demonstration of her unconditional love for France. Weil clearly felt that the truth of God's mysterious ways would emerge at the moment of ultimate affliction suffered for France. She interrelates the issue of divine justice and the issue of self-sacrificial death with the issue of her patriotic loyalty, and thus establishes what seems to be an abstruse connection between her search for divine justice and her relationship with her occupied homeland.

The association between these seemingly unrelated issues of theological and civic nature illuminates the problem of religious identity that the four women confronted at the time of their abrupt, brutal social displacement. The theological discussion of suffering in a world created in the image of divine perfection focuses on God's moral attributes. In a world at war, at the time of terrible suffering of humanity at large, the question of God's goodness, mercy, and justice, and of the nature of God's moral interference in the world, becomes particularly poignant for the believer.

In the reality of the Holocaust, however, the genocide inflicted on the Jewish people raised a further question about the identity of the Divine – that is, the Final Solution raises the absurd issue of God's religious denomination. The question is absurd, because the monotheistic notion of God's ultimate perfection can hardly be defined in terms of a specific religious dogma. Yet the Final Solution implied destruction of the Jewish God. The plan to exterminate the Jews signified the intention to obliterate the God of the Chosen People.

It is true, of course, that the Nazi regime condemned Jews to death on the basis of racist anti-Semitism. People were sent to concentration camps because they were descended from Jewish families and therefore, in terms of their genealogy, were identified as Jews. When confronted with the decree, the assimilated Jews had to face their Jewish identity, which declared them outcasts in their native social surroundings. The predicament of Jewish identity brought forth the issue of Jewish faith. As the writings of Stein, Weil, Frank, and Hillesum show, the plight of anti-Semitic persecution elicited a search for God as a source of consolation and support in the moment of terrible social exclusion. This search followed a universalist pattern that is characteristic of assimilated enlightened Jews. Their quest for the meaning of their persecution elicited questions that were not specifically Jewish but rather imbued with the spirit of Christian humanism.

The four women never gave up on the world that had outlawed them. From their seclusion, in their writings, they continued to struggle to maintain a "humanizing discourse," as Arendt calls it, with a world that had ceased to be humane. However, in the reality of exile, degradation, deprivation, and imminent death, adherence to the ideals of humanism and enlightenment was not sufficient to fend off despair. The people who had been declared subhumans needed a concept of the Divine that would support them in their struggle to maintain a sense of dignity and of belonging.

It might be plausible to conjecture that because the genocide of the Jews was conceived and implemented by Christians, the Christian God assumed in Jewish eyes the image of a vengeful, triumphalist God. Yet none of the four women denounced Christianity. Moreover, while seeking the compassionate Divine, none of them turned to the Jewish religious tradition for solace and comfort. Even in the terrible distress of impending death, none sought the love of the Jewish God. To a larger or lesser degree, all four continued to adhere to the Christian idea of divine love.

Stein, who is said to have declared that she saw "the truth" after having read the life of Saint Teresa of Avila,[1] took the vows of a Carmelite in 1933, retiring from the world at the time of daily intensifying persecutions against Jews. Weil, the unbaptized Catholic, related in her 1942 "Spiritual Autobiography" how in 1938, while "concentrating all my attention" on Herbert's poem "Love," "Christ himself came down and took possession of me."[2] Weil concludes the letter with a confession that reiterates her desire for martyrdom: "Every time I think of the crucifixion of Christ, I commit the sin of envy."[3] Hillesum clearly identified with Jesus when she wrote in Westerbork: "I have broken my body like bread and shared it out among men. . . . We should be willing to act as balm for all wounds."[4] And Frank's search for God led her to realize that the evidence of God's benevolence is found in nature: "Anyone who is afraid should look at nature and see that God is much closer than most people think."[5]

In order to explore the significance of this persistent inclination toward Christianity, we need to return briefly to the formative, post-Emancipation upbringing of the four women. At this point, we can begin to understand Weil's unflinching loyalty to France, which not only had accepted her as an equal citizen but also drew her to the Christian faith. In the context of the history of Western Jewish Emancipation, Weil's national and religious adherence reflects, at the ideological level, the prewar general tendency of assimilated Jews to identify with the Christian world.

The post-Emancipation, prewar cultural Jewish milieu exerted on Jews a strong attraction to Christianity. Enlightened Jews perceived Christianity as a universal religion whose message of forgiveness, compassion, and love for humankind made it appear preferable to the apparent rigidity and severity of the Jewish Law.

In the atmosphere of humanism based on equality and brotherhood, the accultur-ated Jews felt free in Christian circles, away from the restricting forms of Jewish life. Many of them embraced Christianity.

Conversion was common: Heine converted and so did Rahel Vernhagen, and both Husserl and Scheler were converts. Judaism was considered to be the religion of the past, superseded and complemented by Christianity. Henri Bergson, for instance, saw Catholicism as "the complete fullfilment of Judaism" and claimed that Judaism, "a religion which was still essentially national," had been "replaced by a religion [Christianity] that could be made universal."[6] Martin Buber, in his early writings, considered Jesus "a great brother" and a "messianic personality" because, according to Buber, Jesus worshiped the eternal Thou instead of focusing on a dogma-centered faith. Buber claimed that Jesus, "seen from the standpoint of Judaism, is the first in the series of men who, stepping out of the hiddenness of the servant of the Lord, . . . acknowledged their Messiahship in their souls and in their words."[7]

Some thinkers were trying to reconcile the differences between the two reli-gions. After his famous "re-conversion" to Judaism, Franz Rosenzweig focused on the Sinaitic Revelation as the connecting link between Judaism and Chris-tianity.[8] Rosenzweig compares Judaism to the "fire" of the Revelation, and Christianity to the "rays." Judaism moves inward. As the Chosen People, the "Jewish nation's concern [is] for and with itself." Christianity, on the other hand, moves onward.[9] Rosenzweig claimed: "Rootedness in the profoundest self . . . had been the secret of the eternity of the eternal [Jewish] people. Diffusion throughout all that is outside—this is the secret of the eternity of the eternal [Christian] way."[10] Thus the roles of the two religions are balanced.

Rosenzweig, who died in 1928, before the rise of the Nazis, did not consider, as Richard Cohen explains, the history of the oppression of European Jews to be a genuinely Christian behavior. Rosenzweig argued that anti-Semitic attitudes come from the part of the Christian world which is still pagan—that is, not yet touched by the love of the Revelation.[11]

It is interesting that the converted Catholic thinker Jacques Maritain saw the Christian oppression of Jews in a similar way.[12] Maritain claimed that anti-Semitism "de-Christianizes Christians and leads them to paganism."[13] Anti-Semitism, according to Maritain, is anti-Christian, "a pathological phenomenon which indicates the deterioration of Christian conscience. . . . The bitter zeal of anti-Semitism always turns in the end into a bitter zeal against Christianity itself."[14] As James Schall claims, "Maritain maintained that the destiny of the world itself was concerned with, dependent on, the reconciliation of Israel and Christianity."[15]

Not all Christian and Jewish thinkers of the post-Emancipation era were as ecumenical and tolerant as Rosenzweig and Maritain. Lionel Gossman reminds us that the anti-Judaism of the neohumanists, and especially of Hegel, was often indistinguishable from anti-Semitism. In Hegel's efforts to reconcile Hellenism and Christianity, Gossman says, Hegel denigrated Judaism. For instance, Hegel claimed that "the holy was always outside [the Jews], unseen and unfelt," that "the Jews [were to be] equal [as subjects of a tyrant] because they were all incapable of self-subsistence," and that "an essential of their religion was the performance of a countless mass of senseless and meaningless actions."[16] Writers such as Richard Wagner and Paul Anton de Lagarde in Germany and Emile Burnouf in France "imagined a Christianity completely cleansed of Judaism," and theologians such as Adolf von Harnack "argued for the independence of Christianity from a petrified and legalistic Judaism and advocated the removal of the Old Testament from the Bible."[17]

Some thinkers of Jewish origins were as intolerant and as slanderous toward Judaism as their Christian counterparts. For Ludwig Feuerbach, "Jewish 'particularism' is sheer 'egoism.' " Feuerbach claimed that the Jew worships himself rather than God and that Judaism is therefore "egoism in the form of religion."[18] Karl Marx argued that "the profane basis of Judaism . . . [is] practical need, self-interest," that the "worldly cult" of the Jew is "huckstering," and that his "worldly god" is "money."[19]

This brief outline of post-Emancipation approaches to Judaism, both Jewish and Christian, illustrates the diversity of anti-Judaism positions. This polarity establishes a spectrum of the Christian-Jewish relationships and thus helps situate the varying responses of the four women to their Jewish identity in their historical settings.

Despite their strong Christian affinities—in a reality that declared them Jewish—the encounter these four women had with their Jewish identity was unavoidable. We therefore need to explore their self-assertion in the face of the terror as both Christians and Jews—Christians by choice, Jews by decree. How did they relate to such an ambivalent religious position? Did they accept the imposed Jewish identification, or did they rebel against it? Did they try to reconcile both, or did they opt to deny their Jewishness?

Stein and Weil seem to occupy opposing poles of the spectrum. Through her phenomenological view of empathy, Stein asserted an identity that encompassed both her Christian self and her Jewish self. Weil, on the other hand, saw herself as Christian. Openly hostile to Judaism, she rejected her Jewish origins and strove desperately to obliterate herself as a Jew. Hillesum and Frank never denied their Jewish identities; they acknowledged their Jewishness and identified with their fellow Jewish victims of the Final Solution. Although both, especially Hillesum, demonstrated closeness to the Christian idea of God, each developed a concept of a deity whose universality transcended religious dogmas. The next chapter explores their contrasting attitudes to their Jewish selves.

5

STEIN AND WEIL:
DIVERGING RESPONSES TO JEWISH
AND CHRISTIAN TRADITIONS

> I was almost relieved to find myself now involved in the common fate
> of my [Jewish] people. . . . I spoke to our Saviour and told Him that I
> knew that it was His Cross which was now being laid on the Jewish
> people . . . [and that] those who did understand [it] must accept it
> willingly in the name of all. I wanted to do that, let Him only show
> me how.
>
> —Edith Stein

> I . . . have certainly inherited nothing from the Jewish religion. . . .
> If . . . the law insists that I consider the term "Jew," whose meaning I
> do not know, as applying to me, I am inclined to submit. . . . But I
> should like to be officially enlightened on this point.
>
> —Simone Weil

The Problem of the Jewish Self

Edith Stein converted to Catholicism in 1922 and took the vows of the Carmelite
Order in 1933. As painful as it was to her family and Jewish friends, and as baffling
as it was even to her Catholic advisers, Stein's conversion seems, by all accounts,
to be authentic. There is therefore no doubt that Stein died a Christian. At the
same time, as a considerable body of evidence demonstrates, Stein remained loyal
to her Jewish roots and publicly proclaimed her Jewish identity. She never
denied her Jewish origins. On the contrary, in the aftermath of the outburst of
German anti-Semitism in the 1930s, she adamantly and consistently admitted her
Jewish identity.

In her memoir of 1938, Stein recalled her response to the intensifying anti-Jewish hostilities in 1933: "God's hand lay heavy on His people, and [the] destiny of this people was my own." She submitted two requests for a private papal audience in order to intercede for German Jews, but was refused.[1]

In 1936, having completed her magnum opus, *Bounded and Unbounded Being*, Stein learned that the treatise could not be published under her name, but she refused to adopt a name eligible for the guild of Aryan writers.[2] During a Nazi plebiscite, when the Nazi Party members who did not know she was Jewish offered to drive her to the voting place, Stein courageously stated her position on the National Socialists, replying, "Well, if the gentlemen attach such importance to my 'No' vote—I can oblige."[3]

Years later her fellow nuns recalled the pain and anger Stein expressed "when Jews were blackened." They compared Stein and her sister Rosa to Judith and Esther, "the great women of the Old Dispensation [who] . . . by prayer and penance rescued the people of Israel."[4] Stein's final testament, which she composed in 1939, concludes with a prayer for "the Jewish people, . . . for the deliverance of Germany and peace throughout the world, . . . for all my relatives. . . . May none of them be lost."[5] In 1942, when deported from the convent to Westerbork, Stein was heard comforting her sister: "Come, Rosa. We're going for our people."[6]

As these eyewitness accounts—all of them produced by Christians or by Jews who converted to Christianity—demonstrate, Stein's sense of solidarity with the Jewish people intensified with the increasingly dangerous situation for Jews. Simone Weil, on the other hand, presents a painful case of virulent anti-Jewish sentiments. The extent of her intense, hateful attitude toward the Jewish people emerges in one of the final entries in her *Notebooks:*

> The Jews—that handful of uprooted individuals—have been responsible for the uprooting of the whole terrestrial globe. The part they played in Christianity turned Christendom into something uprooted with respect to its own past. . . . Capitalism and totalitarianism form part of this progressive development of uprooting; the Jew-haters, of course, spread Jewish influence. The Jews are the poison of uprooting personified.[7]

Weil did not restrain herself in her condemnation of the role of Judaism in world history. Even though in 1942 the facts about the extermination of the European Jews were well known,[8] she did not change her negative perspective on Jews and Judaism. Weil was still in France when she heard about a detention camp in the Ruhr. She reports about the deported Jews of the Rhineland who "fell quickly into filthiness, an indescribable degradation. Women who had only a little time previously been ladies relieved themselves anywhere, in front of the barracks, within them." In his biography of Weil, Thomas Nevin comments on the "almost sardonic tone" in this description of a most "piteous" scene.[9]

Simone Weil's anti-Jewish sentiments also emerged conspicuously in her vision of postwar France. When in London, the Free French Committee asked Weil to comment on a project entitled "Basis for a Statute Regarding French Non-Christian Minorities of Foreign Origin," which dealt with the problem of the Jewish minority in France after the war. In her remarks, Weil supported actions toward the disintegration of the Jewish community, be it religious or atheistic, in order "to prevent contagion." She claimed: "The existence of such a [Jewish] minority does not represent a good thing; thus the objective must be to bring about its disappearance . . . [through] the encouragement of mixed marriages and a Christian upbringing." In her comments, Weil talks about a homogeneous Christian society that would exercise "protective measures against those who are incapable of participating [in Christian society]."[10]

In Weil's vision of postwar France, the Jews who will not become Christians will endanger the "authentic spirituality"—that is, the Christian spirituality of the country. Weil expresses the stereotypical xenophobic attitudes toward Jews: after the war, in her view, they will be an ethnic-religious minority that will constitute a threat to the majority and will therefore have to be eliminated either through conversion or through other "protective measures."

Weil did not merely theorize about the future of the Jewish minority in France. Her own conduct at the time of the war reflects an unequivocal disassociation from her Jewish origins. Weil's repudiation of her Jewish identity culminates in a letter she wrote in 1940 to the Vichy minister of national education concerning the Statute on Jews, which barred Jews from teaching positions. Weil wrote not to express any objection about the statute itself, which deprived Jews of their basic right as citizens, but to protest the fact that the statute defined her as a Jew. The letter is an angry, vehement denial of both her religious identification and her ethnic Jewish identification. Insofar as Jewish religion is concerned, Weil wrote, the statute, which defined a Jew as "a person who has three or more Jewish grandparents," did not apply to her because two of her grandparents were free-thinkers. Insofar as the Jewish race is concerned, she felt no affiliation with "the people who lived in Palestine two thousand years ago." Weil denied any Jewish connection when she argued: "If there is a religious tradition that I regard as my patrimony, it is the Catholic tradition. In short: mine is the Christian, French, Greek tradition; the Hebraic tradition is alien to me, and no Statute can make it otherwise."[11]

This letter is a rare and probably unique instance of Weil's open admission of her Jewish parentage, even if only to repudiate it. In view of the Nazi racist definition of Jewish identity, her protest identified her as a Jew. In a world ruled by the "irresistible logic of destruction" (to recall Fackenheim), Weil's denial ironically reasserted her Jewish origins and acknowledged the rules of destruction. Indeed, two years later Weil and her parents were fleeing to Casablanca to escape "registration," which would have doomed them to deportation and concentration camps.

Even though her enforced exile confronted her unequivocally with the fact that in the eyes of the world she was Jewish, Weil refused to see herself as a Jew. As her letter to the education ministry demonstrates, Weil's anxiety to deny her Jewishness outweighed the risk of drawing attention to herself as a Jew. Considering the consequences that such an act might have entailed, her letter indicates the extent of her desperation to deny her identity.

Weil wanted to deny her Jewishness, but she yearned to be a Christian as well. Her fantasy of having been born a Christian is clearly expressed in her attempt to rewrite her life story. In her "Spiritual Autobiography," written on the eve of her flight from France, Weil consciously evades the issue of her Jewishness altogether. Although her Jewish parentage is never mentioned in the letter—which, after all, claims to be autobiographical—Weil declared: "I always adopted the Christian attitude as the only possible one. I might say that I was born, I grew up and I always remained within the Christian inspiration."[12]

Weil's autobiographical identification as a Christian underlines her dissociation from her Jewish heritage. She behaved as if the pretense of being a born Christian liberated her from responding to the evolving horror of anti-Jewish persecutions. She seemed completely oblivious to the fact that her Jewish origins accounted for her decision to write the "Spiritual Autobiography." The circumstance that compelled her to write was the prospect of exile—Weil, just as in the case of Stein, who was smuggled to Holland, became a fugitive as a result of the Nazi anti-Semitic decrees.

As we have already seen, however, Stein reidentified herself as a Jew and reasserted her solidarity with the nation into which she was born. Whereas Weil's resistance of terror manifested itself in resisting her Jewish self, Stein's resistance reemphasized her Jewish origins.

The Cross and the Issue of Baptism

Stein did not see a contradiction between the Christian faith and identification with the Jewish people. Clearly, she felt Jewish when she denounced Nazi anti-Jewish policies, but at the same time her solidarity with the Jews was articulated through the Christian symbol of the Cross. After her deportation, she affirmed the Cross in a note from Westerbork to the prioress in Echt: "One can only learn a *Sciencia Crucis* if one feels the Cross in one's person."[13] She wanted to emulate Christ's Passion—his suffering—in her own experience of persecution.

The vision of redemption that Stein strove to find in the Church was indelibly linked to her Jewishness, and ineluctably her Jewishness affected her relationship to the Cross. In fact, it was through her consciousness of Jesus' Jewishness that Stein felt a special connection to the Cross. She saw the Jewish plight as the Cross and was ready to accept it in the name of her people. "I was almost relieved to find myself now involved in the common fate of my [Jewish] people. . . . I spoke to our Saviour and told Him that I knew that it was His Cross which was now being laid on the Jewish people . . . [and that] those who did understand [it] must accept it willingly in the name of all. I wanted to do that, let Him only show me how."[14] Acceptance of the Cross was therefore irrevocably connected with her self-identification as a Jew.

It is possible to conjecture, as some of the Carmelite biographers of Stein do, that Stein intended to sacrifice herself for her people in order to bring forth the conversion of the Jews.[15] But even if the plan of conversion motivated her desire for sacrifice, it should be emphasized that Stein never reneged on her loyalty to her family and to her Jewishness. Her autobiography, *Life in a Jewish Family*, in which she asserted her Jewish origins, proves beyond any doubt her sense of belonging to the Jewish people. Thus, rather than conversion from one identity into another, Stein's Weltanschauung denotes convergence of Christian and Jewish identities.

This ability to reconcile original Jewish identity with adopted Christian identity is completely absent in Weil. As we have seen in her "Spiritual Autobiography," Weil's most comprehensive and most significant self-searching introspection, her desire to be a born Christian outweighs autobiographical veracity. Weil was unable to face her Jewish identity even at the traumatic moment of exile, but despite her unequivocal espousal of Christianity she did not convert to Catholicism. Her rejection of baptism demonstrates that she could not accept formal identification as a member of the Catholic Church. In 1942, while striving to come back to Europe, Weil confided in Maurice Schumann, himself a Jew who converted to Catholicism: "Certainly I belong to Christ. . . . But I am kept outside the Church by philosophical difficulties which I fear are irreducible."[16]

Why couldn't Weil actualize her conversion? What were the "philosophical difficulties" that prevented her from having her autobiographical inventions of Christian birth and Christian upbringing formally recognized? While considering these questions, it is interesting to note an oblique connection that Weil makes between conversion and anti-Semitism. On her niece's birth, Weil strongly advised her brother, who married a non-Jew, to baptize his daughter. She wrote to André: "Sylvie would not have the shadow of a reason to regret having been baptized by a priest. . . . If a more or less anti-Semitic piece of legislation grants advantages to baptized half-Jews, it will be agreeable for her, probably, to enjoy these advantages without having done anything cowardly."[17] Weil seems to allude here to conversion as an act of cowardly escape from anti-Semitic legislation. She expressed this opinion at the time anti-Semitic persecution in France became a legal act. Does she imply that her own baptism would be "cowardly" because it might save her from anti-Semitic persecutions, while unbaptized Jews would continue to suffer?

We remember Weil's agony over the possibility that her departure from France might be seen as an attempt to avoid suffering and therefore as an act of cowardice. We might also recall Weil's agony in London when she struggled for her plans for the nurses' squad to sabotage behind the lines to be approved, so that she could offer herself fearlessly for the afflicted. Could it be that, despite her vehement anti-Jewish sentiments, the fear of committing an act of cowardice when other Jews were suffering was the reason for her refusal to be baptized?

In her discussion of Weil, Anna Freud offers an interpretation of Weil's estrangement from Judaism that might shed light on her refusal to be baptized. Freud claims that Weil "was in danger, as all Jews were, and she wanted to be in danger in her own way, on her own terms! She certainly was not a coward. She didn't want to be curbed because of what others thought she was; she wanted to be curbed because of that which she made clear to others she had become."[18]

In light of Freud's observation of Weil's staunch individualism, the difficulty in accepting baptism might have originated in her refusal to conform as a member of the Christian Church. Becoming a member of the Church through baptism would have restrained her individual freedom, a constriction she could not bear. Neither could she accept the allegation that baptism would align her with the "cowardly" others who converted in an attempt to avoid danger.

This interpretation presents Weil's decision not to be baptized at the time of intensifying atrocities against Jews as an act of resistance. In retrospect, of course, we know that baptism did not help Jews to escape the Final Solution. The futility of conversion to Christianity is corroborated by Etty Hillesum, who describes the Jewish converts, among them Stein and her sister Rosa, at Westerbork in one of her letters: "There was a remarkable day when the Jewish Catholics or Catholic Jews—whichever you want to call them—arrived, nuns and priests wearing the yellow star on their habits."[19] Because at the time so many Jews sought the protection of the Church, Weil's decision not to do so can be seen as a refusal to be terrorized into compromising her inner integrity.

If that was the rationale for Weil's rejection of baptism, it reminds us of Stein, who never considered her vocation as a religious as a means of escaping the anti-Semitic danger. It is true that Stein took her vows in 1933, when the Nazis came to power and when the terror against the Jews was increasing in severity. However, her clearly pronounced dismay at the anti-Semitic policy of the National Socialists, her open refusal to vote for them, and her testament all belie the motivation of seeking security in the seclusion of the convent. Moreover, Stein's repeated requests for an audience with the pope to intercede for German Jews, as well as her willingness to "take up the Cross for her people," attest to her openness about her Jewishness. Her unshaken sense of solidarity with the per-secuted Jews, despite her affiliation with the Christian Church, bespeaks a courageous act of resistance.

The resistance in Simone Weil's refusal to be baptized communicates a differ-ent message. Her view of baptism as an act of cowardly escape from anti-Semitic legislation did not signify feelings of solidarity with the Jewish people. On the contrary, her refusal to become a baptized member of the Church communicated her unwillingness to belong to any institutionally defined body, Jewish or Chris-tian. Thus, to Weil, seeking security in the Church would not only signify cowardice but also exact the price of limiting her intellectual freedom. Weil felt that joining the Church would compromise her lifelong condemnation of the collective. Collectivity, according to Weil, is the source of evil; it distances human beings from the grace of the impersonal. The notion of "we," she claims in "Human Personality," is dangerous because collectivity subdues the soul and destroys it, because it is a force that deprives one of the sacred, and, worse, because it is a "false imitation" of the sacred.[20]

Weil saw the negative qualities of the collective structure in the Church. In a letter to Father Perrin, she wrote: "There is a Catholic circle ready to give an eager welcome to whoever enters it. Well, I do not want to be adopted into a circle, to live among people who say 'we' and to be part of an 'us.' "[21] As Weil saw it, the "Catholic circle" – the Church's hierarchical structure – had become the parody of the Church's original objectives: "Christ expressly forbade his followers to seek authority and power, [but] today if a son of Jewish or atheist parents is baptized, this means that he is joining . . . the Church . . . in the same way that by holding a political party's card he becomes a member of the party."[22]

Weil certainly did not want to become a member of the Church in order to gain protection granted by membership in a powerful establishment. Such a member-ship in the collective body would encroach on the practice of what she defined as the "three strictly individual faculties": "love, faith and intelligence."[23] Determined to be free of any social structure that required collective obedience, Weil remained outside the Church.

The fact that Weil did not renege on her convictions at a time when her own existence was increasingly endangered attests to her courage. Her refusal to accept the protection of the Church for ethical and spiritual reasons reminds us of Hillesum's refusal to go into hiding. In both cases, the two women preferred to risk their lives rather than submit to the exigencies of the situation.

But Weil did not stop at refusing the Church on the grounds that it was a collective and, as such, a dogmatic body that limits the freedom of the individual. She also set herself as a critic and a reformer of the Church, while at the same time being aware of the radical and therefore unacceptable nature of the changes she proposed.

Weil knew that the Church could not accommodate her "philosophical difficulties" and would therefore not grant her the privilege of the sacraments. Her predicament in relation to the Church thus represents a double-bind situation. She could not be baptized because her philosophical queries would lead to the injunction of excommunication, the *anathema sit*. Ironically, this authoritarian injunction, which forbade intellectual thinking except within the bounds of defined dogma, was the main target of her attack on the Church.[24]

What were the heretical "philosophical difficulties" that precluded Weil's integration into the Church? Weil's thought undermines the Church by invalidating its historical-revelatory connection to Judaism. In place of the principle of the historicity of human moral and spiritual evolution, she substitutes the principle of humankind's ahistorical development. While the Church grounds its authenticity by declaring itself to be the pinnacle in human-evolving spirituality, Weil repudiates the Christian notion of the inferiority of the pagan religions that preceded the Church. In other words, Weil dismisses the dogma that the Christian religion superseded other, heathen religious systems, which were not subject to the Revelation.

Weil believed that "one identical thought is to be found . . . in the ancient mythologies," a thought that exists "in the philosophies of Pherekydes, Thales, Anaximander, Heraclitus, Pythagoras, Plato, and the Greek Stoics; in Greek poetry of the great age; in universal folklore; in the Upanishads and the Bhagavad-Gita; in the Chinese Taoist writings; in what remains of the sacred writings of Egypt; in the dogmas of the Christian faith and in the writings of the greatest Christian mystics . . . and in certain heresies, especially the Cathar and Manichean tradition."[25] Therefore, "for Christianity to become truly incarnated . . . it must first of all be recognized that, historically, our profane civilization is derived from a religious inspiration which, although chronologically pre-Christian, was Christian in essence."[26]

The idea of a Christ who coexisted with God since the creation of the world is not new. For example, the hymn in the Prologue to the Gospel of John utilizes the concept of the *Logos* to name "the preexistent mythical wisdom figure from the realm of Light." The hymn presents Jesus as the preexistent Redeemer.[27] Not unlike the early church fathers, Weil claimed that "Greek geometry and the Christian faith have sprung from the same source."[28] In this respect, she emphasized the archetypal timelessness of the Christian faith.

According to Weil, the Christian faith needed to be restored to its own truth. The reformation of Christianity that she proposed was not merely the reaffirmation of the universality of the essential nucleus of Christian thought across time, but rather the excision of its Jewish roots. The Church, Weil claimed, had inherited the ambition for greatness from Israel and Rome, but under the influence of these powers, the Church, through its missionary zeal, had become a totalitarian, colonizing power in its own right.[29] To remedy this evil, Weil planned to rewrite history. Without any evidence to support her claim, she asserted that history had been willfully falsified in the early Christian period[30] and argued that "any [Christian writings] in which Israel's privileged position was not recognized . . . have been suppressed."[31]

Weil's approach falters because the idea of Christianity being corroborated in all true (especially Greek) philosophy, not in Israelite and Judaic thought, ignores the commitment to a history of salvation that unites Judaism and Christianity and erases the distinction between Christians and the pagan *gentes*.

Every attempt to make Christanity into an ahistorical, "gnostic" system of salvation—and, we might imagine, Weil's attempt to do so as well—has been judged by historical Christendom to be heretical. All branches of Christianity have consistently claimed an absolutely unique connection between New Testament (Christian) and Old Testament (Jewish) revelation. To cite one example among many, according to the eighteenth-century Christian thinker Giambattista Vico, the chosenness of Israel validates Christianity, which arose out of Judaism. The existence of the Christian religion, according to Vico, is predicated on the Hebrews "[who] were the first people in our world and . . . [who] in the sacred history truthfully preserved their memories from the beginning of the world."[32]

The theological concept of the universal prefiguration of Christ's Passion, which, Weil proposed, would have severed Christianity from its Jewish sources. Weil was fully aware of the enormity of her proposed reform. Indeed, she admitted that her baptism, if actualized, would constitute "a break . . . with a tradition which has lasted at least seventeen centuries."[33] Note that Weil proposed this break within the Christian tradition at a time when the Jewish people were being systematically annihilated. It is almost too painful to appreciate the irony that the demand that the Jewish component of the Christian doctrine be eliminated was made at the time of the Holocaust by a Jew as a condition for her baptism. However, this seems to be what Weil considered a burning issue at that particular time:

> If this break [from the dogma] is just and desirable, if precisely in our time it is found to be of more than vital urgency for the well-being of Christianity— which seems clear to me—for the sake of the Church and the world it should then take place with bursting impact and not with the isolated initiative of one priest performing one obscure and little known baptism.[34]

Weil ostensibly refused baptism on the grounds of the larger interests of the Christian Church and of the world as a whole, but it is important to remember that, had it been actualized, the reform she proposed would have served her needs of self-obliteration as a Jew. If baptized under the existing dogma, she would still be maintaining links with Israel through the Church. The reconstruction of the Christian doctrine through an acknowledgment of its pagan roots would have given her a new identity, free of any trace of her Jewish origins. Such transformation would have defined Weil's baptism literally as an act of spiritual rebirth in that she would have rerooted herself in the heritage and tradition of universal, ahistorical mythologies.

The Self-Denying Jew and the "Catastrophe Jew"

On the paradigm of ecumenism and anti-Judaism, Weil's theological thought is diametrically opposed to that of both Rosenzweig and Maritain, who certainly believed in the historical evolution of religious-ethical values. In fact, we shall recall both thinkers' perception of anti-Semitism as the vestiges of a pagan element in Christianity. They also maintained that cultivation of the view that the two religions complement each other is the only way to actualize the true meaning of the Sinaitic Revelation.

Weil's view of a Christianity *sans* its Jewish foundations—a Christianity that finds its roots in pagan traditions—seems to stem from an anti-Jewish tradition represented by the neohumanist thinkers. As we mentioned before, such thinkers as Hegel and Wagner sought to establish an affinity between Christianity and

Hellenism by disparaging the Jewish tradition or eliminating it from the Christian dogma altogether.

Weil's attitude toward Judaism has disturbed both her critics and her admirers. Even her most inspired readers have been trying to come to terms with what appears to be a serious flaw in the overall picture of her saintly dedication to the oppressed. Almost all students of Weil's religious thought express reservations regarding her anti-Jewish attitude. For example, Weil's closest Catholic advisers remember being surprised at her clearly pronounced animosity toward Jews. Father Perrin recalls that at their first meeting he "was struck by her hostility towards the Jewish people," and G. Thibon remembers that Simone Weil had "a kind of ideological and religious repulsion regarding the Jews."[35]

Some critics felt the need to account for what seems to be a blatant lack of moral integrity. J. Viard's argument that Weil's lack of sympathy for the Jewish people is attributable to her universalist politics[36] is supported by Conor Cruise O'Brien, who explains Weil's anti-Jewish attitude and her refusal of baptism as a "significant expression of what I call her antipolitics; her radical rejection of all limited associations."[37] Robert Coles claims that Weil's "outrageous, unqualified generalizations—about . . . the Jews of Old Testament times—seem at least understandable in the context of a world almost ready to destroy itself, hence in need of a thoroughly radical penetration of intellect."[38] J. M. Cameron deplores Weil's misinterpretation of the biblical tradition, yet he claims that, despite it, Weil "remains one of the most remarkable women of our time, one who can be placed with Teresa of Avila and with the two Catherines, of Genoa and of Sienna."[39] Betty McLane-Iles subscribes to the notion that Weil's repudiation of Judaism was a rejection of the linear notion of history as opposed to the Greek conception of cyclicity of time that she embraced."[40]

Even some of Weil's Jewish critics have attempted to attenuate the extremity of her anti-Jewish pronouncements. Wladimir Rabi claims that Weil's attitude generated from a lack of knowledge about Judaism that was typical of French Jewry and insists that, despite everything, "she is ours"—that is, she belongs to the Jewish people.[41] Emmanuel Levinas concedes: "Simone Weil has been accused of ignoring Judaism—and, my word, she has ignored it in a royal way."[42] Yet he claims that "no doubt she was more Jewish than she believed she was."[43]

The tragedy of the Holocaust, claims Nevin, "made Judaism the cross Weil refused to carry." In his attempts to explain Weil's refusal of the Cross that Stein was so eager to bear, Nevin even claims Weil as a *tzeddik* [*sic*], the righteous person, "kicking against the pricks of Judaism" and struggling for the oppressed.[44]

But the truth is that Weil can claim no affinity with the tradition of the rebelling *tzaddik*. She did not "kick against the pricks of Judaism"—she did not protest against injustice to God, as did the great Jewish *tzaddikim,* Abraham, Jeremiah, Rabbi Yitzchak of Berditchev, and others. She certainly did not protest the horrible crimes committed against the Jews. There seems to be little righteousness or justice in Weil's indubitable intention to obliterate both Judaism and herself as a Jew.

Despite the attempts to account for her conduct, Weil's unbroken silence regarding the ongoing extermination of the Jews remains incomprehensible in view of her lifelong advocacy of the oppressed and her devotion to the afflicted. Referring to her silence, George Steiner asks poignantly, "Has there ever been a philosophic thinker on love, at often compelling and originating depths, more loveless?"[45]

It is clear that this "lovelessness" toward her afflicted people cannot be fully, and perhaps not at all, accounted for in terms of the post-Emancipation atmosphere of assimilation. It is true that the desire for acculturation undermined the sense of Jewish identity and, with it, affinity with the Jewish tradition. However, a juxtaposition of Weil's adamant denial of her Jewish connection with the conduct of her two prominent and no less assimilated contemporaries, Marc Bloch and Henri Bergson, demonstrates Weil's atypical extremity.

Like Weil, Marc Bloch, an eminent French Jewish historian, demonstrated unflinching devotion for France. During the war, he joined the French Resistance and was caught and executed by the Gestapo. An assimilated Jew, he was clinging to the ideals of human liberty and equality and endeavored to affirm the motto "civis gallicus sum," despite the unfolding persecutions of the Jews.[46] He considered himself a "good Frenchman" and refused to subscribe to any group that claimed solidarity on the basis of race or ethnicity. Nonetheless, unlike Weil, Bloch never denied his Jewish origins. He acknowledged that he had been "born a Jew," and, in total opposition to Weil, maintained that "the generous tradition of the Hebrew prophets, which Christianity . . . has adopted and expanded, [as] one of the best reasons to live, to believe and to fight."[47]

The great French Jewish philosopher Henri Bergson presents an even more poignant example of identification with the Jewish victims. As mentioned before, Bergson embraced the Christian faith. He openly and unequivocally identified with Catholicism. Unlike Weil, however, who denied her Jewishness in her letter to the Vichy minister, Bergson reaffirmed his Jewishness in view of the anti-Jewish position of the Pétain government. He returned all his awards and medals to the French government, refused to accept the dubious title of an "honorary Arian," and insisted on wearing the yellow star. As early as 1937, Bergson wrote: "My reflections have led me closer and closer to Catholicism, in which I see the complete fulfillment of Judaism. I would have become a convert, had I not seen in preparations for years a formidable wave of Antisemitism, which is to break upon the world. I wanted to remain among those who tomorrow will be persecuted."[48]

It is important to emphasize that Bergson, Bloch, Weil, Stein, Hillesum, and Frank were all to varying degrees affected by the post-Emancipation religious climate that encouraged their affiliation with the Christian faith. Nonetheless, at the time of the historical breakup, Weil was the only one among them who refused to admit any closeness or any relationship with the suffering Jews. Steiner suggests that the problem of Weil's anti-Semitism in view of the unfolding Holocaust is "not only immensely complicated, requiring in any approach the most scrupulous delicacy of inquiry, [but] at many points, highly unpleasant, indeed repellent." The reluctance to explore this issue, Steiner claims, resulted in the predominantly hagiographical approach to Weil.[49]

Indeed, the examples above demonstrate clearly the tendency of Weil's critics to attenuate, excuse, and justify the discrepancy between Weil's love for the afflicted in general and her hostile indifference with regard to the Jewish victims.

Yet, we find an exception to the deferential if disapproving treatment of Weil. In his often mentioned study *Simone Weil ou la haine de soi,* Paul Giniewski dwells on the repellent aspects of Weil's anti-Jewishness and refutes all claims to her sainthood. He sees her philosophy as an erroneous escape from the "Sinaitic revelation into the adoptive family of hierogliphs and pagan idols."[50] Giniewski's portrayal of Weil is that of a pathologically imbalanced, deeply disturbed, self-hating Jew.

Just as the hagiographical approach seems to be an evasion of the issue, so the explication of Weil's anti-Semitic sentiments as mental disturbance seems too facile and hardly accurate. However increasingly eccentric and ill, Weil undoubtedly remained coherent and creative to the very end. Her best-known final work, *The Need for Roots,* reveals a systematically developed and cogently presented analysis of the moral downfall of Europe and a thoughtful proposal of spiritual social reform in the postwar France. *The Need for Roots* was highly praised by the existentialist philosopher Sartre, among other thinkers.[51]

Weil's work has drawn the laudatory attention of some of the foremost minds of our age. She was praised as "the only great spirit of our time" by none other than Albert Camus, who wrote about her work: "Western political and social thought has not produced anything more penetrating and prophetic."[52] T. S. Eliot declared that reading Simone Weil exposed him to "the personality of a woman of genius, of a kind of genius akin to that of the saints."[53] Such exuberant and enthusiastic assessments of Weil as both a thinker extraordinaire and a saintly soul reecho in the considerable body of appraisal of Weil by those who knew her personally[54] as well as by those who studied and responded to her life and work. She influenced many men and women of letters, such as Susan Sontag, Mircea Eliade, Iris Murdoch, and was compared to George Orwell, Dorothy Day, and others.[55] It seems, therefore, quite implausible to explain Weil's anti-Semitism in terms of pathological disturbance and insanity.

It is precisely the long-lasting effect that Weil's work imprinted on the foremost minds of this century that makes the explanation of her anti-Jewish sentiments in terms of her ignorance of Jewish sources quite implausible. Had she wished, Weil, who was erudite in Greek philosophy, Christian theology, and Marxist ideology and who studied the Cathars, the Albigensians, and Far Eastern cultures extensively, could have acquired some rudimentary knowledge of Jewish theology. So the problem seems to lie not in ignorance but in the almost deliberate choice to remain ignorant. For assimilated Jews educated in Christian colleges and universities, the Jewish Law, ritual, and observances represented a rather primitive, backward tradition that had no relevance for their professional and public "enlightened" lives.

In this sense, Weil was not alone: all four women—all extremely well educated—knew very little about Judaism. But at the time of the Final Solution only Weil manifested total incompatibility with her Jewish self. Stein was able to reconcile her Jewish and Christian identities in her desire to carry the Cross for her people, and Frank and Hillesum identified with the Jewish victims. What, then, caused Weil to single herself out in her unmitigated hatred of her Jewish self?

Jean Améry's notion of "catastrophe Jews" might illuminate more the peculiarity of Weil's problem with her Jewish identity. A Viennese intellectual and writer born in 1912, Améry was the son of a Catholic mother and a Jewish father, and during the war he was an inmate of Buchenwald, Auschwitz, and other concentration camps. Only with the rise of Nazis to power in the 1930s did he become aware of his Jewish identity. Because of its elucidatory power, Améry's coming to terms with his Jewishness under the duress of anti-Semitic persecution belongs in this discussion of Jewish identity at the time of the Final Solution.

In Jean Améry's definition, a "catastrophe Jew" claims loyalty to her ethnic roots because of anti-Semitism. A "catastrophe Jew," is "the Jew without positive determinants,"[56] says Améry, who admits that "solidarity in the face of threat is all that links me with *my* Jewish contemporaries, the believers as well as the non-believers, the national-minded as well as those ready to assimilate."[57]

Améry's distinction between a connection with his "Jewish contemporaries," as opposed to a connection with his Jewish ancestors, is illuminating. "Positive determinants" would have established solidarity through connections with Jewish learning, religion, and heritage. The assimilated Jews, however, knew almost nothing about their tradition, so they could establish only contemporary linkage—

that is, connections created under the circumstances that gave them the collective identity of the haunted Jew. In Améry's view, with the rise of the Nazi terror the assimilated Jews had to face their Jewishness "without God, without history, without messianic-national hope."[58]

Améry's notion of "catastrophe Jews" linked by the negative determinant of communal danger seems to portray quite accurately the responses of Stein, Hillesum, and Frank to the Final Solution. When confronted with their Jewish identity, they were capable of actualizing it through strong feelings of solidarity and compassion. The uniformity of the Jewish fate under the Nazi terror infused meaning into the identity, which until then had been meaningless or even nonexistent.

It is noteworthy that Stein, Hillesum, and Frank were capable of incorporating their sense of Jewishness into their Christian Weltanschauung. Their Christian universalist perspective of love, mercy, and commiseration with the suffering of humankind seems to have facilitated their affinity with other Jews on the basis of the "catastrophe." To ignore their affinity with their suffering brothers and sisters would in this sense be a transgression of the Christian spirit, as they understood it. The concept of Christian love clearly shaped Stein's desire to bear the Cross for the Jewish people. The ideas of loving-kindness and attention that we observed in Frank and Hillesum certainly helped to ground their Jewish identity in solidarity with their afflicted fellow Jews.

The notion of a "catastrophe Jew" implies a sense of a community—the community of Jews, who discover their common fate of persecution and exclusion and death. Weil, who in principle rejected the collective, was hardly prepared to accept her identity as a Jew—an identification that classified her as a member of a community unified by the common fate of the Final Solution. And, for that matter, neither could she redefine herself as a "catastrophe Christian"—a Jew who joins the Christian community to avoid anti-Semitic persecution. By contrast, she had discovered that she was herself a Christian in her intellectual pilgrimage uncondi-tioned by historical events.

As we have seen, one reason Weil rejected baptism was that she was reluctant to become a member of a Christian collective. Furthermore, the decision to accept baptism would imply her Jewish origins and, by inference, affirm her kinship with the Jewish community. Her adamant dissociation from her Jewish identity ir-revocably separated her from the community of the Jewish victims, but her refusal to become a member of the Church placed her outside both the Christian commu-nity and the Jewish community.

Améry's notion of the "catastrophe Jew" therefore clarifies the dramatic impli-cations of Weil's desire to escape her Jewish identity. Her self-denial as a Jew precluded connection with Jews; the denunciation of the Jewish religion, history, and heritage also precluded affiliation with the Christian community. Thus, Weil's negation of her Jewish roots ensues in her uprooting, in her total alienation from all social or religious environments. Her existence became the "catastrophe" of self-inflicted estrangement—in a sense, a death to the world. Weil is aware of this situation when she writes to Father Perrin: "I feel that it is necessary and ordained that I should be alone, a stranger and an exile in relation to every human circle without exception. . . . To be lost to view in it is not to form a part of it, and my capacity to mix with all of them implies that I belong to none."[59]

Weil's response to the world, which excluded her as a Jew, was to exclude herself from all social connections. In a paradoxical way, Weil's defiance of the forces of terror complied with the oppressors' plan for eliminating the Jewish people. By constructing a life of loneliness and solitude, Weil attained a tragic state of self-liberation from all human contact. Her self-imposed alienation allowed her to ignore the fact that, as a Jew, she had become the object of destruction. At the same time, her social exclusion corroborated the despotic decree that set Jews apart from human society.

Paradoxically, Weil's desire to become a martyr for France and a reformer of the Catholic Church separated her from the world she so eagerly wanted to mend. In another paradoxical twist, Stein's desire to bear the Cross for her people defined her as both a Christian and a Jew; "the Cross" claimed her part in both communities. Whereas the confrontation with her Jewish self was a devastating blow to Weil's sense of identity, for Stein the reencounter with her Jewish self turned into progression toward inner wholeness.

The historical reality of anti-Jewish terror affected not only patterns of socioreligious behavior, such as Weil's refusal of baptism and Stein's acceptance of the vows. On the emotional level, the predicament of religious identity effected the anguish of the fragmented self and therefore the need for inner reconciliation and peace.

6

STEIN AND WEIL:
BETWEEN SELF-AFFIRMATION
AND SELF-RENUNCIATION

*Only the person who has faith in himself is able to be faithful to others
because only he can be sure that he will be the same at a future time as he
is today and, therefore, to feel and to act as he now expects to.*

—Erich Fromm

*One can resist only in terms of the identity that is under attack. Those
who reject such identifications on the part of the hostile world may feel
wonderfully superior to the world, but their superiority is then truly no
longer of this world.*

—Hannah Arendt

Edith Stein's great-niece, Waultraut Stein, maintains that Stein's "life consists in affirmation and not in renunciation." In agreement with Waultraut Stein, I suggest that Stein affirmed herself by striving to reassert her presence in society. She attempted to do so by reconciling the seemingly irreconcilable aspects of her self—her Christian and Jewish identities. Having been repudiated as a Jew, Stein decided to take the vows, only to face the world once again, now both as a Carmelite and a Jew. The discipline of her phenomenological thought helped her to remain faithful to her past by acknowledging its presence in her unfolding self.

Simone Weil, on the other hand, displayed a growing passion for self-effacement. Having rebelled against both Jewish traditions and against Christian traditions, she intended to terminate her existence by offering her life for suicidal missions for the afflicted. But she did not merely want to die a sacrificial death. As a mystic, she aspired to de-create herself in reconnection with the Divine. Her aspiration for complete — both physical and spiritual — self-renunciation signals an inner conflict, the intensity of which countervails the desire to live. She sought salvation from the torment of exclusion and solitude in the identity of "no longer of this world" — namely, in the nonbeing of submersion in God's love.

Edith Stein: Affirmation of Jewish Self

Edith Stein followed a different path from Weil's. In contrast to Weil, she sought to reconnect with the world in an act of both affirmation and self-affirmation. By "taking up the Cross," she wanted to affirm the link between her Christian and Jewish affiliations. By searching her past, she wanted to attain a sense of wholeness in her dual religious identity. Her attempts to reach inner peace emerge especially in her autobiographical self-reaffirmation as a Jew.

Waultraut Stein maintains: "There seems to be a love in evidence in the figure of Edith Stein that transcends the barriers of prejudice built up over centuries so that the Christian and the Jew may live in peace together to fulfill the biblical prophecy that the lion shall lie down with the lamb."[1] Indeed, the ideal of a world free of both violence and hatred figures prominently in Stein's life and work. Yet Stein does not present us with a vision of the messianic age in which, as Rosenzweig saw it, both religions will become united.[2] Her insistence on her dual Christian-Jewish identity does not seem to lie in an impassioned subscription to eschatological ecumenism. She focuses on the here and now. Rather than raising the vision of distant redemption, she applies her thought and act to the unfolding reality of the terror and persecution of the Jews.

At one level, Stein wanted to save the world through the Cross. She affirmed the Cross and wanted to carry it as a representation of Christ's Passion in her own suffering. By taking up the Cross, she perceived her own suffering as a self-sacrificial act for the sake of her people. In her joining the Carmelites, she saw the possibility of an identification with Christ's Passion, a hope that drew her closer to identification with Jewish suffering.

It is not surprising that Stein's intention to become a Carmelite was completely misunderstood by her family, who thought she was taking the vows to escape persecution: "What I was planning seemed [to them] to draw a yet sharper line between me and the Jewish people — at the moment when it was being so oppressed. [They] could not understand that from my point of view it seemed quite different."[3] Her reason for entering the Carmelite Order was that "it always seemed to me that our Lord was keeping something for me in Carmel which I could find only there." She appeared to reassert her will to take up the Cross when she commented on entering the convent: "It is not human activity that can help us but the Passion of Christ. It is a share in that that I desire."[4]

Stein wanted to penetrate the mystery of the Passion and thus assert her affinity with Christ both as a Jew and as a Christian. Furthermore, she insisted on sacrificing herself for the Jewish people by emulating Christ's Passion. But she did not respond to the plight of her people only on the theological-mystical level. She also sought to rehabilitate the deteriorating sociopolitical reality in practical application of her philosophical findings concerning human interaction. On this level, her identification with the plight of Jews motivated her striving for an empathic encounter among people in which hostility against the Jews had no place.

It is interesting to note the predominant influence of phenomenology on Stein's thought. As a thinker and a writer, Stein was first and foremost a phenomenologist. Even her later theological work demonstrates her indebtedness to phenomenology. Her biographer, Hilda C. Graef, complains about Stein's misinterpretations of mystics, about her "cool and critical language about what is generally considered to be . . . priceless gems of mystical writing." Graef attributes Stein's unsatisfactory approach to mystical theology to "her lack of acquaintance with the relevant theological literature." But there is a more important reason for Stein's inadequacy at mystical writing, according to the biographer. Stein's article on the Greek mystic theologian Dionysius the Areopagite, as well as her last book, an unfinished interpretation of Saint John of the Cross, shows that Stein "was a contemplative, and [that] she necessarily tended to interpret her contemplative experience not as a theologian, but as a phenomenological philosopher which she remained."[5]

The phenomenological—and, may we add, the rational, as opposed to the mystical—in Stein's response to the plight of the Jews emerges in the autobiographical account that she began precisely at the time she decided to make religious vows. She began writing in 1933, at her mother's house, while awaiting her acceptance to Carmel. Stein's autobiographical work represents a practical application of the conclusions concerning empathy that she had reached in her dissertation. Entitled *Life in a Jewish Family,* the account represents a courageous step toward mending the sociopolitical crisis through an empathic act.

It is important to remember that, because of her Jewishness, Stein had just been dismissed from Münster, where she had taught educational theory and worked on the feminist reform of Catholic education. Thus, Stein's decision to write about her Jewish life at that particular moment seems to have been motivated by both moral and emotional needs powerful enough to supersede the compounded anxiety of the expulsion from the Institute and of the decision to take the vocation of a Carmelite.

The foreword to *Life in a Jewish Family* demonstrates Stein's understanding of the gravity of the Jewish situation. Her book, she writes, constitutes a response to the "horrendous caricature" of Jews, which, "as though from a concave mirror," emerges in "the programmed writings and speeches of the new dictators." The memoir, she states, is meant to counteract "the battle on Judaism in Germany" launched by the Nazis.[6] Stein is specific about the readers for whom the memoir is intended, addressing the account to those who lack the formative education for tolerance – mainly "the young [who] are being reared in racial hatred from earliest childhood" and are therefore in need of an adequate lesson in civic ethics.[7]

Recognizing the severity of the crisis, Stein asserts that teaching the young is not a matter of choice but rather, under the circumstances, a vital act of social responsibility. Turning to her Jewish compatriots, Stein argues: "We who grew up in Judaism have an obligation to give our testimony." Her own testimony, as she defines it, "is intended as information for anyone wishing to pursue an unprejudiced study from original sources."[8]

Carefully outlining her educational strategy, Stein eliminates the option to write "an apologia for Judaism," unwilling to justify, defend, or explain Jewish thought, religion, or history. Her stated purpose is to demonstrate – that is, "to give, simply, a straightforward account of my Jewish life as one testimony to be placed alongside others,"[9] to offer a factual, unadorned description of Jewish life.

Under the circumstances, this testimony constitutes an empathic act. Empathy enables a person to relate her experience to another person's experience, and Stein's recollections of her childhood are bound to evoke the readers' childhood memories. Those who were programmed to consider anything Jewish as hateful and hostile will be confronted with Jewish family lives that will undoubtedly remind them of their own families. The measure of identification will determine the extent to which the deprogramming of racist education can be accomplished. The element of empathic intersubjectivity is extremely important for the development of the person's ethical potential, which will unfold in the reader's recognition of the sameness of her experience in Stein's testimony.

In his study of the reading process, Wolfgang Iser analyzes the phenomenology of the act of reading. He claims that "the efficacy of a literary text is brought about by the apparent evocation and subsequent negation of the familiar," a process that "[prepares] us for a re-orientation." Through the text, the readers open themselves to the unfamiliar. Exposure to the new, however, is not an end in itself, but a strategy to change the reader's attitudes. In inducing the reader to be "thinking the thoughts of another," the text causes the reader's own individuality to recede "temporarily." At the same time, our ability to "decipher" the meaning of the text brings forth the consciousness of "our own deciphering capacity" – the awareness of "an element in our being of which we are not directly conscious."[10]

As Iser presents it, the notion of the "familiar" is crucial to meaningful reading. Integration of the unknown is made possible by the ability of recognition. Only by gaining the consciousness of the new as it differs from the old can an innovating perspective develop. The interrelationship that Iser detects between the familiar and the novel illuminates Stein's rationale for her autobiographical undertaking. It enhances Stein's stipulation that for the memoir to become educationally effective "it was essential to create enough order and clarity to enable an unfamiliar reader to understand the stream of reminiscences."[11] Stein claims that the people who have personally come into contact with Jewish persons recognize the falseness of anti-Jewish propaganda on the basis of their experience. However, those who do not know Jews must be exposed to the Jewish experience in an orderly and clear manner. Only then will they be able to assess the degree to which their lives are similar to Jewish lives, and consequently to reject the negative stereotype of the Jew. Familiarity with the Jewish experience will effect a sense of identification, and that identification will in turn bring forth a "re-orientation" that will render the "horrendous caricature" of the Jew unacceptable. Stein thus offers an honest testimony of her Jewish life as the antidote to Nazi discourse containing anti-Jewish hysteria, distortion, and demagoguery.

Commenting on the nature of memories, Erik Erikson maintains that memories are "an intrinsic part of the actuality in which they emerge [connecting] meaningfully what happened once and what is happening now"[12] and thus points to the "presence" of the present in the process of recollection. This observation draws our attention to the central role that memories of her Jewish past played in Stein's present. The horrible reality of anti-Jewish atrocities compelled Stein, a Christian on the threshold of her vocation as a Carmelite, to re-create herself as a Jew. Her conception of her memoir as a weapon against the intensifying "battle on Judaism in Germany"[13] attests to the significance she attached to her Jewish origins.

Erikson's notion of memories as a meaningful connection between the past and the present is important in this context. It draws attention to Stein's loyalty to her heritage, especially in view of her radically transforming religious identity precisely at that time. Let us recall that Stein was writing her memoir while awaiting her acceptance to the Carmelite Order, which she ardently desired. Ostensibly, this desire indicated a powerful wish to withdraw from the world, but the actuality of the rising anti-Jewish terror must have been acutely present in this prospective nun's consciousness, and in her efforts to recollect her Jewish past.

Indeed, the reason for the autobiographical project, as Stein defines it, attests to the degree of Stein's solidarity with the victims. In her foreword, Stein responds to what she calls "the condemnation of [the Jewish] people to a pariah's existence."[14] By recalling her own Jewish past, Stein, who had become a Christian, consciously joined the pariahs of her "old" faith. Instead of using her Christian religious identity to escape the fate of the Jewish people, she displayed her Jewish identity in public, with full awareness of the consequences.

It is impossible to ignore the correspondence between Stein's consciously assumed position of the pariah and Hannah Arendt's notion of the Jewish pariah as a "conscious rebel." In her *Jew as Pariah,* Arendt postulates that the emancipated Jew must become aware of her position as a socially excluded pariah and "become a rebel against it." This rebellion places her in "the arena of politics," where she becomes "the champion of an oppressed people."[15] The intention underlying Stein's memoir identifies Stein as a rebellious pariah who wants to reenter the social scene as a reformer of the unjust social exclusion of her people. The objective of her work leaves no doubt that Stein was aware of the pariah status to which she was condemning herself. Intended for German readers, the memoir not only defied the silence imposed on the Jews by the Nazi laws, but also, as an autobiographical act she intended to publish, amounted to a public acknowledgment of her situation as a condemned outsider.

Weil's intentions, as outlined in her letter to the Vichy ministry of education, were quite different. Whereas Stein drew attention to her Jewishness by affirming it, Weil exposed herself as a Jew in an attempt to renounce her Jewish parentage. While Weil rebelled against her Jewish identity, Stein's rebellion asserted her Jewish identity despite her conversion. The memoir thus demonstrates Stein's need to reconnect with her people on a level different from that of a mystical emulation of Christ's Passion. Here we witness resistance through active defiance of the rule of terror in a socioeducational context. The form of Stein's resistance implies the intensity with which she desired to redress the terrible injustice committed against her people. Her choice to resist by returning to the memories of her Jewish self implies a suspension of her Christian identity.

As an empathic act of a "catastrophe Jew," Stein's life story reconnects her with her people. At the same time, as an educational message from a "rebellious pariah," her life story reconnects her with the German people. In contrast to Weil, who was devastated over her social exclusion as a Jew, Stein used her Jewish identity to reenter the "arena of [the] politics" of social education. Her autobiographical project indicates her need to raise a voice of protest against the crime of Jewish persecution as well as against the crime of racist education for German youth.

Edith Stein: Toward Inner Wholeness

In its social aspect, Edith Stein's autobiographical act represents the courageous stance of a moral thinker-educator at the time of atrocity. However, the decision to tell the "Jewish part" of her life story at that particular time in her life also signals an underlying emotional motivation. As the author goes back to her Jewish self, the text indicates a quest for self-knowledge under extreme personal circumstances.

Georges Gusdorf points to a particular function of self-representation when he states: "In autobiography . . . the narrative offers us the testimony of a man about himself, the contest of a being in dialogue with itself, seeking its innermost fidelity."[16] I suggest that Gusdorf's notion of autobiographical representation as an inner dialogue in search of self-knowledge illuminates the subtext of Stein's memoir as an honest and unsparing self-re-vision. In this respect, the memoir functions as a channel toward self-understanding, an understanding of the self needed to achieve a sense of inner wholeness. A "straightforward account of my own experience of Jewish life," as Stein defines it,[17] this personal account illustrates her philosophical theory of inner growth through self-evaluation. Her recollection of herself in family surroundings represents her self–re-vision in formative stages of her life. Such re-vision of the past self is vital to the understanding, evaluation, and consequently growth of the present self. Stein's need for self-writing as a means to self-understanding becomes even clearer in light of Gusdorf's additional observation that "autobiography . . . assumes the task of reconstructing the unity of a life across time. . . . The recapitulation of ages of existence, of landscapes and encounters, obliges me to situate what I am in the perspective of what I have been."[18]

At no point had Stein encountered a greater threat to the "unity of her life" than in 1933. As a Jew, she was declared an outcast in the German social environment; as a Carmelite candidate she had alienated herself from her family. The complete—social and personal—exclusion signals shattered life patterns and indicates identity displacement and disorientation. At that particular juncture of her life, which seemed to be falling apart at its seams, the autobiography emerges as an attempt to restore the sense of "life unity." A search for unity, the undertaking of self-writing signals an attempt to deal with both aspects of exclusion. As an educational discourse directed to German youth, the memoir creates a short-lived illusion of participation in German society. As a testimony of a Jewish family life, the memoir claims the author's part in the life she is leaving.

Stein was fully aware that her decision to become a religious signified severance from her old self, from her family, and from her people. The full implications of Stein's decision emerged in an extremely painful confrontation with her mother. Stein recalled the terrible ordeal of trying to make her mother accept her decision: "Time and again, I asked myself during those weeks, 'Which of us is going to break first—me or my mother?' " When she departed for the convent she noted that, although her fervent desire to become a Carmelite had been granted, "I had just been through something too terrible [to experience any sense of enthusiasm]."[19]

Begun at the time of this heart-wrenching struggle for her mother's approval, the memoir in one sense reveals the depth of Stein's emotional need to demonstrate her personal attachment to her mother, and thereby her connection to the Jewish heritage. *Life in a Jewish Family* begins with a chapter entitled "My Mother Remembers," which is based on Frau Stein's recollections as told to her daughter. The chapter summarizes the life stories of Stein's parents and grandparents, as well as her mother's. In fact, as she mentions in her foreword, Stein's initial intention was to write an account of her mother's life: "Originally, I had intended to sketch my mother's memoirs. . . . In what follows [are] sketches based on [my] conversations with my mother. . . . I will present to the best of my ability, an account of my mother's life."[20]

Indeed, as presented in the first chapter, the narrative of Frau Stein's life illuminates Stein's own deep feelings of affection and respect for her mother. Frau Stein took over the family business after her husband's death, when Edith was only two years old, and turned it into a successful financial enterprise. Stein describes Frau Stein as "the most capable merchant in the whole trade in town."[21] As the sole supporter of her large family, Frau Stein emerges in her daughter's autobiography as the both loved and feared *mater familias* whose unquestioned authority exerted a strong influence on her children.

The other dominant figure in Stein's memoir is Edmund Husserl, her philosophical mentor and in many ways a father figure. Husserl was Jewish, although late in life he converted to Lutheranism. He is depicted as the revered and admired "master"—clearly an emotional substitute for Stein's deceased father. The concluding episode in the memoir describes Stein's coming of age with the reception of her doctorate, which she wrote under Husserl. In the last chapter, Stein inadvertently reveals what is perhaps an even deeper ambivalence toward the "master." She recounts the moment when he asked her to be his assistant and recalled that when she accepted the offer she "[did] not know which one of us was more elated. We were like a young couple at the moment of their betrothal."[22]

The dominant influence of both Frau Stein and Edmund Husserl on Stein's development is undeniable, and it emerges clearly in Stein's account. It is significant that the memoir, which started with her mother's life story and its message of dignified fortitude in face of life's vicissitudes, ends with a blessing by her philosophical father, an academic degree that affirms her intellectual capabilities. In her study of women's autobiographies, Sidonie Smith observes: "The autobiographer who is a woman must suspend herself between paternal and maternal narratives, those fictions of male and female selfhood that permeate her historical moment."[23]

In light of Smith's comment, the beginning and end of Stein's memoir indicate her attachment to the primal parental figures of her Jewish life. The particular place and role that she assigns them in her memoir indicate their indelible impact on her consciousness. In view of Stein's religious transformation, however, the recollections of her original paternal figures imply a particularly complex identity issue.

The "historical moment" Smith mentions—that is, Stein's lifetime—is permeated with more than one "set" of parents. We must remember that when she converted and joined the Carmelite Order, Stein adopted the Christian faith and, with it, her Christian "parents."

Stein's conversion to Catholicism, followed by her vocation as a Carmelite nun, was inspired by the works of the founding mother of the Carmelite Order, Saint Teresa of Avila—incidentally a descendant of the Spanish Jewish *conversos*. Stein even took Teresa's name when she entered the convent and became Sister Teresa Benedicta of the Cross. Metaphorically speaking, the Christian saint replaced Frau Stein as a mother figure. It is interesting to note the management skills, the determination, the decisiveness, and the willpower that characterized Stein's both natural and spiritual mothers.

Stein adopted a father figure of a thinker whose stature was as formidable as Husserl's. After her conversion, under the influence of Jesuit thinker Father Erich Przywara, she began her work on Saint Thomas Aquinas and accomplished the important task of translating his works into German. Although her initial philosophical orientation was phenomenological, and the thought of Thomas required an altogether different philosophical training, Stein declared that in her "St. Thomas found a reverent and a willing disciple."[24] Yet, in an article she wrote in honor of Husserl's seventieth birthday, Stein wanted to reconcile the philosophical worlds of Aquinas and Husserl. At the conclusion of her treatise, she indicates a necessary detachment from her old master when she observes that "Husserl seeks the 'absolute' point of departure in the immanence of consciousness [but that] for Thomas it is the faith."[25]

Nonetheless, Stein's initial effort to reconcile between the two thinkers implies a perhaps unconscious desire to reconcile her sense of fragmented loyalty toward her philosophical-spiritual fathers. This emotional need to reconcile her own life orientations seems to be reflected in the statement concerning her motivation to write the essay on Husserl and Thomas: "My intellect was no *tabula rasa,* it had already received a definite formation that could not deny itself. The two philosophical worlds that met in me demanded to be confronted and discussed."[26]

It is true that in her recollections Stein suspends herself, so to speak, between her Jewish parents. In terms of the actual moment of her writing, however, the Christian parental figures cannot be dismissed. To recall Erikson's notion of memory as "an intrinsic part of actuality," the recollection of the primal parents, as they emerge in Stein's writing, places them alongside those who "parented" her other religious identity. The primordial act of remembering revives the past by transposing it into the present moment of writing. In this sense, Stein's narrative of her Jewish past in her Christian actuality maintains the doublefold pattern of Jewish-Christian "paternal and maternal narratives."

This subtext of coexisting Jewish-Christian life narratives indicates Stein's intense desire to restore the sense of inner wholeness by acknowledging both her native and her adopted religious heritage. The convergence of all parental figures at the moment of writing represents an attempt to create a synthesis, indispensable to the restoration of inner wholeness.

Stein's search for spiritual and emotional wholeness evolves in consistency with her philosophical orientation. Let us recall Stein's notion of the "kernel," or "the true content of personality." Stein claims that human potential unfolds when "the comprehension of one attribute reasonably motivates progress to the other," that every empathic act is experienced "as proceeding meaningfully from the total structure of the person."[27] The realization of the kernel is therefore predicated on the recognition of the historical self. In *The Autobiographical Consciousness,* William Earle tells us: "The I that experienced the event then and recalls it now must be one and the same, or my past acts would not be the mine now."[28] A recollection of her Jewish childhood and youth, Stein's autobiography is in this respect a reaffirmation of her developing present "I." The continuation of self-actualization is predicated on the acknowledgment of the past "I."

From this perspective, Stein's autobiographical self-re-creation as a Jew was indispensable to her evolving self-identification as a Carmelite nun. To achieve inner wholeness, she had to converge her religious identities by acknowledging the vitality of her past in her present.

Simone Weil: The Rebellion of Self-Destruction

Stein's integrity generates from her consistent adherence to the ethics of her philosophical thought. Speaking in one voice, the voice of empathy, Stein was able to downplay her Christian affiliation and engage in a public discourse from the standpoint of a Jewish outcast. In contrast to Stein, Weil's life is marked by contradictions. Her discourse reverberates with the alternate voices of engagement with the world and disengagement from it, and the self-image she projects vacillates between that of a brilliant political, social, religious activist and that of a self-tormented, self-destructive "wretch." There is little doubt, however, that the subtext of Weil's rebellious social activities and controversial missions reveals an intensifying disposition toward dramatic self-sacrificial destruction. Weil did not want to die unnoticed. Her death, as she imagined it, was to be a spectacle of absolute fearlessness and selflessness.

We have already examined the motif of the "sacrificial scapegoat" in Weil's planned missions of the nurses' squad and of the parachuted Resistance saboteur, and we also noted Weil's rejection of refuge in the Church, her self-mortification over her "cowardly" departure from France, her return to Europe, and her eventual self-starvation in London. These plans and acts present Weil as a perennial nonconformist and obsessive rebel. It is as if—by positioning herself in dissent from all that was expected and acceptable in social, political, and religious spheres—she had been desperately trying to test her mettle as a courageous fighter, unaffected by social exclusion, danger, and death. Indeed, the notion of rebellion as a state of dauntless single-mindedness preoccupied Weil. In a letter to a student she wrote: "The rebel is morally and materially alone—I speak of true rebels. . . . Only those who are really strong, really pure, really courageous, really generous, will be able to meet the challenge."[29]

In her final work, *The Need for Roots,* Weil discussed the true meaning of rebellious disobedience. While, in general, obedience is an obligation, she claimed, "There is at least one necessary condition, . . . to disobey without being guilty of crime; this is to be urged forward by so imperious an obligation that one is constrained to scorn all risks of whatever kind."[30] The following outline of Weil's activities preceding the climactic, final period of her life in London traces Weil's relentless determination to meet her own definition of "a true rebel" by adhering to her convictions with unflinching fortitude and seeming disregard of social exclusion. This examination of her intensifying proclivity to place herself outside social environment elucidates the peculiar form of Weil's resistance manifested in the increasing eagerness to remove herself from the living.

Weil's social activities were unconventional, and her plans were often quite unrealistic—to say the least—but they were at all times ineluctably connected with her concern with morality and justice. Her unwavering dedication to the victims of social and military oppression, and her vehement denunciation of colonizing, imperialist regimes, are clearly voiced in her early activities and writings. After having passed her *Agrégation* in 1931, Weil taught philosophy in the working-class schools in Le Puy and Auxerre. Her articles in the workers' union newspapers *Libres Propos* and *L'Effort,* as well as her indefatigable political activism at that time, demonstrate her ardent preoccupation with the improvement of the working-class life conditions.

As a revolutionary activist, Weil demonstrated uncommon intrepidity and remarkable political perspicacity. In 1932 she was among the leaders of a miners' demonstration and carried the red flag. In the same year, she went to Berlin and Hamburg to witness the rise of German fascism and came back disillusioned with the German trade unions and the German Communist Party. Both organizations, she found, were guilty of divisiveness and passivity with regard to the rising National Socialists. Weil correctly predicted both the defeat of the German workers' movement and the Nazi victory. At the same time, she demonstrated her political astuteness and foresight in her repudiation of the Stalinist regime, which she found comparable to fascism. She expressed these opinions quite openly in her meeting with Trotsky in 1933 in Paris and expounded them in one of her major essays, "Reflections Concerning the Causes of Liberty and Social Oppression."[31]

During the period 1934–35, Weil worked as a factory hand in order to experience the life of the working class. At the same time, she continued her syndicalist activities and wrote extensively on social and political issues. An ardent supporter of the Spanish anarchists, she went to Spain in 1936 at the time of the Civil War. Her disillusionment with the extent of political hypocrisy that she discovered in both Republican and Communist camps once again proved her political astuteness. Soon afterward, in 1939, Weil abandoned her former pacifist stance on the Hitlerian aggression. With the fall of France in 1940, together with her parents, she fled from Paris to Marseilles, where in the first year of the war she worked as a farmhand. While in Marseilles, she completed the important essays "*Iliad* or the Poem of Force" and "The Great Beast,"[32] in which she repudiated tyrannical regimes and their perpetration of victimization.

Weil's political activity and writing show an enormous concern about the world, and especially about the victimized and the oppressed. Her single-minded dedication to the victims, and her vehement denunciation of, as George Abbott White observes, "each of our oppressive twentieth century *isms*—colonialism, imperialism, state socialism, totalitarianism, nationalism, racism,"[33] leaves no doubt about her absolute sincerity. Weil wholeheartedly worked all her life toward a just, oppression-free world.

But although her intention to construct a better social system is beyond doubt, the manner in which Weil wanted to implement her ideals unequivocally discloses her growing proclivity to extremely perilous ventures. Even her earlier activities demonstrate a streak of unwarranted risk-taking. Her Jewish identity put her in danger during her visit to Germany in 1932, and her journey to Spain in 1936 almost ended in disaster due to her lack of military experience. Weil's parents, who always feared for her safety, followed her to both Germany and Spain and in both cases brought her back to France. They were, however, unable to bar her return from New York to London. That last trip ended in Weil's self-destructive death.

The trips to Germany and Spain show the extent of Weil's readiness to risk her life to fight oppressive regimes. Her self-sacrificial tendencies emerge in her lifestyle as well. Her decision to work in the factories was detrimental to her physical well-being. Of frail constitution and suffering from chronic headaches, she did not stop the physical labor before she went into a state of complete physical collapse. In her private life, Weil became an ascetic who deprived herself of necessities, such as food and clothing and minimal standard conveniences.

This brief overview of Weil's nonconformist conduct highlights the consistency of her rebellious rejection of the affluent bourgeois lifestyle in which she was born and raised. At the same time, this lifelong opposition both to social oppression and to class privileges reveals two contradictory movements. While all of Weil's social activity affirmed the needs of the oppressed, her intentionally inflicted self-oppression disconfirmed her own needs. Weil's struggle against victimization and exploitation of the masses indicates faith in working for a future, better world. By contrast, her increasingly self-destructive attitude reflects a negation of her own future. These contradictory movements emerge perhaps most poignantly toward the end of Weil's life. As Gabriella Fiori observes in her extensive biography of Weil, "The mystery of [Weil's] death begins to raise questions about the meaning of her life."[34]

When in London, Weil was engaged in writing her important book *The Need for Roots,* in which she examined why the enlightened world was disintegrating and envisioned a reformed sociopolitical order in postwar France. At the same time that she was planning for a better future for France and for humanity at large, she was dying of self-inflicted starvation and deprivation in what she deemed a demonstration of solidarity with the suffering French people.

The discrepancy between Weil the brilliant social thinker and rebel, and Weil the sufferer aspiring to self-obliteration as a martyr, raises questions of both identity and identity denial. Stein's autobiographical work as resistance to the Nazi terror affirmed her indelibly as a Jew but also as an educator of German youth. The title of the autobiography, *Life in a Jewish Family,* and the declared intentions to write her mother's memoir bespeak Stein's acknowledgment of her Jewishness as well as her insistence on her responsibility as a citizen and a humanist to mend the deterioration of social moral values. Weil's quest to mend the world, however, bore no indication of her Jewishness, and her activities as a citizen and a humanist were becoming both increasingly out of touch with reality and inexorably self-destructive.

In contrast to Stein's specific mention of Jewishness in her autobiographical title, Weil entitled the autobiographical letter she wrote to Father Perrin as a "*Spiritual* Autobiography." The emphasis on the spiritual component is significant. After all, most autobiographies set out to present, first and foremost, a factually reliable life narration. That certainly was Stein's declared goal.

Why did Weil depart from the autobiographical convention by suppressing the historical aspects of the life story? Was the emphasis on the spiritual an indication of her intention to eliminate the fact of her Jewish birth from the representation of her growth as a Christian? Indeed, except for the letter to the Vichy education ministry in which she talked about her Jewishness in order to deny it, Weil never mentions her Jewish origins. The autobiographical deemphasis of biographical facts clearly reemphasizes Weil's self-denial as a Jew.

But Weil exhibited more than one aspect of self-denial. She denied her Jewish identity and also strove to deny her physical needs. The denial of the corporeal aspect of existence is closely associated with her wish for self-sacrificial death. The desire to obliterate her Jewishness therefore emerges concomitantly with the desire to destroy her body as an offering for the general good. Although Weil never mentioned this connection, in light of these correspondences the likelihood of such an emotional linkage of her self-negating drives deserves attention.

If accepted, this view posits Weil's overwhelming need to efface her Jewish identity as the rationale for her passionate desire to die for France. In other words, the spectacular death for France will irrevocably affirm her indubitable "Frenchness" and thus irreversibly obliterate her Jewishness. As shown earlier, Weil's proposal to reform the Church by obliterating its Jewish roots demonstrated a similar intention of identity effacement.

Is it then possible that the inability to accept herself as a Jew resulted in fixation on sacrificial self-destruction? Is it possible that the desire for self-sacrifice projected erasure of Jewish identity, and with it the erasure of her enforced exile from France? Could we claim that, for Weil, the deliverance from the burden of Jewishness meant a "legitimate," if posthumous, restoration of her identity as a French citizen?

While that is seemingly incongruous, such a hypothesis concerning the "mystery of Weil's death" gains plausibility when examined in the context of Weil's theological-mystical concept of de-creation.

Simone Weil:
The Rebel and the Mystic in De-Creation

We have already touched on the mystical element in Weil's thought in her notion of attention to the afflicted. As Weil saw it, attention does not aim at reciprocal relations with the other, but rather at total receptivity of the sufferer. And the ability to open up in total acceptance of the other amounts to the annihilation of the self. The state of complete self-abnegation transcends the conventions of social intercourse. Attention assumes the dimension of the mystical and comes into being "only by the supernatural working of grace." Then it becomes "pure love."[35]

According to Weil, we can attain "pure love," which is the true ability to love God, only by disclaiming our self. We need to become like "the mystic, whose whole effort . . . always has been to become such that there is no part left in his soul to say 'I.' "[36] According to Weil, the ultimate act of love—the act that will connect us with the Divine—lies in the annihilation, or de-creation, of the self. When God created the world and humankind, he reduced the divine self by giving us, in an act of love, an autonomous self. But true existence is in God, so the personal, or autonomous, aspect of the self separates the individual from God. Because, as individuals, we live in separation from God, our being is an illusion.

Once we realize that "to say 'I' is a lie,"[37] Weil says, we have approached the truth of our existence, which is really nonexistence. Human existence is "the greatest crime against God," says Weil.[38] When we acknowledge our crime of existence, we understand that "expiation is desiring to cease to be; and salvation consists for us in perceiving that we are not."[39] The true act of love of God is therefore to restore to God the autonomy that was given us in divine love. This act of self-negation amounts to the annihilation of our "I." Truth lies in reconnection with God. By willed de-creation of the self, we reconstitute the original unity with God that existed before the act of creation.

The argument that the ultimate act of love of God lies in becoming reconnected with the Divine is characteristic of the mystical thought in both Judaism and Christianity. But Weil's theory of de-creation actually departs from the Christian notion of reuniting with the Godhead and with the kabbalistic notion of restoring closeness to God. Weil has her own peculiar theory of reconnection with God in self-annihilation. The particularity of her mystical approach provides a rationale for her twofold denial of physical existence and of Jewish identity.

In the essay "Simone Weil's Concept of Decreation," J. P. Little places Weil in the context of the Christian mystical tradition, especially in connection with the mystical thought of Meister Eckhart. She maintains that Eckhart's idea that to know God one must forget oneself and all the creatures and that "all creatures are pure nothing" clearly echoes again in Weil.[40] On the other hand, H. L. Finch connects Weil's concept of de-creation with Isaac Luria's "kabbalistic idea of creation as withdrawal (in Hebrew, *tsim-tsum*) or making-room-for-the-world."[41] In the kabbalistic lore, God withdrew from the universe so that the creation could take place. Wladimir Rabi, in his attempt to both attenuate the malevolence of Weil's rejection of Judaism and reclaim her Jewish roots, also maintains that Weil's premise that the creation of the world as God's intentional withdrawal stems from the kabbalistic principle of *tsim-tsum*. Although he cannot account for Weil's knowledge of the Kabbalah, Rabi conjectures an affinity between Weil's mystical thought and Jewish mystical thought.[42]

In contrast to the proponents of Weil's affinity with Jewish mysticism, Martin Buber rejects any connection between Weil's idea of de-creation and the kabbalistic notion of *tsim-tsum*. In Jewish mysticism, God's withdrawal posits the human being as God's partner in the ongoing act of creation. Weil's idea of the destruction of the "I" is foreign to Judaism. Judaism, claims Buber, does not reject the individual self; on the contrary, the individual "is a bridge which spans across two firm pillars, man's 'I' and the 'I' of his eternal partner."[43]

Buber asserts that "Judaism . . . affirms the 'I' of the real relationship[,] the 'I' of love. For love does not invalidate the 'I'; it binds the 'I' more closely to the 'Thou.' "[44] Buber's notion of the partnership of the individual and the Divine relates to the kabbalistic concept of mending the world (*tikkun olam*). The divine perfection of the world in the moment of creation will be restored through good deeds and moral improvement. The moral perfection of the world, which fell apart due to human imperfection and inclination to evil, can be mended through human aspiration to virtue. In kabbalistic thought, therefore, the proximity to the God-head is predicated on the emulation of the divine perfection and love in everyday acts of justice and kindness.

The view that love of God requires annihilation of individuality is not typical of Christian thought either. According to most Christian theologians and thinkers, because the human being is God's creation the individual's task is to imitate the Creator. And since God created human beings in love, imitation of the love of God is the reason for human existence. In his discussion of love in Christianity, Scheler contends that because "God bent down to man in the incarnation, . . . love now becomes bowing down [and] losing oneself in all others." Love is therefore the imitation of God's existence in all his creatures. The task of humans becomes "as much as possible . . . to love the things as God loves them."[45] According to Scheler, love of God is to disseminate God's love.

To quote an example that is at one remove from both Judaism and Christianity, Spinoza's thought also disconfirms the notion of love of God as an act of "un-becoming," or "un-existing." Spinoza proposes loving God through self-affirmation. He claims that human self-affirmation signifies participation in God's self-affirmation. Since human beings are part of God, God's love for human beings amounts to God's love of himself. Self-affirmation is therefore the affirmation of God's love for his creatures and thus the affirmation of God himself.[46]

In the Spinozistic sense, participation in God's self-affirmation does not suggest self-annihilation. On the contrary, self-preservation, which affirms God, defies the option of self-annihilation. As Tillich observes, "both self-preservation and self-affirmation logically imply the overcoming of something which, at least potentially, threatens or denies the self."[47]

The above-mentioned views between the affirmation of self and the affirmation of God highlight the peculiarity of Weil's postulation that "we participate in the creation of the world by de-creating ourselves."[48] Her position contradicts the Christian thinkers who see the love of God in the individual's self-identification as God's sacred creation. It also contradicts the Jewish thought of the partnership of the Divine and the individual in the labor of love intended to re-create the original purity and perfection of the world. Both Christian and Jewish theologies accentuate both the physical and the spiritual existence of the human being, whether in self-reaffirmation as God's creation or in the common goal of the individual and the Divine of constant creation of a better world.

Why, then, would Weil see divine love in the negation of human existence? Why did the intensity of Weil's self-denial outweigh the affirming self-preservation? The rhetoric of the "I" underlies the tension of the highly personal and emotional involvement in Weil's meditations on de-creation. It is by no means an abstract speculation on de-creation that emerges in the dictum "I must love being nothing, I must love my nothingness, love being a nothingness."[49] And in another revealing instance, Weil claims that "if only I knew how to disappear, there would be a perfect union of love between God and the earth," since "I disturb the silence of heaven and earth by my breathing and the beating of my heart."[50]

Weil rejects the value of self-preservation when she writes that at the lowest rank of created beings "is *the most wretched one that is capable of loving [God]*" and that "the love of the most wretched one is the most precious love; for when such a creature has become transparent—transparency indicating the way in which God can love himself—the creative act has been completed."[51] Weil's notion of "transparency," of human being as God's love for himself, contrasts with those thinkers who see God's love for himself in willing human existence. God's self-affirmation through creation stands in contradiction with the view that the existence of God is proven through transparency—that is, through the loss of shape and texture, the markers of creation.

"Transparency" signifies, in Weil's terminology, uncreation, but also the absence of the ability to distinguish one person from another or to imprint the uniqueness of each individual. "To consent to being a creature and nothing else," says Weil, "it is like consenting to lose one's whole existence."[52] The wretch's "transparency"—that is, her depersonalization, is redemptive because it removes the barriers that separate her from loving reconnection with God.

Once the suffering individual ceases to claim her uniqueness and de-creates herself, she reunites with the Creator. In this moment, the wretch's love for God becomes one with God's love for the wretch. Then the cycle of the re-creation of God's perfection through human de-creation is complete. In a cryptic comment she adds to her description of the wretch's capability of loving God, Weil identifies herself as such a transparent wretch: "How grateful, therefore, I should be that fate has placed me in the lower ranks, with those that are most wretched."[53]

Why would Weil, a well-educated daughter of a loving, well-established family that doted on her and granted her every wish, feel herself to be a "transparent wretch"? Was it the sense of "being a stranger and an exile" in a society that could not tolerate Jews that motivated Weil to seek the love of God in social invisibility? Or was it her inability to tolerate the exclusion that Jewish identity signified that prompted Weil to seek the love of God in the state of "transparent wretchedness"? Or was it perhaps her repulsion of the body and bodily existence that caused her to aspire to the invisibility of the transparent, the privilege of the wretched?

Before attempting to determine the affinity of Weil's theory of de-creation with her self-denial(s), we must emphasize that her theory of de-creation never ostensibly signified an exhortation for physical self-destruction. In fact, Weil considered suicide a false imitation of de-creation.[54] She rejected suicide as an *ersatz* of de-creation, because suicide is an act of will. As we did not create ourselves, she claimed, we are not allowed to destroy ourselves.[55] Nevertheless, her language of immense inner ambivalence speaks for itself. Weil's self-image as a "transparent wretch," her self-exhortation to love her nothingness, and her desire to disappear—all these reiterate the notion of self-negation.

Although probably used consciously in the metaphorical sense, Weil's rhetorical strategies convey intensity that implies the physical aspects of self-destruction. The desire not to be is further reinforced by explicit references to self-inflicted violence. We find such affirmations as "Duty is given us in order to kill the self. And I allow so precious an instrument to grow rusty" and "The necessary energy dwells in me, since I live by it. I must draw it relentlessly out of myself, even though I should die in doing so."[56] The imagery of self-inflicted agony, as well as the self-portrayal as a wretch, communicates an unbearable sense of being that seeks relief and joy in nonexistence.

Even if used metaphorically, such violent images of self-annihilation confirm that, in Weil's case, this "something" that, in Tillich's terms, "threatens or denies the self" has prevailed. Clearly, the propensity to denial of the self emerges stronger than the need for self-preservation. The underlying desire for self-destruction that propels Weil's self-denial motivates her portrayal of the love of the Divine as de-creation rather than uniqueness, as passivity rather than active partnership, as self-renunciation rather than self-affirmation.

In "Example of Prayer," Weil's desire for de-creation assumes the concreteness of complete physical dysfunction. The text presents a most terrifying imploration "to be paralytic—blind, deaf, witless and utterly decrepit." The ultimate act of de-creation emerges in an almost ferocious, cannibalistic image of incarnate attention to the afflicted. "May all this [body, faculties, mind, sensibility, love]," Weil pleads, "be stripped away from me, devoured by God, transformed into Christ's substance, and given for food to afflicted men."[57]

The prayer for numbness, immobility, and inertia begs for death in life. The first-person narrative indicates the directness of Weil's wish for incapacitating affliction. Yet, despite the horrific misery that such supplication signifies, the specific entreaty to be transformed into the body of Christ signals the desire to die a privileged death.

As mentioned before, Weil wanted to die, but she did not want her death to go unnoticed. A death in emulation of Christ's agony for humanity would conflate Weil's love for God with God's love in the most anguished and most ennobling act of de-creation. As imitation of Christ's self-sacrifice for humanity, the sacrifice of Weil's transparency—her social invisibility—carries the reward of merging with the Divine and thus partaking in divinity. Conceived as the ultimate act of love for the afflicted, the transparency of alienation, humiliation, and suffering assumes the form of a mystical and heroic martyrdom.

Weil means her martyrdom to be an emulation of Christ's absolute self-offering to the afflicted. Her wish for Christ's Passion reminds us of Stein's similar wish for martyrdom when she asked her Mother Superior for permission to offer herself "to the Heart of Jesus as a sacrificial expiation for the sake of true peace." For Stein, however, her self-sacrifice signified continuing presence in the world in the vocation of a rescuer of the world's peace. Weil, on the other hand, wished for a martyrdom that would sever her from society. As she indicated in her prayer, she wished that all sensory and emotional channels of communication with the world would cease to function.

Identity is a function of social interaction. Outside society, identity has no meaning. Could it be that Weil's pleading for deafness, blindness, and muteness actually communicated the desire to neither hear, see, nor acknowledge her identity mirrored in the unfolding affliction of the Jews?

Although a terrible misfortune, the paralysis of senses and emotions also indicates liberation from feeling, experiencing, and suffering. As physical and mental paralysis, de-creation seems to indicate the end of the agonizing interaction with the world. From this point of view, the "transparency" as depersonalized reconnection with the Divine designates identity as the locus of unbearable mental and emotional suffering. As such, de-creation signifies the unbinding of all ties and relations that cause suffering and anguish. Beneath the desire for self-destruction in self-offering for the afflicted, we detect a supplication for nonbeing as a rescue from the impossible torment of life.

May we assume that this impossible torment of life was the consciousness of having been branded as a Jew? If so, how can the supplication of the "wretch" to shed body, mind, love, sensibility, and faculties in total self-annihilation be reconciled with the figure of the social rebel and her tireless defense of the afflicted?

The "wretch" and the rebel seem to meet in Weil's attitude of unmitigated compassion for France. For Weil, France under occupation assumed the identity of the afflicted. "Whoever feels cold and hunger, and is tempted to pity himself," she wrote in *The Need for Roots,* "can, instead of doing that, from his own shrunken frame, direct his pity toward France; the very cold and hunger themselves then can cause the love of France to enter the body and penetrate the depths of the soul."[58]

As we have seen in her self-sacrificial plan of the parachuted Resistance saboteur, Weil was prepared to do more than commiserate with occupied France. She was ready to give her life for the suffering French people. As she saw it, total attention to France would require the martyrdom of physical sacrifice and spiritual de-creation.

Weil's boundless compassion for France motivated her self-offering as a scapegoat. The mystical element of this sacrificial offer emerges in the connection that she draws between her compassion for France and Christ's compassion for Jerusalem. Weil maintains that the "authority" for our compassion is Christ, who "wept over [Jerusalem], foreseeing . . . the destruction which should shortly fall upon it. . . . Even as he was carrying the cross, He showed once again the pity He felt for it."[59]

The reference to Christ's Passion evokes Weil's prayer and her desire to emulate Christ by becoming his body fed to the afflicted. Was she implying that soon enough she would, indeed, offer her body in the ultimate, Christlike sacrifice for the hungry in France?

Weil's identification with Christ as food for the afflicted and as an aggrieved petitioner for the afflicted brings together the aspects of the self-de-creating mystic and of the self-sacrificial rebel. These aspects of the self display the common traits of self-exclusion, willingness to undergo extreme suffering, and above all, self-denial. Both rebel and mystic aspire to the dissolution of individuality, the former in the acceptance of France's affliction, and the latter in the acceptance of God's love. In this sense, therefore, the self-sacrificial rebel and the self-de-creating mystic demonstrate a common desire for elimination of the ego. The struggle to fend for France fills the self with boundless compassion, whereas the struggle to reconnect with God empties the self of individuality.

Strangely enough, however, the self-obliteration of the rebel and the mystic seems to offer protection against the affliction Weil feared most. In her essay "The Love of God and Affliction," Weil defines the mechanism of affliction: "There is not real affliction unless the event that has seized and uprooted a life attacks it . . . in all its parts, social, psychological, and physical. The social factor is essential. There is not really affliction unless there is social degradation or the fear of it in some part or another."[60]

The emphasis on the "social factor" of "social degradation" as essential to affliction is extremely significant. It brings forth the distinction between the martyrdom of self-inflicted exclusion and the degradation of decreed exclusion. This distinction illuminates Weil's preference to sever herself from the world, as rebel and mystic, rather than subject herself to the humiliation of the tyrannical rule that branded her as a subhuman outcast.

If the degradation of social exclusion is the ultimate stage of affliction, is it possible to understand Weil's designation of her Jewishness, which excluded her from society, as the main source of her affliction? In this respect, her self-abnegation indicates resistance to the Nazi dictate of a Jewish outcast. By excluding herself on her own as a sacrificial martyr, Weil repudiated the authority of those who excluded her as a Jew.

At the same time, Weil's choice of physical and spiritual martyrdom signals the intensity of the desire to escape the social exclusion that Jewishness signified. A woman of extremes, she paradoxically chose complete social exclusion over a relative banishment from society. We shall recall that Weil saw affinity with any collective, even the collective of the Church, as affliction. May we then surmise that she saw physical martyrdom and self-denial as means of self-affirmation—an affirmation in the true immortality of submersion in God and of devotion to humankind? Paradoxical as it may seem, Weil's desire for self-immolation indicates a search for immortality not only in God but among humans as well.

7

FRANK AND HILLESUM: IDENTITY AND THE SEARCH FOR GOD

> I find life beautiful and I feel free. The sky within me is as wide as the one stretching above my head. I believe in God and I believe in man and I say so without embarrassment.
>
> —Etty Hillesum

> The best remedy for those who are afraid, lonely or unhappy is to go outside, somewhere where they can be alone with the heavens, nature and God.
>
> —Anne Frank

Our discussion has focused and will continue to focus on religious (self-) identification as a means of resistance. It may be helpful to summarize our analysis of Edith Stein's and Simone Weil's divergent approaches to their own self-identity before going on to explore the approaches of Anne Frank and Etty Hillesum.

Edith Stein opposed the political climate of anti-Jewish propaganda by trying to acknowledge and converge her Jewish past and her Christian present. She resisted the terror as a Jewish daughter who shared her Jewish family story with German youth, and as a Carmelite nun who wanted to bear the Cross for the Jewish people. Her insistence on raising her voice in the "public arena" situates Stein's defiance of the silencing persecution in the context of the enlightened humanizing discourse.

Simone Weil's response to the fact of her Jewishness raises the problematic issue of denial of religious identity as a means of resistance. Her dissociation from anti-Semitic measures by defining herself as Christian, French, Greek, but certainly not Jewish, is hardly palatable for us today, and I venture to say that her silence about the horror of the Jewish mass murder is appalling. Our historical retrospective viewpoint makes it difficult to condone Weil's behavior. At the same time, however, we must admit that our consciousness of the Holocaust makes it difficult to avoid anachronism. It is necessary to consider Weil's response to her Jewishness in the context of the ideological climate in which she was raised.

Despite our objections, we must admit that, in resisting the imposed identification as a Jew, Weil claimed her equal status when choosing to identify herself as a French citizen and a Christian. Although not consonant with the evolving situation, the identity she wanted to maintain was quite characteristic of the social integration that many assimilated Western Jews in the post-Emancipation, prewar era had taken for granted.

The interpretation of Weil's desire to reform the Church and of her desire to die for France as compensatory mechanisms related to her denial of her Jewish identity seems valid when considered in the context of the unfolding Final Solution. At the same time, despite the risks and the danger involved, her preoccupation with social, political, and religious issues represented a defiant claim to freedom of speech and action, as promised by the Emancipation. In a reality of boundless violence and brutality, and of the direct threat of annihilation, Weil, through her thought, her writings, and her plans, however unacceptable they appear to us today, remained within the tradition of the European Enlightenment.

Stein's and Weil's religious self-identifications therefore do not stand outside the range of options allowable within the framework of the Enlightenment intellectual tradition, even though their self-identifications appear in a sense as polar opposites. Despite the eccentricity and radicality of their life choices, their self-constructions fall into recognizable categories that serve well in describing other assimilated Enlightenment Jews of their times. Whereas Stein can be identified as both a "rebellious pariah" and a "catastrophe Jew," Weil chose to construct her identity as a self-sacrificing rebel and—this makes Weil unique—a mystic of de-creation.

The realities of Nazi terror compelled both Stein and Weil to grapple with their identity as Jews. Stein's discourse affirmed her Jewish-Christian identity in her connectedness with the world. Weil's discourse negated her identity *in toto* in a redemptive gesture toward the world. These parameters—social affirmation and sacrificial negation—help us characterize the other two women's self-perceptions as Jews and the role their religious self-identifications played in their resistance of the terror.

The proximity of Anne Frank and especially Etty Hillesum to the atrocity of the Holocaust shapes their identities as victims. Weil never directly experienced the Nazi anti-Jewish persecution, and Stein enjoyed a relatively normal convent routine until the very moment of her deportation.

This is not to minimize the sense of anxiety, fear, and even panic that both Stein and Weil must have experienced when witnessing the growing terror and when fleeing their native countries. However, neither of them left records of experiences of exposure to the horror comparable to either Frank's two long years of hiding, or Hillesum's more-than-a-year-long service at Westerbork.

Imminent destruction evokes uncertainty, anxiety, and fear, emotions that produce the diverse responses of both the search for inner strength and the quest for salvation beyond the self. The constant threat of annihilation produces moods that vacillate between hope and despair, between a sense of relative potency and the agony of total disempowerment. We have seen this dynamic at work in Stein, and especially in Weil. The examples of Stein and Weil elucidate the two-tiered religious response of Frank and Hillesum to the encroaching threat of despair.

At one level, both Frank and Hillesum approach closely Stein's pole of the "rebellious pariah," or "catastrophe Jew." Despite their virtual lack of knowledge about Judaism, both women identified in complete solidarity and sympathy with Jewish suffering. In this respect, they affirmed themselves as Jews. At another level, however, the pain of the worsening hardship and the growing awareness of unavoidable death created a need for support that solidarity in common suffering could not offer. In their search for spiritual sustenance, both women reached into spheres beyond the reality of the horror that they shared with their fellow Jews. Their inclination to seek consolation in communion with the Divine points to affinity with Weil.

It must be added that neither Frank nor Hillesum ever reached the extreme of Weil's self-destructive de-creation. They both wanted to live. However, the experience of suffering affected their view of the self in interaction with the Divine. Hillesum's growing vision of God in suffering humanity and Frank's discovery of the closeness of God in nature deemphasize the boundaries that separate self and God. In their yearning to commune with the Divine, both Frank and Hillesum remind us of Weil's desire to reconnect and attain oneness with the God of love.

Identification with Jewish Suffering

Both Frank and Hillesum were fully aware that their Jewish identity made them targets of the Final Solution. Unlike Weil, who denied her Jewish identity and kept silent about the Jewish genocide, the two women acknowledged their Jewishness and openly empathized with the suffering that befell the Jewish people.

As was typical of "catastrophe Jews," both Frank and Hillesum claimed their common fate with their people and pronounced their indignation about the humiliation and the suffering inflicted on Jews. In fact, we observe in their diaries that both Frank's and Hillesum's identification with Jewish suffering *as Jews* intensified with the aggravating situation of persecution.

Frank's and Hillesum's association with the persecuted Jews as their people needs to be reemphasized, especially in light of the critical views that question the genuineness of their Jewish response to the Final Solution. Thus, Lawrence Langer tells us that although Hillesum "does not repudiate her Jewish identity, neither does she particularly acknowledge it; it lies uneasily on her shoulders like a burden she might wish to discard." Langer goes on with evident disapproval that Hillesum's diaries "are virtually unique among victim and survivor memoirs dissociating her Jewish heritage and her fate and searching for sources of strength and consolation in a Christian vocabulary and attitude that to many will seem alien to her special dilemma."[1]

A similar kind of argumentation pertaining to identity and language appears in the criticism that questions Frank's Jewishness. For instance, Sander Gilman maintains: "Anne Frank was typical of assimilated Jews. . . . [Her language] is of no specific marker for her identity. . . . She does not speak with a Jewish accent, does not mix bits of Hebrew in her discourse."[2] Gilman's view is corroborated by James Young, who stresses the Jewish authenticity of the diarists who wrote in Hebrew and in Yiddish, as opposed to "Anne [who] was assimilated, non-Zionist, and wrote in Dutch." According to Young, Frank emerges as "a member of the human community and not as one who identified herself as part of a collective Jewish tragedy."[3]

It is true that both Frank and Hillesum grew up in an assimilated atmosphere, as did Améry, Bergson, Bloch, Weil, Stein, and many other "catastrophe Jews." Their responses to the Nazi anti-Jewish terror therefore ineluctably reflected their ideology, their beliefs—in short, their formative Weltanschauung. It is therefore impossible to ignore the irony in postwar scrutiny and critical assessment of the degree of Jewishness in the responses of Jewish victims to the Final Solution. This self-righteous position of the critics implies that there was a pattern of "correctly Jewish" response to the Nazi persecution, which some of the Jewish victims failed to follow.

Such judgments of Frank and Hillesum are clearly inappropriate. These women were doomed to death for their Jewishness and struggled heroically to make some sense out of their fate and thus to maintain their humanity against terrible odds. Besides, the claim that they did not sense connection with the Jewish collective is far from being accurate. While it is true that, like most of the Western Jews, neither Hillesum nor Frank was a Zionist and that neither of them knew much about her Jewish heritage, it is difficult to dismiss either their genuine identification with the fate of the Jews or their sincere expressions of Jewish pride.

Frank communicates her sense of solidarity with Jews in no uncertain terms, affirming her faith in the chosenness of the Jewish people and acknowledging the uniqueness of her Jewish identity:

> We are Jews in chains, chained to one spot, without any rights, with a thousand duties. . . . If we bear all this suffering and if there are still Jews left, when it is all over, then Jews instead of being doomed, will be held up as example. Who knows, it might be even our religion from which the world and all the peoples learn good, and for that reason and that reason only do we have to suffer now. We can never become just Netherlanders or just English or any nation for that matter, we will always remain Jews, we must remain Jews, but we want it, too. . . . God has never deserted our people; right through the ages there have been Jews, through all the ages they have had to suffer.[4]

Frank's sense of pride in her Jewish heritage, and her faith in the future mission of the Jews to the world, are echoed in Hillesum's affirmation of her Jewish identity. In a poetic image, Hillesum compares Jewishness to a cloud that envelops her, making her feel "so warm and protected and safe."[5] She tries to gain perspective on the present by placing it in the context of the long history of Jewish persecutions: "But does it matter if it is the Inquisition that causes people to suffer in one century and war and pogroms in another? To suffer senselessly, as the victims would put it? Suffering has always been with us, does it really matter in what form it comes?"[6]

Like Frank, Hillesum envisions the Jewish mission to the world. A redemptive lesson of a new moral understanding will ensue from the suffering of the Jewish people: "It is not easy — and no doubt less easy for us Jews than for anyone else — yet if we have nothing to offer a desolate post-war world but our bodies saved at any cost, if we fail to draw new meaning from the deep wells of our distress and despair, then it will be not enough."[7]

As "catastrophe Jews," both Frank and Hillesum place themselves in the context of Jewish suffering over centuries. They establish affinity with Judaism by identifying with the history of Jewish persecution. At the same time, they acknowledge the particular role of the Jewish people in the world. They accept the concept of Jewish "chosenness" as responsibility to serve as an ethical model for the world. It is significant that at the time when their own lives were in constant danger these assimilated Jews, who spoke neither Hebrew nor Yiddish, spoke unknowingly in the language of the old Jewish tradition of *tikkun olam,* mending the world, combining its universal message with their Enlightenment heritage.

The notion of moral responsibility even in a time of catastrophe indicates the desire to fend off the senselessness of the suffering. The "Jewish component" that emerges in their struggle against despair clearly communicates both a consciousness of Jewish identity and an acceptance of it.

As both diaries show, Frank's and Hillesum's sense of Jewishness was not confined to reading a historical-eschatological meaning into the unfolding Jewish destruction. Both Frank and Hillesum were completely aware of the unfolding Jewish genocide. In contrast to Geoffrey Hartman's claim that during the Holocaust "few could hope to make sense of the events, . . . [could] discern a normal pattern that could eventually be expressed in the form of a story,"[8] these women lucidly read the horrible narrative of the systematic destruction of the Jews in the events they witnessed.

Like the diaries from the Warsaw ghetto discussed in the Introduction, the diaries of Hillesum and Frank prove that the victims were capable both of understanding and of articulating in writing the implications of the atrocities they witnessed.

Thus Hillesum notes that "the surface of the earth is gradually turning into one great prison camp" and that Jews are being buried alive or exterminated with gas.[9] She writes about the concentration camps, about the deaths and suicides of her professors and colleagues, about "the world . . . in the process of collapse,"[10] about the bombings and the houses that have been destroyed.[11] She records how "the threat grows ever greater, and terror increases from day to day," how everyday further measures against Jews are imposed, how Jews are going to be transported to Poland, and how hundreds of thousands of Jews have already perished.[12] Finally Hillesum reaches a "new certainty that what they [the Germans] are after is our total destruction."[13] This certainty is reconfirmed in her poignant depiction of Westerbork: "The sky is full of birds, the purple lupins stand up so regally and peacefully, . . . the sun is shining on my face—and right before our eyes, mass murder. The whole thing is simply beyond comprehension."[14]

Frank demonstrates her understanding of the global scope of the disaster in similar terms, when she writes: "No one is able to keep out of it, the whole world is waging war."[15] She deplores the destruction of the city in the bombings, the wounded, the dead, and the lost children.[16] She talks specifically of the catastrophic situation of the Jews, and tells of Jewish friends deported to Westerbork, and about the news of Jews murdered and gassed.[17] She refers to stories "so gruesome and dreadful that one can't get them out of one's mind."[18] She has nightmares of Jews "sent to filthy slaughterhouses like a herd of poor sick, neglected cattle."[19]

Her sense of solidarity evokes tremendous guilt for being safe when other Jews are exposed to persecution. Forgetting her own incredibly precarious situation, Frank reports, "I saw two Jews through the curtain yesterday, I could hardly believe my eyes; it was a horrible feeling, just as if I had betrayed them and was now watching them in their misery."[20]

These painful observations convey a full consciousness that the existence of Jews was coming to its end. They also clearly disconfirm the critical views that question Frank's and Hillesum's identification with the fate of the Jewish people. It is precisely the extent of their identification with Jewish suffering that raises the more pertinent issue of emotional adjustment to their horrific entrapment for being Jewish.

How did they cope with the unfolding narrative of total Jewish destruction? How did they fend for their sanity in a situation of mass murder "beyond comprehension," which one "can't get out of one's mind"? How did they contend with the awareness that their own death was inevitable?

Attempts at "Psychological Survival"

We have observed Stein's psychological defenses in her insistence on staying in the world as an educator of empathic tolerance to German youth. This path of self-assertion as a useful member of society was no longer open to Frank and Hillesum. For them, even a semblance of normal life was diminishing inexorably. To maintain normalcy in a world that had gone insane, they needed to construct an immune system, so to speak, that would protect them from growing fear and despair.

Indeed, Hillesum observes everywhere "signs barring Jews from the paths and the open country." She knows that these "vexatious measures which interfere with daily life" are not meant just to cause inconvenience, but to humiliate and degrade the victim. While, unlike Stein, she can no longer reach out to the world in an attempt to educate it, Hillesum turns inward in an attempt to educate herself.

As Hillesum observed, the oppressors work on the assumption that their restrictive treatment would elicit "feelings of being persecuted, humiliated and oppressed" in their victims. By giving in to despondency, Hillesum claims, we comply with the oppressor. The response to persecution should therefore be refusal to take the position of a humiliated victim. "Humiliation," Hillesum contends, "always involves two. The one who does the humiliating, and the one who allows himself to be humiliated. If the second is missing, that is, if the passive party is immune to humiliation, then the humiliation vanishes into thin air."[21]

A similar approach of refusing to internalize the disgrace and shamefulness of the persecution emerges in Frank's *Diary*. On August 10, 1943, Frank writes down "a new idea." She will make believe that things are different from the way they are. She has decided to keep silent at mealtimes and pretend that the food she "simply can't stand" is delicious – and so, she writes, "before I know where I am it is gone." She applies the same technique to getting out of bed in the morning, which she had found "also a very unpleasant process." She gets up thinking "You'll be back [in bed] in a second," breathes some fresh air, turns the bed down quickly – and by then she would realize that "the temptation is removed."[22]

In his insightful essay on Frank's psychological growth, John Berryman notes that in the entry just cited Frank aims at the two worst problems in her situation: the humiliating and exasperating situation of the meager and tasteless meals in the company of the irate others, and the hopelessness and fear to which she has to rise every morning. Berryman sees in Frank's responses to these morally debilitating problems an "ability to alter reality, to create a new reality, . . . one of her greatest mental strengths," which she puts "at the service of her psychological survival and tranquillity."[23]

At its psychological level, Frank's and Hillesum's resistance to the increasing degradation takes the form of constant, disciplined modification of behavioral and perceptual patterns. To overcome the emotions of fear and distress, Frank and Hillesum employ intellectual sophistication and the freedom of imagination. For example, Hillesum talks about the humiliation of being harassed in stores by those "who want to clear society of all Jewish elements." Despite her sadness and sense of "utter defenselessness," she is determined not to let these feelings take over. "I have my inner strength," she maintains, "and that is enough, the rest doesn't matter."[24]

Frank's celebrated statement that "in spite of everything . . . people are really good at heart" offers another example of a conscious attempt to modify the perception of a despair-provoking situation. In its context, the sentiment Frank conveys certainly does not confirm the naive message of hopeful faith in humanity that has been commonly attributed to this statement. In the sentence that follows, Frank admits that her belief in people "seem[s] so absurd and impossible to carry out." She confesses that she holds on to her ideals about the good in the world because she "simply can't" build her hopes on "a foundation consisting of confusion, misery, and death."[25]

These disciplined attempts to modify emotional and intellectual responses represent extraordinary strategies of psychological survival. At the same time, it is important to emphasize that the two are women fully conscious of the situation against which they were erecting their defenses. Neither suppressed her understanding of the hopelessness of her position as a persecuted Jew. In a valiant attempt at what we might call "lucid self-deception," they tried to fend off the specter of despair. Their awareness of this self-contradictory psychological "game," which they nevertheless "played," communicates the extent of their determination not to give in to despair. At the same time, the paradoxical nature of this "game" of self-conscious self-deception signals both the vulnerability and the inadequacy of psychological means of survival.

To accept Frank's and Hillesum's attempts at character reformation at face value would attest to our reluctance to comprehend fully their desperation and fear, to our need to evade the enormity of their mental suffering. To perceive these attempts as the definitive evidence of the prevailing inner strength of the victims "despite everything" would trivialize the horror of the Holocaust experience. It is important to recognize that, even while trying to construct the "new reality," their efforts reveal the enormous odds against which they were trying to re-form their psychological selves.

Inner strength is "all that matters," claims Hillesum, reacting to the sense of "utter defenselessness"; I simply can't live with a sense of "confusion, misery, and death," asserts Frank. It is precisely the definitive tone of these statements that reveals the abyss of defenselessness, confusion, misery, and death that made it indispensable to construct a make-believe set of ideals to live/survive by.

Thus, the texts reveal the fragility of these mental defenses in the reality of deportations and concentration camps. The conscious efforts to erect barriers against fear communicate, in fact, the immensity of despair. In order to gain a measure of understanding of their hardship, we must try to fathom the fear that both women were striving to fend off. Only then will it be possible to gain insight into the images of God they construct in their distress.

Confronting the Apocalypse of the Timeless Present

The similarity of the imagery that Anne Frank and Etty Hillesum use is striking. Says Hillesum: "From all sides our destruction creeps up on us and soon the ring will be closed and no one at all will be able to come to our aid. All the little loopholes that are still left will soon be stopped up."[26] And Anne Frank has a nightmare in which "the clouds gather more closely about us and the circle which separates us from the approaching danger closes more and more tightly. Now we are so surrounded by danger and darkness that we bump against each other, as we search desperately for means of escape."[27] The rhetorical patterns in these two quotations provide an inkling of the enormity of the fear and despair of the two women awaiting their fate. The emphasis on their complete, hermetic entrapment conveys the impossibility of redemption.

It is noteworthy that both Frank's and Hillesum's images evoke a global, all-encompassing catastrophe rather than a personal disaster. The emphasis on the totality and irrevocability of the approaching end in both descriptions evokes a sense of a universal, cataclysmic event that precludes any hope for survival. The images of the closing ring and the diminishing circle convey the sense of a sealed decree of complete destruction that will not spare a soul. Both writers represent their sense of approaching death in imagery that implies the apocalyptic ending of the world.

Frank Kermode tells us that the consciousness of the eventual apocalypse has always been present in human perception of time. The fear of the end of time has shaped humanity's historical narrative. But, while the paradigm of world history begins with the creation and ends with the eschatological vision of total destruction, the assumption has always been that the apocalypse "is disconfirmed without being discredited"; that it is "immanent rather than imminent."[28] As Kermode sees it, however, the Third Reich produced a "consciously false apocalypse which projected death upon others."[29] Through fascism, Kermode says, "the world is changed to conform with a fiction, as by the murder of Jews."[30]

The Final Solution represented the (im)possibility of the apocalypse actualized. It literally denoted the final stage in Jewish history and thus placed the mythical, immanent notion of the apocalypse in the sphere of the imminent. The presence of the apocalypse in the historical rather than mythical sphere spells the end of history and therefore the end of time. Both the hiding Jews in the Annex and the imprisoned Jews in Westerbork faced a world in which their history had stopped evolving. Their past irrevocably erased, their future brutally denied, the Jews were doomed to the apocalyptic present of an imminent destruction.

For both Frank and Hillesum, the evolving awareness of being trapped in a timeless present produced paralyzing fear and despair. In her description of an air raid, Frank shows her full awareness of the hopeless situation of the trapped Jews: "The house rumbled and shook, and down came the bombs. I clasped my 'escape bag' close to me, more because I wanted to have something to hold than with an idea of escaping because there's nowhere we can go and if the worst came to the worst, the street would be as dangerous as an air raid."[31] The sense of hopelessness and entrapment in an incomprehensible situation emerges in Hillesum's observations on the night before a deportation:

Tonight I shall be helping to dress babies and calm mothers—and this is all
I can hope to do. I could almost curse myself for that. For all we know that
we are yielding up our sick and defenseless brothers and sisters to hunger,
heat, cold, exposure, and destruction. . . . What is going on, what myste-
ries are these, in what sort of fatal mechanism have we become enmeshed?
The answer cannot be that we are all cowards. . . . We stand before a
deeper question.[32]

The "deeper question" of the "fatal mechanism" is that of a world in which the
notion of choice had ceased to make sense. The entrapment is complete because it
applies not only to the notion of limited space and physical restriction, but also to
the mental activity of weighing issues and making decisions. Death awaits the
Jews whether they try to escape or not, whether they help each other or not. Their
predetermined fate rendered all decision-making, all moral acts, completely
meaningless. Making decisions implies the sense of the future that might be
affected by the choice of action. The fate of the Jews had been sealed regardless of
their decisions or actions. Their destruction had already been determined by the
Final Solution.

As for all Jews in Europe, for Frank and Hillesum, history has assumed the
apocalyptic dimension of timelessness, of death-in-life. Frank was very much
aware that her life had become devoid of meaningful memories and purposeful
planning. "I do talk about 'after the war,' " she says, "but then it is only a castle in
the air, something that will never really happen. If I think back to our old house,
my girl friends, the fun at school, it is just as if another person lived it all, not
me."[33] Time that lost its meaning—it alienated her from her past, and therefore
from the sense of self. Because there was nothing to expect, life turned into a
depressing routine underlain by constant dread of the end.

The dread of the end, as Frank experienced it at times, was overwhelming. In
poetic, metaphorical language, she communicates the oppressive atmosphere,
which is "as heavy as a lead," and "a deadly close silence [which] hangs everywhere, catching hold of me as if it would drag me down deep in an underworld."
She sees herself as "a songbird whose wings have been clipped and who is hurling
himself in utter darkness against the bars of his cage."[34] At a later date, the
desperation becomes even more pronounced, when she wonders, "How long have
we still to put up with this almost unbearable, ever increasing pressure" and asks to
"let the end come, even if it's hard."[35]

Hillesum's desire for an end comes with the "almost uninterrupted flow" of
Westerbork inmates on the endless transports to Auschwitz. She confesses to have
"sometimes" thought "it would be simpler to put yourself on transport than have to

witness the fear and despair" of the deportees. The "mathematical regularity" with which "the quota must be filled" and the train loaded[36] has reduced any consideration of the past or the future to the absurd. Time is measured by the repetitive, ever-recurring event of the "transports," which precludes any sense of progression but which evokes the ever-increasing sense of horror.

To overcome fear and depression, Frank attempts to sleep, "to make the time pass more quickly, and the stillness and the terrible fear, because there is no way of killing them."[37]

To overcome growing fatigue, anxiety, and distress, Hillesum tries to concentrate only on the present. She quotes from the Gospel of Matthew, "Take therefore no thought for the morrow. . . . Sufficient unto the day is the evil thereof," and tries to deal only with the here and now. This, she claims "is the only attitude that allows you to carry on at Westerbork."[38]

The practical resolutions of "sleeping it off" and "taking one day at a time" reflect the "low" moments in which both Frank and Hillesum are desperate for some release of the pressure. But these solutions can help for only a short time. Other means are needed to maintain the struggle against the forces of terror that "drag them down into the underworld" of despair.

Frank, Hillesum, Stein, and Weil all sought support in their sense of responsibility for the world and for the other. We also observed resistance in Stein's self-affirming voice of an educational action, and in Weil's plans of sacrificial self-annihilation. We saw how Frank and Hillesum, both "catastrophe Jews," resisted through proud association with the painful past and the redemptive future of the Jewish people, the heritage they shared with other suffering fellow Jews.

Yet in view of the intensifying terror of the apocalyptic destruction, these ways of resistance were not sufficient. The horrific news about mass murder, the air raids that shook the attic and its inhabitants, and the incessant transports from Westerbork to Auschwitz presented Hillesum with the traumatic landscape of unendurable human misery. Compassionate rationality and a sense of responsibility toward the world could hardly protect the victims from mental and emotional collapse. The need to withstand the increasing fear and despair required a perspective reaching beyond the reality of the human world.

The pervasive sense of the destruction all around them brought forth the question of the Divine, its potency, and its relationship to the world. Even as they tried to maintain their faith in ethics and humanitarianism, both Frank and Hillesum were struggling with the question of their relationship with God at the time of fear and despair.

In view of their humiliating and degrading exclusion from humanity, the two women needed to reaffirm their humanity in the consoling presence of the Divine.

Despite the increasingly imminent end, and perhaps because of it, they searched with growing intensity to establish a sense of a God, which would offer meaning and consolation at the moment in which, paradoxically, the world—God's creation—was coming to its end.

Weil too was seeking the Divine as refuge and consolation in the affliction of degrading exclusion. Like Weil, Frank and Hillesum conceptualized relationships of loving interdependence between God and the self. Unlike Weil, however, who saw these relationships culminate in the disintegration of the self, both Frank and Hillesum conceived of the empowerment of the self in the restructured relationship with God.

Images of God in the World Approaching the Apocalypse

Both Frank and Hillesum seek consolation and comfort in the Divine. Frank sees the consoling presence of God in nature: "Only then does one feel that all is as it should be and that God wishes to see people happy, amidst the simple beauty of nature. . . . Nature sets all fear at rest for every trouble, even when there are bombs or gunfire."[39] Hillesum feels the presence of God as part of her inner self:

> I shall always feel safe in God's arms. They may well succeed in breaking me physically, but no more than that. I may face cruelty and deprivation the likes of which I cannot imagine in even my wildest fantasies. Yet all this is as nothing to the immeasurable expanse of my faith in God and my inner receptiveness.[40]

These declarations of faith diverge from commonplace notions of the powerful, rescuing God. Frank does not pray to God to save her from the reality of "bombs or gunfire." Hillesum does not plead with God to save her from the experience of unspeakable "cruelty and deprivation" that, as she is well aware, await her in the near future.

The absence of the expectation that God might actually save from death, or at least alleviate the suffering, leads to a twofold realization. It communicates the two women's consciousness of the irrevocable apocalyptic reality they are witnessing and experiencing, and the uncompromising straightforwardness about the unfolding cataclysmic horror that will inevitably engulf them brings forth a concept of God who saves them *in* but not *from* the terror in which they live and die.[41]

Because history had reached an apocalyptic point of no return, the God of Revelation could no longer fulfill his traditional providential role. In the reality of the Holocaust, the commanding God of history seemed to have absented himself from the history of the Holocaust. The God that both Frank and Hillesum invoke and pray to is not a God revealing himself as powerful, authoritarian God, but rather a God of loving attention and consolation. It is a God who does not rescue the lives of the victims, but one who sustains the sufferers in their struggle to maintain, as long as possible, a life of dignity and self-respect.

It seems important to reiterate that, as pictured by Frank and Hillesum, the Divine is not a reflection of the Jewish God. Against the critics who questioned their Jewish "authenticity," we discussed the pride that both Hillesum and Frank have in their Jewishness, as well as their solidarity with their victimized fellow Jews. However, the sense of belonging to the community of persecuted Jews, and their faith in Jewish chosenness to construct a better world, did not signify a conscious subscription to the Jewish concept of God.

At the same time, the God of Frank and Hillesum does not conform entirely to the notion of the Christian God. It seems that their discourse with God draws on ecumenical theology, which stresses the universalist values of the Enlightenment era, values that emerge from both religious traditions. Both Frank and Hillesum supersede the dogmatic distinctions of religious concepts of God and conceive of a divine entity, the essence of which lies in the ethics of dignity, self-respect, and responsibility. Their God acts in self-revelation by enabling them to transcend their fear and despair in a perspective that reaches beyond the self.

Ostensibly, the ways in which they talk to God, even the position in which they pray, reveal Christian undertones. In one of the hard moments of fear and despair, Frank describes herself praying and crying "with my head on my arms, my knees under me, on the bare floor, completely folded up."[42] Hillesum describes herself repeatedly as "the girl who could not kneel." Finally she describes herself as "the girl who learned to pray" with "folded hands and bended knee." She admits it is a posture that "is not handed down from generation to generation with us Jews."[43]

Who is the God to whom they pray? What is the nature of faith without the hope of survival? How meaningful is this faith on the "different planet"[44] of the Holocaust world ruled by the forces of brutality and evil? "I know," says Frank, "that I am not safe, I am afraid of prison cells and concentration camps, but I feel I've grown more courageous and that I am in God's hands. . . . Without God I should long ago have collapsed."[45] Frank's fear projects an image of a God who inspires faith despite the indubitable reality of the world changing into an enormous prison camp. We must recall that, when writing about Jews who will be held up as an example of the good after the horror is over, Frank did express a hope for the future. But when turning to her everyday reality, Frank discovers the faith that keeps her from "collapsing" in the here and now, amid the bombs, gunfire, and concentration camps rather than in an eschatological promise.

For Frank, the concept of the Divine emerges in her understanding of nature as a reflection of God. Nature becomes the proof of God's existence, and its beauty and serenity attest to God's greatness. Frank finds a source of strength in nature, whose eternity supersedes the course of human history, which had reached a tragic, apocalyptic point of no return. God, who has disappeared at least temporarily from history, reemerges and is nevertheless present in the grandeur of creation.

In probably what is Frank's best and most moving short story, entitled "Fear," her autobiographical narrator finds God in communion with nature. In this story we recognize Frank's fear of being trapped in the Annex at the time of air raids in her fictional representation of the "grip of fear" that took hold of her at the time of shelling, shootings, and explosions. She describes how "fear clawed at my mind and body and shook me," how she escaped "from the fiercely burning mass about me," how she ran "with the image of the burning houses, the desperate people and their distorted faces before me."[46]

In the end, the powerful sense of affinity with nature brings forth feelings of peace and comfort. The inner calm communicates God's loving presence: "When I was alone with nature, I realised . . . that fear is a sickness for which there is only one remedy. Anyone who is as afraid as I was then should look at nature and see that God is much closer than most people think."[47]

The conclusion of Frank's story reminds us of Job, whose quest for God ends in a vision that intends to prove that the glory of creation testifies to God's existence and unfathomable wisdom. Job's God, however, communicates the insignificance of the human being vis-à-vis God's awe-inspiring creation. Frank's God, whose presence she discerns in nature, is the God of loving care and of healing relief of suffering. In the story, the self-revelation of God in nature cures her "sickness." It reaffirms Frank's autobiographical protagonist's humanity at the time of dehumanizing terror. The message from God that she reads in the meadow, in the stars, in the dandelions, and in the clover leaves is healing because it reinstates her dignity and restores her self-respect, which was devastated by the haunting fear that has reduced her to a hunted animal.

In her perception of God, Frank demonstrates her uncommon maturity. Her meeting with God not in history but in the intimate aloneness in nature represents a concept of the Divine released from the strictures of religious denominations. Her concept of God is personal and not just historical. She structures the image of God through contemplation of the natural world, and at the same time redefines God's interaction with humanity.

On the one hand, nature reaffirms the existence of God despite God's temporary absence in history. On the other hand, as revealed in nature, the image of God that Frank discerns in nature differs from the traditional image of an omnipotent, commanding God. She meets God not in the human world but in the sphere of nature. Nature's beauty and tranquillity communicates a divinity that is benevolent, consoling, and healing.

The God that Frank discovers in nature is a God that each of us needs in order to be cured of the terrible "sickness of fear" that humanity has inflicted on itself. It is therefore no longer a communal God, but a personal God; no longer the omnipresent God who demands obedience, but a God whose presence depends on our readiness to find him. It is, postwar theologian John Pawlikowski argues, the "compelling" God—that is, "a God to whom we are drawn" and who signifies "a healing, a strengthening, an affirming."[48]

Frank's perception of the relationships between the individual and God clearly does not reiterate Weil's notion of liberation from degradation through joining God in the transparency of self-de-creation. On the contrary, Frank seeks a God who will liberate her from the degrading fear that has stripped her of human stature. Rather than ending in the annihilation of the "I," as Weil would have it, Frank's connection with God will restore her self. Despite the considerable differences between the two, however, the notion of the individual seeking God seems to establish a measure of common ground between Frank and Weil.

The theological thought of both Frank and Weil emphasizes interdependence of the individual and God. This dimension of the relationship between the individual and God is shared, of course, by the Jewish and Christian traditions. God's love is revealed to those who actively seek communion with the Divine. In both theological concepts, a loving relationship between the individual and God is not a given, but rather created through the individual's affirmation of God's love. For Weil, God's love will be affirmed in the act of de-creation. For Frank, the affirmation of a loving God lies in the confirmation of nature as a healer of the wounded self. Despite their differing views of the self vis-à-vis the divine, both Frank and Weil highlight the potent role of the individual in her interaction with God. It is the active search for God, either through self-de-creation or self-restitution, that brings forth communion with the God of love.

The compelling aspect of Frank's God is therefore the power to motivate the individual to seek morally restoring forces in her distress. As mentioned before, this God is not expected to prevent the conflagration of the world in apocalyptic destruction. Yet God has the power to empower the individual to seek self-dignity and self-respect in the world by recognizing herself as part of God's creation. It is not only the discovery of God in nature that heals the degraded self. It is, first and foremost, the compelling urge to commune with nature and to discern the divine immanence in nature that brings forth a renewed sense of self-worth.

Frank's notion of connecting with God in nature, outside of the reality of war, to an extent corresponds with Hillesum's search for God away from the apocalyptic destruction. Like Frank, Hillesum was capable of creating an imaginary "physical" space that separated her from the immediate surroundings and allowed her to reach the intimacy of communion with God.

While Frank's imagination led her to seek redeeming powers outside her self, Hillesum sets out on an inner journey. Let us recall that in her story Frank liberates herself from the "death-trap" of the Annex, escaping to a pastoral, secluded spot in nature where she is healed from her uncontrollable fear. Hillesum achieves a sense of liberation by imagining her prayer in the shape of a monastic house of worship. When "the threat grows ever greater, and terror increases from day to day," she writes, "I draw prayer round me like a dark protective wall, withdraw inside it as one might into a convent cell."

Like Frank, who maintains that without God she would have collapsed, Hillesum argues that prayer helps "prevent my going to pieces altogether, my being lost and utterly devastated."[49] But while Frank finds the healing God, who restores her dignity, in a direct, sensory encounter with nature, Hillesum's prayer introduces a more complex process of the discovery of God in a spiritual sphere of the self.

Hillesum's dialogue with God proceeds from the traditional supplication for strength, help, and protection to the conceptualization of human responsibility for the Divine. As a supplicant, Hillesum beseeches God to give her the ability to face the world, to find enough courage not to escape from the inexorably increasing horror into the world of dreams. She wants to be strong and to be able to help others. She wants to be the "mediator" to God "for any other soul I can reach."[50]

These prayers reflect Hillesum's anxiety that despair and weakness will prevent her from fulfilling her responsibility toward humanity. They reflect her desire to withstand the trial with dignity, courage, and honor. At this stage, Hillesum's God is the "compelling" God, a God who can draw her to himself in love and help her to maintain her dignity and self-respect as a comforter of the suffering others.

Gradually, however, a different image of God emerges. It is the perception of the divine protector who needs protection, of the divine redeemer who needs to be redeemed. The role reversal posits the victim as the defender of God. Now it is the sufferer who must ascertain God's existence. Paradoxically, in a world in which God is powerless his existence is predicated on the faith of those whom he cannot save. In one of her most moving diary entries, Hillesum pledges help and protection to God, who can neither help nor protect her, in order to preserve the vestiges of a world order that had effectively vanished:

> I shall try to help You, God, to stop my strength ebbing away, though I cannot vouch for it in advance. . . . You cannot help us, but we must help You and defend Your dwelling place inside us to the last. . . . I shall try to make You at home always. Even if I should be locked up in a narrow cell and a cloud should drift past my small barred window, then I shall bring You that cloud, oh God, while there is still the strength in me to do so.[51]

In a dramatic modification of Frank's conception of the sky, the moon, and the meadow as representations of God as the master of creation, Hillesum's offering of the cloud becomes a desperate attempt to heal the ailing God by restoring God's identity as the God of creation. She gradually gains the understanding that her destiny is not confined to helping suffering humanity. Rather, in the reality of the apocalyptic point of no return her responsibility is all-encompassing, because it also signifies caring for the suffering God. In other words, the responsibility lies not only in the concrete, physical support of the victims but also in rescuing the stratum of moral values, the foundations of humaneness, from total destruction.

Hillesum's image of God transcends the notion of the "compelling" God. Beyond the "compelling" God, she discovers a defenseless, yet curiously powerful God. On the one hand, it is a defenseless God, whose survival depends on support from suffering human beings. On the other hand, it is a powerful God, because in a paradoxical way he wields the power of his weakness over the sufferer. It is the power implied in the responsibility for the powerless God, or the destroyed values, which attests to the spiritual strength of the victim.

Hillesum postulates the duty to internalize this strength. She prays, as she puts it, to "what is deepest inside me, which for the sake of convenience I call God."[52] Hillesum thus defines God as the redeeming moral value that needs to be redis- covered and rescued in the reality of total moral collapse. God is the divine spark that constitutes the essence of humanity and therefore must survive. And as the divine spark in us, God is more powerful than ever, because the illuminating spark of the Divine compels us to resist the dehumanizing logic of destruction and affirms our courage in the reality of the apocalypse. What emerges, therefore, is the absolute, irrevocable interdependence of God and humanity/humaneness. To remain human/humane, the individual must protect the "God" part in her; to remain divine, God must be protected and guarded by the individual.

"Yes, it is true," Hillesum writes from Westerbork. "Our ultimate human values are being put to the test."[53] Passing the test, according to Hillesum, will amount to demonstrating the fortitude of the sacred in the human in the unprecedented situation of the apocalyptic termination of history.

A brief reference to Weil's theology will help reemphasize the humanistic—that is, humanity-oriented—focus of Hillesum's religious orientation. Let us reiterate that for both Hillesum and Weil, as well as for Frank, the individual is indispensable to the continuity of the Divine. Because the apocalyptic reality in which they were living and dying precluded any hope that God would intervene and avert a global catastrophe, the survival of God is more than ever contingent on the individual. In Weil's perception, God's perfect love depends on the de-creation of the human self. In Hillesum's view, the presence of God is predicated on the re-creation of the humane self, which will enfold the divine spark.

Weil's notion of the sufferer's salvation through communion with a God who is ready to accept her self-sacrifice is reversed in Hillesum's concept of God's salvation in communion with the sufferer who is capable of protecting the notion of the Divine by living up to the "ultimate human values" even at the time of apocalyptic destruction. This reversal is indicative of the pervasive humanism of both Frank's and Hillesum's religious thought. Both have faith that redemption lies in the fortitude to resist the external enemy of terror as well as to fight the internal enemy of fear and despair.

The internal struggle against fear emerges most conspicuously in Frank's understanding of the healing powers of nature. It is her strength to direct her attention beyond the fear for her physical safety that restores her human dignity. The struggle against the external enemy of political terror that deprived the victim of dignity and self-respect is accentuated in Hillesum's metaphorical expansion of the inner self as a dwelling place for the ailing, powerless God. She "passes the test of values" she sets for herself, thanks to the ability to direct her attention to the needy, in whom she discerns the image of the afflicted God as the ultimate emblem of the other. The disempowered God is in essence the representation of the suffering other, whose powerful neediness performs the miracle of humanism restored.

The notions of God, as they emerge in both Frank and Hillesum, are instrumental to their resistance of terror. God reveals himself in the motivation to construct a self potent enough to transcend the inner imprisonment of fear and despair, to break away from self-concern. This ability emerges in Frank's discovery of God in the beauty of nature and in Hillesum's realization of her inner self as the refuge of the defenseless God. God is close, yet he is Other; he is in me, or in my proximity, but it is up to me to find him. In order to give my attention to that which is not me, I must attain a measure of self-detachment that will liberate me from the confinement of the all-consuming terror.

Finding God, or finding the other, is therefore predicated on the ability to dissociate oneself from total absorption in the suffering, tormented self and to progress toward a more objective self-perception. The presence of God emerges in self-transcendence that liberates from fear and despair. How is this liberating self-transcendence attained? The art of autobiographical writing indicates an important avenue of liberation from the tyranny of dehumanizing dread and deprivation. In its employment of the faculties of the imaginative, the intellectual, and the ethical, the artistic quest for form, and the choice of life narrative and self-representation, signal defiance. Writing as self-discovery brings forth a liberating insight that transcends and thus relativizes the apocalyptic reality of the present.

PART THREE

AUTOBIOGRAPHICAL
ACTS OF RESISTANCE

8

WHERE ART AND SELF MEET

Death as the victim of an attempted collective extermination signifies . . . the radical desubjectification of the individual as part of the
collective from which individual subjectivity derives. . . . The interdependence of individual and collective subjectivity is a condition of
human social life.

—Peter Haidu

An utterance includes not only its signification but the act of reaching
across towards others. The bearer of language does not, as it were,
disappear into the meaning of what is said but remains a silent presence
alongside the utterance itself. Language is a non-violent social bonding
between speaker and addressee.

—Edith Wyschogrod

The act of autobiographical writing is, among other things, an expression of the
individual's desire to leave a mark on the collective consciousness. As "utterance,"
it constitutes an act of "non-violent social bonding"; as a personal life story, it aims
to restore the "interdependence of individual and collective subjectivity." The
autobiographical acts of Edith Stein, Simone Weil, Anne Frank, and Etty Hillesum clearly express the desire of the outcast to reenter the collective. Works of
individuals expelled from society as subhuman, worthless, and despicable species, these autobiographical acts are, first and foremost, a loud refutation of their
authors' "desubjectification."

As demonstrated by the literary genres of the four autobiographical acts, the
authors do not protest against the power that doomed them to the horrific exclusion

from humanity with a uniform voice. Whereas Stein and Weil produced autobiographical life narratives, Frank and Hillesum focused on diaristic writing. The
difference is significant: though in both autobiography and diary the narrator and
the principal character are identical, and in both the subject is primarily the
narrator's life, the perspective in autobiography is mainly retrospective, whereas
in diary it is contemporaneous.[1]

If we accept William Howarth's analogy that posits that "an autobiography is a
self-portrait,"[2] we might venture that a diary is a self-portrait "in the making."
Whereas the autobiographer presents us with a portrayal of her life as it had
evolved before the act of narrating took place, the diarist enables us to follow the
unfolding process of self-portrayal.

These distinctions are pertinent especially as indicators of the intentionality of
the text. We have already established the overall intention of these autobiographical "utterances" as attempts to reenter the social sphere of intersubjectivity. In this
sense, the texts illustrate Hannah Arendt's claim that "with word and deed we
insert ourselves into the human world."[3]

Despite the terror of "collective extermination," each woman asserts her
individuality in an attempt to share her life story with the world. But while this
general intention underlies all four "utterances," the distinction between autobiographical and diaristic texts draws attention to varying authorial objectives.

As mentioned before, the act of writing implies a split between the individual
who writes (the author) and the writing persona of the author (the narrator).
Because in autobiographical writing the author and the narrator are identical, the
split takes place in the autobiographer's mental space. The author's consciousness
as the narrator of her story redirects attention from her reality of misery and
dread to the reality of shaping her emerging story. The attention of the victim-
writer at the time of writing focuses on communicating, through the story
construct, the intention to reenter the sphere of intersubjective social bonding,
even though, in the case of Stein, Weil, Frank, and Hillesum, such a reentry
is impossible.

It is perhaps the awareness of the illusionary nature of this autobiographical
intention that best demonstrates the earnestness of the struggle against despair.
Even if eventually proven futile, artistic effort requires detachment from the
surrounding atmosphere. The attainment of such detachment in the reality of
imminent mental and physical annihilation attests to the seriousness of resisting
dehumanization through art.

Wyschogrod's statement that the bearer of the language remains a silent presence
alongside her utterance is of particular significance in the case of autobiographical

writing. It gains further importance in the case of the autobiographical works in question. While under normal circumstances the author's silent presence in her life story that she tells through the construct of the narrator is almost a commonplace, authorial silent presence becomes a poignant reminder of the situation in which the four women authors were writing their autobiographical accounts.

The autobiographical act aims to vocalize the singular identity of the silent author, the self-concealed bearer of the language, through her narrator-protagonist. In the circumstances of the Holocaust, the utterance of the singular identity defies the rule of terror that aimed to silence the bearer of the language. It is precisely the unique voice of the individual story that the dehumanizing system of destruction wanted to destroy.

Whether completed or in the making, the autobiographical acts of the four women are narrative self-portrayals uttered at the time when the world decreed that they be silent. What, then, were the specific messages that these self-portrayals tried to communicate? How did the autobiographical accounts of the *silenced* bearers of the language reflect the underlying intent to break out of the silencing oppression of external terror and of internal fear?

In terms of form and message, the texts reflect the inexorably foreboding position of the authors in face of the menace of the Final Solution. The exacerbating precariousness of Frank's and Hillesum's existence—their lives increasingly on the brink of the disaster—is concomitant with the immediacy and intermittency characteristic of diaristic writing.

In contrast, Stein's and Weil's relative distance from the atrocity—be it historical, geographical, or even mental—allowed them to reckon with their past lives and to construct their self-portrayals as completed narratives.

As the diverse genres, so the intended messages reflect the consciousness of the situation. The self-representations of both Stein and Weil communicate the intention to reach the world through portrayals of their religious self-definitions. Both Stein and Weil nurtured the illusion that the response of religious self-assertion could still be effective at the time of the unfolding disaster. They clearly believed that their "words and deeds" were relevant in the deteriorating situation. It is possible to claim, certainly in the case of Stein, that they may have even hoped that their messages could reach across and leave a mark on the hostile world.

Neither Frank nor Hillesum cherished such hopes. Instead, they chose to pierce the impregnable barrier of silence by focusing their diaristic narratives on their growth as artists. As the story of the past was no longer valid in the apocalyptic present, both women structured their evolving, daily struggle against the terror, fear, and despair as self-portraits of young artists. In a truly remarkable display of inner strength, they strove through their art to transform into a legacy their increasing physical and mental hardship—a legacy for a world that, as they were well aware, was beyond their reach.

9

STEIN AND WEIL:
DISPLACED
AUTOBIOGRAPHICAL SELVES

*Writing is born from and deals with the acknowledged doubt of an
explicit division, in sum, of the impossibility of one's own place.*

—Michel de Certeau

Perhaps nothing is more explicit with regard to the circumstantial background of
the composition of Edith Stein's *Life in a Jewish Family* and Simone Weil's
"Spiritual Autobiography" as the "impossibility" of the two autobiographers'
"places." Barred from teaching positions, their lives in danger for being Jewish,
the two women found themselves to be outcasts in their native countries. But the
decree of the Final Solution displaced them not only in terms of national "placement" but also in terms of their religious "places." These two "Jewish Catholics"
were confronted with their Jewish origins, from which they had deliberately
detached themselves. Their autobiographies were, to a considerable extent, motivated by the predicament of religious-identity displacement.

Barret Mandel draws our attention to the fact that, on the one hand, "most autobiographies include introductory remarks" that proclaim the objective of the autobiographical portrait, while on the other hand "a whole body of unstated assumptions . . . create a horizon in the autobiography"[1] that needs to be discerned through attentive reading of the text. Indeed, the autobiographies of Edith Stein and Simone Weil start with introductory comments that establish their intent and thereby spell out the explicit message for the reader. At the same time, that which they conspicuously leave unstated traces the "horizon" of the displaced religious identity.

In Stein's opening remarks, which indicate her intent to teach German youth about Jewish life in order to counteract the devastating effects of Nazi anti-Jewish propaganda, she does not claim her story to be unique. On the contrary, in a footnote to her foreword, Stein mentions the accounts of Glückel von Hameln and Pauline Wengeroff, thus grounding her own work in the tradition of Jewish women autobiographers.[2] This reference to other memoirs strengthens the declared purpose of this autobiography as an antidote to anti-Jewish propaganda. As Stein sees it, every personal account of Jewish life represents an authentic document that belies the reasons to hate Jews. By adding to the number of existing individual accounts, Stein hopes to dispel the hateful misconceptions about persons of Jewish descent.

Stein's introductory chapter, "My Mother Remembers, 1815–1891," begins with the generation of Stein's grandparents, introducing Stein's parents, especially her mother, and describing Stein's birth and her early years. Arranging the following nine chapters in strictly chronological order, Stein tells the story of her youth as a member of a large, closely related family clan. The story unfolds as a sympathetic yet matter-of-fact dispassionate first-person narrative. In this sense, it fulfills the initial promise of an informative testimony. Against the background of a Jewish family life, the account portrays the personal experience of a young Jewish woman in Germany. The narrative concludes in the tenth chapter, entitled "The *Rigorosum* in Freiburg, 1916," which focuses on Stein's completing her dissertation and the reception of her doctorate.

Weil's autobiography is more personal in nature, as indicated by its letter form: Weil wrote her "Spiritual Autobiography" for Father Perrin on her departure to Casablanca, escaping the threat of deportation. In terms of structure and approach, the autobiographical works of Stein and Weil reveal certain similarities. Weil's narrative, like Stein's, is explanatory. Stein's intent is to enlighten her German readership on the nature of Jewish life. Weil's purpose is to clarify to her addressee the nature of her refusal of baptism.

Weil sets out to explain her "spiritual state" so that Father Perrin can understand her and not be "sorry" that he "did not lead [her] to baptism." And like Stein, who in a systematic way tells the story of her Jewish life, Weil structures her narrative so that it methodically encompasses all the aspects of her Christian Weltanschauung.

Weil divides her autobiographical account into three main parts. First she tells the story of her growth as a Christian, ending with an account of her mystical experiences, in one of which she felt she had been possessed by Christ. The second part explains her theology of ahistorical Christianity and why her opinions "concerning the non-Christian religions and concerning Israel"[3] would not let her accept the historical notion of the Church. Finally, she turns to criticize the Church as a "collective body" and a "guardian of dogma,"[4] because the Church's dogmatic position does not tolerate dissenters and the Church opposes individual voices of love, faith, and intelligence. For these reasons, Weil confesses to being unable to relinquish her refusal of baptism.

Ostensibly, then, Weil seems consistent with what Mandel calls "introductory remarks," in which she declares the purpose of her "Spiritual Autobiography." As she promises, she explains her reasons for refusing baptism, while at the same time claiming fervently her unflinching Christian faith. But, to return to Mandel, what is the "horizon" of "unstated assumptions" that impels her at the time of exile and uprooting to undertake the effort to reclaim herself? What impels her once again, as she did many times before, to justify her rejection as a Christian of the prevailing Christian doctrine?

One passage delineates the implicit message of Weil's autobiographical act as an attempt to "reach across towards the others" and reenter the subjectivity of social bonds. After having recounted the story of her Christian growth and her mystical experiences, and after having enumerated her objections to the historical grounding of the Church, Weil explains the compelling motivation for this explication of her spiritual self:

> And as I am going [away] more or less with the idea of probable death, I do not believe that I have the right to keep it [this autobiographical narrative] to myself. For after all, the whole of this matter is not a question concerning me myself. It concerns God. I am really nothing in it all. If one could imagine any possibility of error in God, I should think that it had all happened to me by mistake. But perhaps God likes to use castaway objects, waste, rejects.[5]

The rationale Weil offers here for her spiritual self-representation differs from the "introductory remark" that presents the text as a self-justification to Father Perrin for not having accepted baptism. As she explains it here, her story is not an apologetic explanation, but rather an act of compliance with a divine command. Indeed, the rhetoric of the analogy to the unworthy bearer of the divine truth suggests the sacred nature of the position that Weil wanted to assume in relation to the world. The drama of exile and her premonition of death reinforces the significance of the message she is carrying. The identification as God's beloved outcast not only elevates her social stature but also places her, as God's messenger, in the ranks of the traditionally mocked, socially rejected prophetic figures. On the one hand, Weil's self-representation as the instrument of God places her in the role of the bearer of God's message. On the other hand, it identifies her as a prophet who cannot disobey the command of God and must communicate the message.

Weil's claim to be God's truth-bearer reveals the "horizon" of a two-tiered intention. The self-representation as God's messenger "legitimizes" her identity as an unbaptized Christian.[6] At the same time, the sense of mission defuses the fear and anxiety of the awaiting ordeal of exile. The sense of avocation in sharing her views with the world allows her to see the exile and the likelihood of death as a ratification of her "chosenness." This implied "horizon" of her autobiographical portrayal is a function of Weil's consciousness of the "impossibility of her place" as both Jew and Christian. It demonstrates the extent to which Weil sought to reduce her fear of loneliness and degradation as an outcast. She attempted to see her isolation, in its suffering and affliction, as a special way of reconnection with the world.

The final sentence, in which Weil tells Father Perrin "Every time I think of the crucifixion of Christ I commit the sin of envy," confirms the underlying intention of the "Autobiography." It brings home her intensity to escape the torment of social displacement through a mystical transformation into a bearer of a new vision to the world. While seemingly writing a retrospective of the evolution of her Christian identity, Weil in effect writes herself toward the vision of the special "place" she would want to occupy in relation to the world.

James Olney suggests that "to redeem time is one of the autobiographer's prime motives, perhaps *the* prime motive—perhaps, indeed, the only real motive of the autobiographer."[7] Compared with Weil's underlying construction of her "future autobiography" as a Christlike sufferer, Stein's self-narrative seems to be a straightforward illustration of autobiographical redemption of the past. Unlike Weil's account as a composite of a life narration and a narrative of ideas, Stein's account focuses on a chronological, factual rendition of her life story.

It would appear that Stein's autobiographical work is marked by the absence of an "unstated horizon," but Olney's emphasis on *time* redeemed in autobiography draws attention to the "unstated horizon" in Stein's self-representation. A closer look at the figuration of time in her text—and, more specifically, the time that remains unredeemed—reveals an interesting subtext of Stein's autobiography. Indeed, the subtext of unredeemed time becomes even more conspicuous when compared with Weil's treatment of time. Both self-portraits display the corresponding traits of muted "religious times." Weil's redeemed time is her "Christian time," which marks the evolution of her Christian consciousness. Stein redeems her "Jewish time," which marks her childhood and adolescence. The intentionality of Weil's dismissal of her ethnic origins precludes the representation of her historical self. The single-minded purpose of Stein's life account as a Jew ignores her present self as a Christian.

We shall recall the epigraph to Chapter 8 and the notion of the utterance as the opening of the silent bearer of the language to others. We note that in the case of these two autobiographical authors the opening of the self is partial, as each of the women deliberately muted an aspect of her narrating self. It is possible to understand why in Weil's case the original Jewish self must be silenced so that her new self as the messenger of a new vision of Christianity can ensure her special "place" as a displaced visionary. But why would Stein silence her legitimate "place"—her identity as a Christian and a Carmelite—while emphasizing the politically discredited identity of the Jew?

The conclusion of Stein's memoir signals that the omission of the story of conversion was not accidental. Stein ends her autobiography with an account of the celebration of her doctorate with Husserl. The last brief scene focuses on her leaving Göttingen with Frau Reinach.

We know that shortly after, Frau Reinach, the wife of the converted Jewish phenomenologist Adolf Reinach, played an instrumental part in Stein's religious conversion. Frau Reinach's pious acceptance of her husband's death at war in 1917 inspired Stein to convert.[8] The presence of Frau Reinach at the closing of Stein's autobiography reinforces the argument of Stein's deliberate decision not to continue her autobiographical story beyond 1916, a year in which she received her doctoral degree. Stein's departure with Frau Reinach constitutes a prolepsis of Stein's subsequent conversion, a development she wanted to keep out of her account. The complete omission of allusions to her future conversion in her life narrative seems to reaffirm Stein's intention to keep her autobiography strictly within the boundaries of her Jewish time.

This is precisely what disturbs Sister Josephine Koeppel, the translator of Stein's account. In her "Translator's Afterword" to *Life in a Jewish Family*, Koeppel raises the issue of the content and the conclusion of Stein's autobiographical narrative. She deplores the absence of the story of Stein's conversion and vocation and questions the abrupt, *in media res* end of the account. Koeppel's disapproval explains the liberty she took with the title *Life in a Jewish Family* by adding the subtitle *Her Unfinished Autobiographical Account.*

Koeppel tries to explain the omissions by arguing that, after the escape to Holland, "it is . . . probable that Edith found no time for that type of writing."[9] At the same time, however, Koeppel undermines this speculation when reporting that the manuscript, left behind in Germany, was smuggled at Stein's request and at great risk across the border to Holland in 1939. The translator thus inadvertently calls attention to the importance Stein must have attached to this text.

It is significant that, despite the risk entailed in smuggling the manuscript, Stein added only one chapter to the account—the chapter concerning the completion of her doctorate and her departure with Frau Reinach. Stein's insistence on retrieving the manuscript draws attention to the final episode, which marks the end of her life story as a Jew.

Is it possible that the risky act of smuggling the manuscript implies a subconscious need of the now Carmelite author to remain close to the Jewish aspect of her self as represented by her autobiographical narrator-protagonist? Could it be that the need for the proximity of her Jewish self-portrait signaled her inability to suppress her Jewish identity, especially in view of the danger her Jewish family was experiencing at the time? It is impossible to verify these conjectures, but it is possible to claim that the intentional incompleteness of her autobiography attests to Stein's ethical integrity and to her commitment to the educational message of her account.

Faithful to her objective to educate German youth in matters concerning Judaism, Stein eliminated components that might have jeopardized the goal of her undertaking. In fact, Stein's clearly stated intent of her work provides a plausible explanation of why she refrained from alluding to her later conversion and vocation. Under the political circumstances, a story of conversion would have undermined her intention to promote tolerance of Jews. To ensure the effectiveness of her project to redeem her Jewish past, it was necessary for Stein to suppress her Christian present.

Both Stein and Weil manipulated the "times" of their religious identities to actualize the intention of their autobiographical accounts. They tailored their self-portrayals to their perceptions of the immediate needs of collapsing humanism. Each in her own way and manner felt that she had a message to the world, a message that would contribute to the morally disintegrating human society. Both used their life stories to get their messages across. Stein and Weil muted the aspects of their selves that might antagonize their readers and make them unreceptive to the social-religious messages they intended to take to the world.

This attitude reveals an optimistic faith that their utterances were relevant and that, consequently, intersubjective social rebonding was still possible. We shall observe in the diaries of Anne Frank and Etty Hillesum that with the growing proximity of the horror this hope for reconnection practically disappears. Instead of opposing the terror by reaching out to the world with a redeeming message, Frank's and Hillesum's diaries turned inward, focusing on articulation of the silent presence of the developing artist. Conscious of the world's absolute repudiation of their existence, they embarked on a process that pitched the prowess of imagination and creativity against the victim's powerlessness and despair.

10

FRANK AND HILLESUM: THE DIARISTS AS GROWING ARTISTS

[Art's] only aim is to give another form to a reality that it is nevertheless forced to preserve as the source of its emotion.

—Albert Camus

The perseverance of Anne Frank's and Etty Hillesum's diaristic writing (in Hillesum's case, also letters sent from Westerbork to her Dutch friends in Amsterdam) affirms the struggle the two women waged to preserve the part of the self that Hillesum named "God" or "ultimate human values."

Both Frank's and Hillesum's diaristic introspections reveal highly self-demanding ethical standards. Their diaries present moving testimonies of the struggle to maintain humanity at the time of dehumanization, of their efforts not to allow the Nazi terror to rob them of their human/humane image. But the diaries are not merely accounts of an ethical nature; they are also testimonies of the development of their authors as young artists. It is important to remember that their artistic identities were shaped by the reality of a historically unprecedented ordeal. At the same time, this reality presented the artist with the unprecedented task of shaping her ordeal in an artistic form.

To begin to grasp the difficulty the two diarists faced, we need only remind ourselves of a famous statement by Elie Wiesel that has been reiterated by many survivors and postwar students of the Holocaust: "There is no such thing as a literature of the Holocaust, nor can there be."[1] While it is true that Wiesel and others believed that a retrospective literary representation of the Holocaust experience is impossible, there remains the problem of how to represent the experience at the time it is occurring. Anticipating the predicament of the post-Holocaust writer, the artist in the Holocaust contended with conflicting emotions: on the one hand, the frustration of the futile search for an adequate language of representation, and on the other hand, the irreducible need to express the horror.

Despite the frustration entailed in the search for the proper lexis to represent the "unreal reality," the diarists continued writing as long as possible. The motivation for self-portrayal against the reality of the Holocaust arose in part as a process of self-education, in part as an illusory attempt to maintain a semblance of discourse with the world, in part as a search for God in the world of the Holocaust.

It seems, however, that a remark of Alfred Kantor, a Holocaust survivor who made hundreds of sketches in Theresienstadt, Schwarzheide, and even Auschwitz, illuminates an important aspect of the motivating force for creating the art of the Holocaust *at the time of* the catastrophe. Kantor claims that, as an artist, "by taking the role of an 'observer' I could at least for a few moments detach myself from what was going on in Auschwitz and was therefore better able to hold together the threads of sanity."[2]

The notion of self-detachment as an observer is of crucial importance for the creative process in the Holocaust. It was precisely the adoption of the identity of the artist-observer that offered a momentary respite from the suffering, degraded, terrorized victim Kantor had become. The intent to represent the experience in art reduced the immediacy of the threat that the experience signified. This ability to detach from the suffering self through artistic engagement proved to be essential to Kantor's survival.

An important distinction thus emerges between the post-Holocaust testimony and the Holocaust testimony. Through her post-Holocaust testimony, the survivor attempts to return to the experience and to relive it, often as an attempt to exorcise the haunting past. But at the time of the unbearable suffering, the victim records the horror in an attempt to distance herself from it.

Kantor's observation provides an insight into the function of art in the lives of the two diarists. It is true that their art did not, could not, touch the ultimate horror of Auschwitz. To create art in the concentration camp was next to impossible, and even Kantor, one of the few artists who worked in concentration camps, destroyed his sketches for fear of being discovered. He reproduced them after the war.[3] It is therefore not my intention to present the diaries as testimonies of the ultimate horror of the Holocaust. However, as works of doomed-to-death authors, the diaries testify to artistic creativity as emotional support in the completely hopeless situation of the Final Solution.

The persistence with which both Frank and Hillesum held on to their writing—we should recall Hillesum's postcard thrown out of the train to Auschwitz, "We left the camp singing"[4]—attests to their perception of art as a safeguard of their humanity and humaneness. The insistence on their vocation as artists is reflected in the search for adequate language and literary forms to represent their experiences. Their vocation resounds with a claim for self-expression at the time of depersonalizing atrocity. At the same time, their consciousness of the historical function of their testimonies evinces the growing artists' sense of the moral significance of their self-writing.

The Improbable Possibility of New Narrative Forms

The notion of history invalidating existing literary forms became quite commonplace in the postwar era. For instance, Paul Ricoeur observes: "Perhaps we are at the end of an era where narrating no longer has a place . . . because human beings no longer have any experience to share. . . . And yet . . . perhaps, in spite of everything, it is necessary . . . to believe that new narrative forms, which we do not yet know how to name, are already being born."[5] In a truly prescient way, both Hillesum and Frank anticipated that the existing literary genres would be inadequate to communicate the experience of the Holocaust. Watching the "unreal reality" of Westerbork, Hillesum wrote: "One should be able to write fairy tales here. . . . The misery here is so beyond all bounds of reality that it has become unreal. Sometimes I walk through the camp laughing secretly to myself because of the completely grotesque circumstances."[6] And Frank commented on the implausibility of any attempt to tell the story of the Annex: "Just imagine how interesting it would be if I were to publish a romance of the 'Secret Annexe.' The title alone would be enough to make people think it was a detective story. . . . Although I tell you a lot, you only know very little of our lives. . . . It is almost indescribable."[7]

The diary as a "new narrative form" seems to be a contradiction in terms. After all, a diary represents a well-established, clearly defined literary genre. According to Lawrence Rosenwald, the diary takes the form of a chronological sequence of dated entries addressed to an unspecified audience and its function is to record events and aspects of the writer's own life.[8] By virtue of its dating system, the diary is a type of historical record. It is intended as a story that might be shared with others, even if posthumously, and verified against the general historical background of the time it was composed.

Hillesum and Frank were highly skeptical about the possibility of sharing their experiences with others. In their attempts to frame their accounts in a literary convention, they deliberated among the genres of "fairy tale," "romance," and "detective story," while characterizing the events they were trying to turn into a story as "unreal," "grotesque," and "indescribable." When contending with the need to articulate the experiences, they encountered the problem of translating the unprecedented into the language of the familiar. What disturbed them, however, was not only that they might be unable to find common ground with potential readers, but also their own bewilderment at the unreal and indescribable nature of the situation they were experiencing.

The existence of the diaries of both Frank and Hillesum demonstrates, however, that despite their shocked bewilderment they felt compelled to record the "unreal reality" of their existence. The intermittency that characterizes the diaristic recording was apparently a viable form of representation for the unpredicted and unpredictable situation. But in the situation of intensifying horror, the closeness of the act of recording to the recorded event raises the issue of an emotional predicament.

The act of diaristic recording requires a re-vision of the immediate past. In both Hillesum's and Frank's situations, such a re-vision signifies a reencounter with degradation, deprivation, and fear. Yet both diarists asserted an irrepressible need to record not only the events but also the feelings and reactions the situation evoked. We have already witnessed Frank's fighting off the nightmares evoked by reports about the atrocities that had reached the Annex, and we have noted her confessions of bouts of terrible depression and fear. The same response to the surrounding horror emerges in Hillesum. She writes how, after a day of work at the camp, "I lay in the dark with burning eyes as scene after scene of human suffering passed before me."[9]

The focus on the mimetic, accurate renditions both of the daily events and of their mental impact raises the issue of the raison d'être of the diaries. Why would both diarists feel compelled to dwell in their writing on the clear signals of the approaching end as well as on the fear those signs evoked? Why would they choose to contemplate rather than suppress the victimization process, the fearful unintelligibility of which undermined all sense of security and stability?

In approaching these questions, we need to consider the problematic of the mimetic representation of apocalyptic destruction. The representation of such a reality subverts the Aristotelian notion of the mimetic plot as a carefully selected sequence of events. Mimesis, "the medium of imitation," as Aristotle defines it,[10] foregrounds the "unity of plot," which is predicated on the appropriate selection of the "probable or the necessary" events clustered around "one action." The unity of action is shaped through selection out of the "infinitely various . . . incidents in one man's life."[11] The narrative is directed at the audience, and if effective the cathartic impact of its mimetic construct, especially in the case of a tragic tale, "will thrill with horror and melt to pity" those who hear the story.[12] Aristotle postulates that in order to be effectively cathartic "the tragic plot must not be composed of irrational parts," because "the poet should prefer probable impossibilities to improbable possibilities."[13]

An invocation of the Aristotelian precepts in the context of the Annex and Westerbork reveals the inadequacy of the classic literary tradition in the unprecedented reality of the Final Solution. In terms of selection of events, the range of options was extremely limited. In the reality of the isolation, the deportations, and the mass murder of the Jews, the response of horror and pity presented a totally implausible expectation. In fact, any response of comprehension would be quite unlikely, because, as both diarists realized, their stories depicted experiences that were beyond comprehension. The unfolding "plots" were so outlandish that even their authors, as we have seen, had difficulty characterizing them in terms of accepted classifications of literary works.

The authors' ambivalence concerning genre is indicative of the breakup of literary convention with regard to the Holocaust event. The "new narrative," to recall Ricoeur, adumbrates disrupted communication between the work and the audience whose members can no longer recognize familiar generic markers in the text.

In contrast to Aristotelian tenets, in the testimonies of the Jewish genocide by Hillesum and Frank the factual emerges as improbable and irrational. Both diaries deal with the unprecedented problematic of the "improbable possibility" of the Holocaust.

The consciousness of the unfolding "possibility" of such a catastrophe confronts the diarist with a situation whose finality precludes any referential framework. As a rule, life presents the artist with a myriad of viable options, out of which she can select those that will forge her story. Improbably, in the situation of the Holocaust, life became an artifact carefully staged by the perpetrators: it became a stagnant existence in the shadow of apocalyptic destruction by helpless waiting for a horrible death in a "no-exit," limbo-like entrapment.

In the Aristotelian *ars poetica,* the function of art is to reshape and refigure life through conscious selection and compression. In the reality of the apocalyptic destruction of history, the entrapment in terror has ineluctably reduced the life of the victim to the torpor of the complete lack of choice. As a consciously made choice, writing thus becomes a sign of vitality that counteracts the inertia of fatalism and fear. We note an inversion of the Aristotelian paradigm that designed art as a mimetic construct—a highly contrived representation of the infinite and endless possibilities of life.

In the reality of life immobilized by the external terror of persecution and by the internal torpor of fear and anxiety, the Aristotelian precept of "probable impossibility" is inverted. The diaries of the victims of the Jewish genocide present the "improbable possibility" of art-as-life in the death-in-life reality of the implacable decree of the Final Solution.

Art as the Safeguard of Mental Survival

For both Hillesum and Frank, the act of writing transcended its historical function of testimony. It became the emotional support, the sole raison d'être, and the rescue from despair. As Hillesum writes: "The worst thing for me will be when I am no longer allowed pencil and paper to clarify my thoughts—they are indispensable to me, for without them I shall fall apart and be utterly destroyed."[14] Frank reiterates Hillesum's feelings when she notes: "The brightest spot of it all is that at least I can write my thoughts and feelings, otherwise I should be absolutely stifled."[15]

The act of recording the "improbable possibilities" of the "stillness" of the Annex entrapment and of the regularity of the departing trains from Westerbork to Auschwitz defines artistic creativity as a life-sustaining system. The act of art is restorative because it counteracts the "stifling" passivity of awaiting the unavoidable end. Writing becomes a lifeline, because it validates thoughts and feelings and thereby highlights the relevance of the individual in a reality in which the individuality of the Jewish victim had been obliterated.

The acknowledgment of fear, anxiety, and despair attests to an emotional vitality that counteracts the deadening negativity of the depicted feelings. At the same time, the deintensification of feelings in the process of writing deflects, to an extent, the immobilizing premonition of the imminent end.

Focus on art saves from despair because it transcends the constant anxiety about physical survival. In fact, artistic creativity becomes the safeguard of mental survival. Writing becomes a moving, vital force that contravenes the consciousness of death. This perception of the therapeutic function of the artistic process illuminates Frank's claim, "I can shake off everything if I write; my sorrows disappear, my courage is reborn."[16]

Hillesum echoes Frank's sense of freedom from the compulsive anxiety about survival when she says, "I know how to free my creative powers more and more from the snare of material concerns."[17]

Writing signifies communication through language. The consciousness of engaging in an act of communication erected a mental defense against the ordeal that condemned the victim to silence. But under the decree of isolation from the world, the process of communication transfers to the inner self. The dialogue with the self through self-writing alleviates the threat of self-estrangement, of mental disintegration. When, after the burglary, the terrified inmates of the Annex discuss burning Frank's diary, she responds vehemently, "Not my diary; if my diary goes, I go with it!"[18] Clearly perceived by its author as the anchor of sanity and of the sense of wholeness, the diary becomes indispensable to maintaining her will to live.

For Hillesum, communication as a lifeline need not take a written form; it just needs to be conceived in her mind as a prayer to create a sense of protection. In the reality of the camp, the ultimate grace is the poetic word: "Give me a small line of verse from time to time, oh God, and if I cannot write it down for lack of paper or light, let me then address it to you softly in the evening to Your great Heaven. But please give me a small line of verse now and then."[19] A "line of verse" has the power to appease fear by restoring the dialogue with God, who resides in her inner self. This communication bestows a sense of serenity that transcends the pandemonium of the deportation camp.

Paul Tillich claims: "The most fundamental expression of [every encounter with reality] is the language which gives man the power to abstract from the concretely given and . . . to return to it, to interpret and transform it. The most vital being is the being which has the word and is by the word liberated from bondage to the given."[20] As testimonies of the "concretely given" of the Holocaust, both diaries present poignant illustrations of the word as a liberating force. The words the diarists find to describe the horror of their reality also free the writers, if only for a moment, from the reality of horror. In a curious way, words erect a protective barrier against fear and despair.

In this sense, the creative ability "to abstract, to interpret and to transform" the reality of death through words amounts to affirmation of life. Putting the situation in words empowers the victim, because her voice breaks the stillness of apocalyptic destruction. At the same time, the word that shapes reality endows a sense of control that distances the horror.

The Liberating Voice of Art

Saul Friedlander's apt observation elucidates the importance of the artistic quest even at the time of an overwhelming tragedy: "It is the reality and significance of modern catastrophes that generate the search for a new voice and not the use of a specific voice which constructs the significance of these catastrophes."[21] In the reality of the Holocaust the terrible signification of the uttered word paradoxically engenders a sense of liberation, control, and even consolation. The concreteness of the reality is relived in its immediate diaristic rendition. For a short while, the menacing reality is transformed into the subject of an artistic interest.

How can artistic activity possibly displace the overpowering concern about immediate physical survival? How does the need to record life defuse the ever-present threat of imminent annihilation? I suggest that the way the artist uses the time that elapses between the actual experience and its diaristic record-ing is essential to the process of emotional liberation from oppressive reality through writing.

As "a book of time,"[22] the diary points to two durations of time: the duration of the occurrence and the duration of its recording. In the unprecedented situation in which the diaries unfold, the duration of the recording—the time of the writing activity—contravenes the consciousness of the timeless stagnation of the Annex and of the uninterrupted routine of deportations from Westerbork. Even more significant, the intention to record affects the writer's perspective on the experi-ence. The observer's perception of the reality as raw material to be shortly shaped in writing engenders an attitude that obviates the sense of hopelessness the experience evokes.

Henri Bergson observes an interesting correlation between the inspirational stage of artistic creativity and the actualization of the work of art: "To the artist that creates a picture by drawing it from the depths of his soul, . . . the duration of . . . the time taken up by the invention is one with the invention itself. . . . It is a vital process, something like the ripening of an idea."[23]

According to Bergson, a work of art is the product both of the time in which the genesis of the artistic idea is conceived and of the time during which this vision shapes itself into an artistic form of expression. In this sense, the particular mode of the diary—an intermittent recording of events as they evolve—indicates a continuous, almost uninterrupted, creative use of time. The experience engenders the intention to record it. Transformed in the artist's creative imagination into a narrative, the experience is almost instantly transcribed into a diaristic entry. As the art of "microscopic literary writing,"[24] each entry of the diary becomes a distinct, creative act, conceived in the short time that separates the experience from its recording.

For each of the diarists, the daily preoccupation with her art infuses the concreteness of her experience—be it hiding in the Annex, or taking care of the needy in Westerbork—with an ongoing, subterranean artistic activity. The consciousness that anything that happens can be used as subject matter for the creative act of writing infuses a sense of meaning and continuity in daily existence.

Steven Kagle claims: "The life of a diary is often born of tension . . . in the life of its author, [which] is a sustaining force of a diary."[25] He suggests that the vicissitudes of life engender the ongoing need for diaristic recording. In the context of Hillesum's and Frank's particular situations, however, the existence of inertia and mental paralysis does not produce tension that leads to creativity; the creative impetus arises from the diary itself. By virtue of its existence in the reality of the Final Solution, the diary generates tension that upholds life. The determination to engage in diaristic writing creates life-sustaining tension, because the activity of re-creating life in art clashes with the terrible alternative of passive surrender to the lifelessness of despair.

The diary thus becomes indispensable to its author's sense of meaningful being. Frank personifies the diary as her other self when she admits, "Although I can't express myself properly anywhere else, . . . in my diary I can completely. It cries with pain or joy as I sometimes do myself!"[26]

While the restrictions of life in the Annex suppress Frank's genuine, impulsive reactions, the art of writing provides a sense of freedom and spontaneity. The recognition of her self and the innermost feelings, emotions, and reactions that she finds in the process of writing is revitalizing because it validates her sense of relevance as an individual.

Hillesum moves even further, beyond the notion of writing as a reaffirmation of the meaningful self. As she perceives it, writing does not reveal meaning in life, but is, rather, the force that shapes her life as a meaningful whole. "Such a longing to jot down a few words!" she writes. "Such a strong sense of: here on these pages I am spinning my thread. And a thread does run through my life, through my reality, like a continuous line."[27]

The sense of continuity that every entry creates infuses a "strong sense" of control. Shaping the sense of her existence through writing is empowering. Even further, Hillesum seems to indicate that life can gain meaning only *as* a narrative.

The diaristic life-narrative sustains meaning in the meaninglessness of apocalyptic destruction by creating an illusion of historical continuity. By virtue of their calendric recording, the diaries delineate progression from the past into the future, a progression that offsets the sense of the apocalyptic hour. In the diary's "microscopic" writing, today's entry follows yesterday's and presupposes tomorrow's. Every entry produces anticipation of the next entry and thus creates future expectations. It is precisely the intermittent and dated form of diaristic writing that infuses the recorded life with a sense of vitality.

The diary is never a finished book, but always, as Rosenwald tells us, "a manuscript by necessity. During the life of the diarist, the diary remains unfinished and open; something can always be added."[28] Not only added—we could continue Rosenwald's observation—but also reread and reconsidered. New perspectives can be gained, and the past can be reevaluated. As an evolving record, the diaries enable the diarists to, so to speak, read "backward" and write "forward"; to draw analogies to formerly described events and thus to reconstruct the historical flow of their lives, which were excised from history.

For instance, Frank writes that on turning some pages of her diary she found her previous behavior selfish and inconsiderate and therefore decided to change in the future. The diary has become both the record and the motivating force of her personal development. As she observes, "I have been trying to understand the Anne of a year ago and to excuse her, because my conscience isn't clear . . . without being able to explain, on looking back, how it happened." She then adds: "This diary is of great value to me, because it has become a book of memoirs in many places."[29] Hillesum expresses a similar need for a retrospective self-evaluation when she writes: "I shall read through my old diaries. I have decided not to tear them up after all. Perhaps later on they will help reacquaint me with my former self."[30] For her too the diary becomes the book of personal history, the story of her constantly changing self. Despite the decree of terror that robbed the victims of their past and their future, the diary reaffirms, even in its limited, "microscopic" form, the historicity of the diarist.

But the diaries are not merely records of private lives. Both Frank and Hillesum knew that their personal experiences represented an unprecedented historical event. And so, while the diaries attest to the individual's defiance of her dehistoricization, they also demonstrate the diarists' search for a language of art to represent the apocalyptic context of their experience.

The Art of Holocaust Testimony

Frank's sense of the testimonial value of her diary is manifest in her decision to recopy the diary for publication after the war. Responding to the announcement of the Dutch government in London that after the war private documents will be needed to write a comprehensive history of the war, Frank confided in Kitty:

"You've known for a long time that my greatest wish is to become a journalist someday and later on a famous writer. . . . I want to publish a book entitled *Echt Achterhuis* after the war. Whether I shall succeed or not, I cannot say, but my diary will be a great help." As the editors of the Critical Edition of the diary indicate, Frank started recopying and editing the existing entries on May 20, 1944.[31]

Frank's diary was therefore intended not only as a personal life narrative. Its author saw it as a testimonial of the ordeal of hiding directed at a general readership. Methodically and painstakingly, Frank tried to create a record of a life in a world that, as she observed, was "indescribable." As she turns to her addressee, Kitty, she struggles with the language to give accurate descriptions of situations that are "beyond belief."[32]

Kitty, whose persona determines the epistolary form of the diary, is the key to the understanding of Frank's self-motivation as a recorder of history. Kitty is an imaginary bosom friend placed outside the reality of occupied Europe. This construct of the distant addressee functions on a number of narrative levels.

On the most evident level, Kitty's characterization serves as the model of the readership to which *Het Achterhuis* will be addressed. The addressee-outsider designates the text as a testimonial for those who did not experience the menace of the Final Solution. The typology of an addressee who knows neither about the horror of the raging war nor about the systematic destruction of European Jews presents Frank as a self-appointed chronicler writing for an audience that is ignorant of the unfolding cataclysmic war. Thus, Frank describes in detail the rumors about deportations, the air raids on Amsterdam, the news about the advancing Allied armies. She contextualizes her personal story in the reality of the world at war:

> Everything has upset me again this morning, so I wasn't able to finish a single thing properly. It is terrible outside. Day and night more of those poor miserable people [Jews] are being dragged off, with nothing but a rucksack and a little money. On the way they are deprived even of these possessions. Families are torn apart, the men, women, and children all being separated. . . . The earth is plowed by bombs, and every hour hundreds and thousands of people are killed in Russia and Africa. No one is able to keep out of it, the whole world is waging war and although it is going better for the Allies, the end is not yet in sight.[33]

At this level, Frank's intention to share her experience with an addressee-outsider approximates the intent of Holocaust survivors-writers—for instance,

Elie Wiesel, Pelagia Lewinska, Primo Levi, and others—who wrote after the war because they felt compelled to leave their testimony for posterity. Like them, she writes for a distant reader who is unfamiliar with the situation.

At another level, the position of the reader as an addressee communicates Frank's need to tell her story not only for posterity but also for an existing though distant audience. This need is further conveyed in the "conversational" narrative of the diary. The existence of the addressee is not only dramatically reaffirmed in each entry by the heading "Dear Kitty" and the signature "Yours, Anne," but often by directly addressed statements, comments, and references, such as "I must tell you," "I think you should know," and "You asked me . . . so I must reply."

As demonstrated in its epistolary form, this diary is intended to be read. The consciousness of writing for a reader "over there" highlights the therapeutic function of the addressee. The creation of a special friend—a confidante ready to hear but not to condemn—indicates Frank's artistic strategy of searching for an outsider whose sympathetic ear would alleviate her fear and despair. The consciousness of being listened to helps to unburden the frustration of the hopelessness of the situation. However, the construction of a *naive* listener evinces an even more sophisticated strategy of a search for proper self-representation in the context of the reprehensible historical time.

As mentioned, Kitty is a mind unaffected by the war. In many instances, the awareness of the *tabula rasa* consciousness of the recipient of the story affects the manner and the voice of the narrative. The intention to convey the story to the naive addressee necessitates innovation, diversification, and often comic relief, in order to create interest and attention. In her "good"—that is, hopeful—moments, Frank realizes that a representation of such a terrible reality requires a rhetoric appropriate for the "uninitiated" person.

Frank's deliberate search for means and ways to depict the "indescribable" attests to her growth as an artist. Even more significant, writing to edify both her immediate addressee and the postwar reader of history affords a sense of empowerment that permits her, even if for a moment, to minimize the seriousness of her situation. She writes: "I regard our hiding as a dangerous adventure, romantic and interesting at the same time. In my diary, I treat all the privations as amusing. . . . I am young and strong and am living a great adventure."[34]

The sense of potency that Frank achieves through writing allows her to assert the identity of an aspiring artist, whose art, as she claims in a curiously prescient statement, will outlive her: "I want to write later on. . . . I want to go on living even after my death! And therefore I am grateful to God for giving me this gift, this possibility of developing myself and of writing, of expressing all that is in me!"[35]

In appreciating Frank's moments of exuberant artistic potency, we should remember that these were rare instances of hopefulness offset by times of despair and paralyzing fear. Her claim to "be expressing all that is in me" is by no means a euphemism; her self-portrayal is characterized by honest representations of youthful optimism as well as vivid depictions of hopelessness and depression. She confesses that fear makes her turn white, get "a tummy-ache and heart palpitations." Her anticipation that she would go on living through her art even after her death is contravened by premonitions of the approaching horrible, devoid of all greatness end: "I see myself alone in a dungeon. . . . Sometimes I wander by the roadside, or our 'Secret Annexe' is on fire, or they come to take us away at night. . . . I see everything as if it is actually taking place and it gives me the feeling that it may all happen to me very soon."[36] The shifting moods elucidate the tremendous hardship of the uncertainty and tension endured in the Annex. "Am I only fourteen?" Frank wonders, "I have been through things that hardly anyone of my age has undergone."[37]

The moments of panic illuminate even more clearly the heroic struggle that Frank, the aspiring writer of her war story, was waging with and in her diary. For even though the overpowering fear made her want to "go and lie down under my bed in despair,"[38] the account proves that she did not give in. She went on writing, recopying, and editing her entries, hoping in hopelessness, to become the writer who would tell the tale of the "indescribable" experience of the global war against humanity and the total war against Jews.

I would suggest that the eloquently and straightforwardly recorded vacillations between "high" and "low" moments constitute undeniable evidence of Frank's calling as an artist. The responsibility of the artist to shape her fear into a testimony for the unimplicated world, as represented by Kitty, proved stronger than fear itself.

For Hillesum the overriding sense of artistic calling is as compelling as Frank's and perhaps, owing to the circumstances, more dramatic. Exposed to the terrifying reality of Westerbork, Hillesum never ceased to struggle for words to describe the atrocity she was witnessing, and of which, as she knew very well, she would soon become a victim. In her letters to her Gentile friends in Amsterdam, she acknowledged both the difficulty and the imperative to record the unimaginable. On August 24, 1943, the night of yet another transport, she wrote:

> I have told you often enough that no words and images are adequate to describe nights like these. But still I must try to convey something of it to you. One always has the feeling here of being the ears and eyes of a piece of Jewish history, but there is also the need sometimes to be a still, small voice. We must keep one another in touch with everything that happens, . . . each of us contributing his own little piece of stone to the great mosaic that will take shape once the war is over.[39]

Hillesum appears to identify herself as "a still, small voice" of a writer searching for adequate words and images to portray the sights and the sounds of Jewish history at its apocalyptic point of no return. Both Frank and Hillesum predicated their prospects as writers on effective representations of the evolving reality. Let us recall Frank's editing of her diary in preparation for publishing it under the title *Het Achterhuis* after the war.

Frank, as we have seen, admitted the limitations of her descriptions of the "indescribable, incredible, beyond belief" reality and acknowledged the inadequacy of accepted literary conventions to classify her story. Hillesum was more articulate about the need for "new forms" of art for the unprecedented enormity of the disaster. In another letter to her friends, she tried to explain the objective difficulties of becoming the chronicler of Westerbork:

> It would take a great poet [to write the chronicle of Westerbork]. . . . The whole of Europe is gradually being turned into one great prison camp. The whole Europe will undergo this same bitter experience. To simply record the bare facts of families torn apart, of possessions plundered and liberties forfeited, would soon become monotonous. Nor is it possible to pen picturesque accounts of barbed wire and vegetable swill to show outsiders what it's like. Besides, I wonder how many outsiders will be left if history continues along the paths it has taken.[40]

It is interesting to note that Hillesum's observation of the atrocities inflicted on Jews and of the totality of the world war echo Frank's description of the terrible situation outside the Annex. But Hillesum's approach highlights her preoccupation with the problematic of literary representation. Her tone conveys a self-directed bitter irony that, as the world is coming to its historical ending, recording becomes superfluous and ineffective. In the monotonous repetitiveness of the atrocity, time stands still. In the unbroken uniformity of the prison camp, lack of choices precludes narrative. No selection of events can be made to create, in the Aristotelian sense, a gripping, cathartic plot. Because the whole world is being gradually engulfed in the terminal phase of its own apocalyptic destruction, no audience is left to experience cathartic relief. The mundaneness of the disaster displaces the pathos of tragedy. The totality of the oppression turns suffering into commonplace.

Nonetheless, Hillesum strives to record the "unreal reality" of her world, and in this sense she reaches further than Frank, who combatted the inertia of despair through vivid descriptions of her fearful fantasies and nightmares. Hillesum fights the fearful "monotony" of the disaster by turning it into an artistic challenge. To a remarkable degree, her writing can be seen as a search for a rhetoric that would measure up to the reality of horror. Indeed, she unequivocally proclaims her artistic dedication:

> And I shall wield this slender fountain pen as if it were a hammer and my words will have to be so many hammer-strokes with which to beat out the story of our fate and of a piece of history as it is and never was be-fore. . . . A few people must survive if only to be the chroniclers of this age. I would very much like to become one of their number.[41]

The metaphor of language as a hammer communicates the seriousness of Hillesum's artistic undertaking to become the chronicler of her time. Perhaps even more clearly, the hammer metaphor communicates the difficulty in narrating a history "as it is and never was before." Long before post-Holocaust skepticism about the art of the Holocaust, Hillesum realized that the event of the Holocaust had locked art and life in an asymmetrical relationship.

The dimensions and the brutality of the destruction had overridden artistic possibilities. The chronicle, a straightforward narration of events, remains the only compatible form of representation. But even the genre of the chronicle assumes a different signification in the un/reality of the Final Solution.

Walter Benjamin, incidentally a victim of the Holocaust who terminated his life to escape the horror of the Nazi persecution,[42] defined "chronicle" as "histori-cal tales" concerned "with the way in which [events] are embedded in the great inscrutable course of the world."[43] In the reality of the Final Solution, however, was it still possible to presuppose sense in history? It is death, Benjamin claims, that sanctions everything the chronicler as the history-teller can tell. In other words, death, or the sense of ending, to recall Kermode, infuses meaning in the sequences of historical happenings.[44] In the reality of the mass murder of the Jews, however, was it still possible to attribute meaningfulness to death?

The chronicler of the Holocaust can no longer use a language that communi-cates either the sense of natural order in the individual life that ends in death, or the eschatological course of history that, in the indefinite end of time, will conclude in the Apocalypse. The actualization of apocalyptic destruction defies the traditional concept of the chronicle as affirmation of meaning in history. This reality requires a "new narrative," a narrative that is capable of contending with the "improbable possibility" of the destruction of the European Jews. Indeed, Hillesum was conscious of the task she faced as a Holocaust chronicler:

I shall become the chronicler of our adventures. I shall forge them into a new language and store them inside me should I have no chance to write things down. I shall grow dull and come to life again . . . until life begins to bubble up in me again and I find the words that bear witness where witness needs to be borne.[45]

To bear witness to the cataclysmic reality of the Holocaust, the artist must give birth to a new art. Toward the end of her diary, Hillesum arrives at a realization that she will never be able to measure up as an artist, that the apocalyptic horror of history will forever escape the language she commands. "I shall never be able," she laments, "to put down in writing what life itself has spelled out for me in living letters."[46]

The living letters are too overwhelming to be transformed into a literary text. The chronicle the living letters of the destruction tell is not informed by the unstated presence of death. This chronicle is the narrative of death, and there is no language for the writer to articulate the terror of the "monotony" and the absurdity of live lifelessness.

Yet, despite her frustration, indeed despair, at the failure to transform the Holocaust experience into a chronicle, it is important to consider Hillesum's conceptualization of the art of the Holocaust. Her images of an art fit to represent the Holocaust are extremely powerful. The language of this art is *new*. As a writer, she must *forge* the words and *beat out* the story, she will turn her pen into a *hammer*, her testimony will be *borne* when life begins to *bubble* once again. By no means will the art of the chronicle be lethargic and passive. As the images indicate, this art will exhibit both potency (the hammer) and potential (birth).

The forcefulness of these images elucidates Hillesum's notion that only a "great poet" could become a chronicler of the destruction. Only an artist of incomparable stature can engender a new art that will restore the lost symmetry between art and life. As both Aristotle and Benjamin contend, the art of telling or chronicling infuses life with meaning. The construct of a chronicle as a work of art implies life's wholeness and order. The complementation of art and life was destroyed by the rule of terror that erased all sense of order and wholeness. The great poet must therefore be able to do the impossible to reaffirm wholeness in collapse and disintegration and rediscover hope in despair and fear.

Despite the proclamation of her failure, Hillesum seems to be able, even if only in her private sphere, to restore symmetry between art and life. The sense of harmonious complementation comes in the realization that the force of love merges art and life into one whole:

Surrounded by my writers and poets and the flowers on my desk I loved life. And there among the barracks, full of hunted and persecuted people, I found confirmation of my love of life. Life in those draughty barracks was no other than life in this protected, peaceful room. . . . There was simply one great, meaningful whole.[47]

We should therefore not concede Hillesum's failure too hastily. As reflected in her writing, Hillesum's ethics indeed represent a "new narrative" told in a "new language" that speaks of love of life in the midst of unprecedented horror. In this sense, her diary and her letters are evidence of the love that affirms life in the reality of mass death.

At the same time, however, we must not trivialize Hillesum's ethics in a sentimentalized version of "love conquers all." Hillesum wanted to become the "thinking heart of the barracks, . . . the thinking heart of a whole concentration camp."[48] This self-image as the "thinking heart" highlights the emotional identi- fication with the suffering, as well as the imperative of "thinking" even in a situation beyond reason. Indeed, the intention to feel and to reason in the concentration camp situation illuminates Hillesum's writing as a "new" narrative-chronicle. This narrative does not present us strictly with a chronicle of camp events. Written amid the horrific misery of the camp, the diary does not merely record; it *is* a chronicle of reasoning compassion. It is an act of writing shaped by creative reasoning, which chronicles humanity in the reality of in- human suffering.

"A camp needs a poet," Hillesum claimed, "one who experiences life there, even there, as a bard and is able to sing about it."[49] Even though Hillesum did not see herself as such a poet, this statement establishes a meeting of her art and ethics. Being a poet signifies the ability to live the horror as an artist—that is, to erect the protective barrier of detached observation against fear and despair. At the same time, the ability to "sing" about the experience demonstrates an extraordinary extent of sensitivity and empathic identification controlled and shaped by the new language of Holocaust testimony.

One can therefore claim that both Hillesum and Frank fulfilled the promise to bear witness. In her "song" about the world of suffering and imprisonment, each became a poet. In a supreme act of defiance, each transformed the experience that she knew aimed to destroy her and her people into a source of artistic creativity.

Both autobiography and diary are genres of personal writing. The four life accounts discussed here present four self-representations as responses to the traumatic encounter with the rule of despotic terror. As such, the accounts demonstrate valiant self-assertion in the face of oppression. Stein's and Weil's autobiographical writings demonstrate the importance they attributed to the narrative of the past in their attempts to transform the present. Stein wanted to deprogram German anti-Semites through her life story as a Jew, even though she no longer belonged to the Jewish fold. Weil desired to re-form the Church by sharing the story of her growth as a Christian and a Christian mystic, even though, or perhaps because, she positioned herself outside the Church.

Through their diaristic writing, Frank and Hillesum represented themselves in the unfolding present, devising their narratives for the future that would not be theirs. Frank's rewriting her diary addressed to a reader-outsider, and Hillesum's searching for a new language of art, communicated their sense that they had a responsibility to produce testimonies of the world coming to its end.

At the same time, it is important to keep in mind that these autobiographical accounts were not written exclusively for the sake of their sociohistorical impact. Autobiographical exploration constitutes its author's self-introduction to the world. As a personal life story directed to the world, the autobiographical account perforce is informed by the gender of its author-narrator-protagonist. Indeed, the story of the author's growth as a young woman or young man constitutes the core of autobiographical writing. The consciousness of female/male identity ineluctably affects the subject's self-perception, while consciousness of the surrounding world and its social structures shapes gender-oriented interaction with the environment.

In the reality of the Final Solution, the four self-accounts raise the issue of the feminine gender of the authors. To what extent, if at all, does their femaleness determine their confrontation with the reality of the Holocaust as feminine? Is it possible to perceive their responses to the situation as gender-specific—that is, affected by feminine sensibilities?

While the questions are pertinent, the answers remain elusive. On the one hand, it would be impossible to attribute modes of social interaction to sexual differentiations, and impossible to prove gender-particular sensibilities. On the other hand, we cannot deny the signification of gender consciousness in the individual's interaction with the self and with the world.

Recall James Young's postulation that each victim's response to the Holocaust depended on her Weltanschauung, as it had been formed by the ideological, religious, ethical atmosphere of her upbringing. I suggest that the response of each woman was affected considerably by consciousness of her female gender. The ways in which each perceived woman's position in relation to the world affected the mode of her resistance. In fact, it is possible to detect patterns of interdependence between their views on womanhood and woman's destiny and the ways in which each woman asserted her uniqueness under the rule that aimed first to dehumanize and then to annihilate its victims.

PART FOUR

RESISTANCE AND WOMANHOOD

11

GENDER CONSCIOUSNESS IN THE RULE OF TERROR

The outside world probably thinks of us as a grey, uniform, suffering mass of Jews, and knows nothing of the gulfs and abysses and subtle differences that exist between us. They could never hope to understand.

—Etty Hillesum

Etty Hillesum's assertion of individuality against the politics of Jewish deperson-alization is pertinent to this discussion of the function of femininity in the response to the rule of terror: Whereas in terms of their sexual identification Edith Stein, Simone Weil, Anne Frank, and Etty Hillesum were all women, their perceptions of womanhood and of themselves as women vary considerably. All four communi-cated a two-tiered perspective: each had a view on the social role of women and each articulated a particular attitude to her own womanhood.

The range of views on the social role of women extends from Stein's perception of women as the moving force behind moral reform, to Weil's mainly derogatory view of womanhood; from Frank's view of the unlimited possibilities of women's social self-actualization, to Hillesum's skepticism about the ability of women to free themselves from their inherent limitations. The gamut of their views of their own womanhood ranges from Stein's self-assertion as a woman to Weil's absolute denial of her femininity; from Frank's self-affirmation as an emotionally independent growing woman-artist, to Hillesum's transformation from a "weak," dependent woman into a woman liberated by her love for humanity.

In her consideration of Frank's and Hillesum's diaries, Yasmine Ergas claims that although both women "repeatedly attempt to fashion and review their ways of being women, gender ultimately recedes to second place. As Nazism casts them, they must cast themselves: first and foremost as Jews."[1]

It is true that the Final Solution confronted all Jews with the implacable reality that their Jewish identity sentenced them to death. In this sense, the horrible decree turned the Jews into the "grey, uniform, suffering masses" in Hillesum's depiction. But how did the condemned Jews respond to the sentence of death? While the terror imposed uniformity, was the response to the terror uniform, or did it reveal, in Hillesum's terms, "gulfs and abysses and subtle differences"?

Assimilated post-Emancipation Western European Jews, the four women were confronted with their Jewish identity, which indiscriminately condemned them to banishment and death. Despite the common fate of persecution for an identity with which none of them had much sense of identification, each woman demonstrated a different approach to the situation. The intellectual activity of writing that each undertook attests to independent modes of thinking; their self-writing asserts individuality. The issue of gender, therefore, should not be considered from the point of view of the perpetrators, who reduced the Jewish people to a monolithic target of genocide. From the point of view of the victim, the issue of gender identity occupies an important place in the victims' individualistic responses to the persecution.

As discussed before, the confrontation with Jewish identity elicited ambivalent reactions. Because the four were raised in an assimilated milieu, the awareness that their Jewishness amounted to a death sentence initiated responses that ranged from rejection of Jewish identity to sacrificial identification with the Jewish victim, from silence about the catastrophe to self-affirmation as a "catastrophe Jew." We observed Stein's open espousal of her Jewish past and Weil's anti-Semitic attitude, we saw Frank's guilt at being "safe" when other Jews suffered, and we saw Hillesum's voluntary service at Westerbork.

What role did gender consciousness play in the four women's responses to the Final Solution? Did they identify themselves as Jewish women, as Jews of female gender, or, rather, as women who happened to be Jewish? In what way was the sense of vocation in the world of each of them—educator (Stein), religious reformer and social rebel (Weil), a future famous writer (Frank), the chronicler of Westerbork (Hillesum)—shaped by their perceptions of woman's responsibilities toward the world? To what extent did they feel obligated to the world as women despite their degrading social exclusion as Jews?

Stein's and Weil's views on gender and on Jewishness illuminate the polarization of their self-identifications as women and as Jews. Whereas Stein's notion of gender equality communicates a self-assertion that elucidates her self-affirmation as a daughter in a Jewish family, Weil's view of women's inherent inferiority explains her self-denial as a woman, an attitude that sheds light on her self-denial as a Jew.

The spectrum of Stein's and Weil's contrastive standpoints facilitates an understanding of the developing notions of femininity in Frank and Hillesum. In their diaristic self-representations, these two "catastrophe Jews" never ceased to explore the signification of their femininity. Even in the inexorably restricting circumstances of the Annex and Westerbork, their consciousness of being women was pertinent to shaping their self-images, aspirations, and responses to the world. We shall observe how their beliefs in women's particular social responsibility fueled their insistence on independence and on moral development in the reality of the Final Solution.

12

STEIN AND WEIL:
WOMEN'S NATURE AND DESTINY

I would like to tell women about my life in terms of my own sexuality because it is not just a personal matter, but a political one, too.

—*Simone de Beauvoir*

The Signification of Female Role Models

An interesting correspondence emerges between ethno-gender identities in Edith Stein and Simone Weil and their references to other female figures. As already mentioned, in the preface to her autobiography Stein aligned herself with the tradition of autobiographies by Jewish women by associating her work with the two Jewish women memoirists, Glückel of Hameln and Pauline W. Wengeroff. Stein stated that she would like to have her account of Jewish life "as one testimony to be placed alongside others, already available in print or soon to be published."

In a footnote, Stein offers bibliographical information on Glückel of Hameln's memoirs (published by Alfred Veilchenfeld, Jüdischer Verlag, Berlin, 1920) and

Wengeroff's *Bilder aus de Kulturgeschichte Russlands* (published by Verlag Pop-
pelaner, Berlin, 1913). Stein's placement of her Jewish life story in the tradition of
Jewish women's self-writing, and her providing the detailed bibliographic information about their books, indicates her sense of common denominator with these
Jewish women's life narratives.

Who were these women? We know that Glückel of Hameln, the better known of
the two, chronicled her life as a child, wife, widow, and mother in a well-off
merchant Jewish family in seventeenth-century Germany. Besides its life narrative, the book also contains Glückel's meditations on spiritual and religious
matters. She often affirms her faith in God in spontaneously composed prayers.[1] A
rare example of a memoir written by a woman at that time, Glückel's autobiography demonstrates her outstanding intelligence and religious education.

We also know that Pauline Wengeroff, who wrote memoirs in which she
portrayed her life as a member of a wealthy Jewish family in the nineteenth-
century Russia, is also a rare example of an educated Jewish woman writer.[2]
Wengeroff described with much love and affection the traditional Jewish life, and
she deplored the destruction of Jewish values with the advent of the Haskalah
[Jewish Enlightenment] movement, which caused many Jews to abandon the
Jewish tradition.[3] Stein must have had some of this information when she associated herself with pious Jewish women who asserted their intellectual capacities in
their autobiographical writing. As demonstrated in her own writing, Stein identifies with both Glückel's and Wengeroff's intentions to share the experience of
Jewish life with others. By referring to their memoirs as precedents that define her
own, Stein legitimized her autobiographical effort and affirmed the educational
value of Jewish women's self-narratives in teaching the world about Jewish life.

Weil demonstrates a diametrically opposed position. The one woman who
exerted the most influence on Weil was Rosa Luxemburg. As a socialist, Weil
admired and endorsed Luxemburg's notion of antimilitarist, international solidarity, although she lacked Luxemburg's optimism about the success of the
working-class pacifist cause. In the late 1930s and early 1940s, Weil could not
possibly share Luxemburg's optimistic faith in the workers' attainment of revolutionary consciousness,[4] although she subscribed to her socialist principles.

It would seem possible to read in Weil's admiration for Luxemburg's ideas an
acknowledgment of women's participation in the world akin to Stein's endorsement of women's intellectual activity of self-writing. Such an attitude would be
plausible, especially in view of the fact that both Weil and Luxemburg were
women socialists of Jewish origins. The following comment by Weil, however,
disconfirms the ethno-gender common denominator as the basis for Weil's sense
of affinity. In her review of Luxemburg's writing, Weil asserts that Luxemburg

"was profoundly pagan" and claims that Luxemburg "emanates a feeling for the Stoic conception of life . . . [as well] as the virile attitude toward misfortune, which is what is ordinarily meant by the term Stoicism."[5]

In what seems quite an unfortunate choice of epitaphs, Weil emulates Luxemburg as "pagan" and "virile." But this mispresentation of Luxemburg, who was a Jew and a passionate woman, is not incidental in view of Weil's self-denial as both woman and Jew. Luxemburg was a revolutionary, an assimilated Jew, and a woman who, as Arendt notes, had a "distaste for the women's emancipation movement" and who admired "masculine" qualities.[6] Except for the value of chastity, which, as we shall see, was extremely important to Weil, Luxemburg seems to provide an excellent model for Weil.

Stein's and Weil's choice of female models is indicative of their self-images as women and Jews. Whereas Stein's selection of Glückel of Hameln and Pauline Wengeroff affirms her affinity with traditional Jewish life, Weil's admiration for Luxemburg reflects her desire to dissociate from Jewishness by adopting the identity of the cosmopolitan, international fighter for the working class. The notion of Luxemburg's "paganism" and "Stoicism" alludes to Weil's desire for pagan, especially Greek, ethics to replace the Jewish origins of the Church. Furthermore, the choice of these particular female figures indicates opposing concepts of woman's position in society. Whereas Stein's endorsement of the autobiographies validates both the lives and the life narratives of women, Weil's image of Luxemburg signals the desire to cast her role as a "virile" female, or, more precisely, as a female who acted as a male, as she understood herself to be.

Between Mythical Equality and Biological Inferiority

The diverging attitudes indicated by Stein's and Weil's choices of female models reflect profound differences in their conceptual outlook on the genders. In Stein's view, men and women are distinct but equal; according to Weil, women are different from and inherently inferior to men. The attempts of Stein and Weil to substantiate their conceptual views led them back, respectively, to the mythical and biological origins of gender differentiation. Stein asserts gender equality in her rereading of the biblical story of creation; Weil grounds gender inequality in her interpretation of female sexuality.

Stein's lectures on women, delivered between 1928 and 1933 when working for the Münster Institute, delineate her perspective on the condition of women. The theology of her reading of the story of creation is constitutive of her view of man-woman relationships. Stein sees the Edenic nonhierarchical existence of Adam and Eve as evidence of gender equality. In Stein's view of pre-Fall condition, Adam and Eve were equal counterparts. Eve was destined as *Eser kenegdo,* which Stein interprets as "a helper as if vis-à-vis to him." The Edenic man and woman were not identical but complementary "as one hand [complements] another."[7] The Fall shattered the perfectly balanced positions of man and woman, and "the relationship of the sexes . . . has become a brutal relationship of master and slave" whereby man uses woman to satisfy his lust.[8]

Stein's reading of the story of creation is prototypical of today's feminist theology. The interpretation of the story of creation by Phyllis Trible, a contemporary feminist theologian, seems to validate the portrayal of Stein as a forerunner of the subsequently developed feminist religious thought. Trible's view of *Eser kenegdo* as "a helper who is counterpart" and her conclusion that "woman is the helper equal to man"[9] reconfirms Stein's perception of the initial harmoniously balanced relationship between man and woman.

Trible reiterates Stein's view of male supremacy as the distortion of the ideal Edenic order, which was based on equality between sexes. She claims that "the suffering and oppression we women and men know now are marks of our fall, not of our creation."[10] Furthermore, Trible claims that the feminist biblical interpretation "opens possibilities for change, for a return to our true liberation under God."[11] This view reechoes Stein's intent to explore the sources of social oppression in order to restore the initial harmonious existence.

Stein and the feminist theologians today see man's superiority over woman as an unnatural state of being which corrupts the original order of perfect balance between the sexes.[12] For Weil, however, woman's inferiority is an inbred condition that is evident in her sexuality. Unlike Stein, who grounds her argument in the balanced coexistence of pre-Fall Adam and Eve as man and wife, Weil establishes her view of the sexes on the premise of sexual abstinence, claiming that "chastity becomes a source of holiness [and] is compared to Grace."[13] Sexual abstinence redirects potency toward objects that are more valuable than sex objects.

According to Weil, men, especially artists, are capable of generating artistic energy through abstinence, "but the satisfaction of the sexual instinct . . . takes away from them a part of that energy thus developed."[14] Weil maintains that "if the semen . . . is destroyed within the body of man, . . . man disposes of a higher form of energy than he could possibly acquire in any other way. Chastity is this laying up of high-grade energy."[15]

Male chastity, therefore, becomes the source of Grace, and a channel of creativity and holiness. When she turns to consider female potential of creativity and holiness, however, Weil offers the following query, in parentheses (!): "(Haven't women any such [comparable to chastity] source of energy? Does their inferiority in the matter of genius and even as regards aspects of sainthood proceed from this?)."[16] These rhetorical questions take for granted the natural inferiority of women regarding "genius" and "sainthood." Women lack the values of abstraction and objectivity, which are components necessary to maintain chastity because "there is no such thing as chastity without detachment."[17]

Eventually, Weil proffers the dubious reassurance that "women, too, must possess a transcendent source of energy, . . . otherwise conception would not necessitate the union of the sexes."[18] Thus, in Weil's view, it is conception, not chastity, that constitutes the source of energy in women. While she allows that women are not devoid of energy, she certainly does not attribute to them the highest form of energy accumulated through sexual abstinence. Furthermore, the notion of "conception" clearly implies a nonchaste, less-than-"pure" relationship.

Stein and Weil present disparate approaches to the feminine condition. While Stein sees inequality of women as the distortion of the Edenic, ideal order, Weil sees it as the natural order of things determined by biological differences between the sexes. These differences illuminate the stances that the two adopt with regard to the social condition of women. Here we find that Stein's outspoken support of women's equal rights and equal duties in the political life of their country contrasts with Weil's complete silence regarding women's social oppression and exploitation.

Perspectives on Women's Inequality

Stein's lectures on women relate directly to the catastrophic sociopolitical situation of Germany at the time. She responds to the economic crisis and to the threatening rise of the National Socialist Party, a situation she calls "the beginning of a great cultural upheaval."[19]

Stein demonstrates a lucid view of the arising rule of terror, which perceives society as "a mechanistically ordered structure . . . [determined] merely on a biological basis."[20] The foreboding political climate contributes to "the breakdown of married and family life" and to total moral dissolution.[21] She observes how Nazism has nullified the emancipatory "gains during the past decades"[22] by seeing women's role as limited to the biological function of "[bearing] babies of Aryan stock."[23]

Measures must be taken, Stein claims, to remedy the situation she describes as "the great sickness of our time and of our people."[24] Women are by no means excused from assuming an active role in defending the nation's democratic freedom. Every person, according to Stein, is a "co-sufferer as a member of the vast national body" and a *"jointly responsible* member of the whole nation." Therefore, women too must become politically active. Furthermore, as Stein sees it, the situation is "a matter, of immediate concern to women. . . . Wives and mothers, sisters and daughters must needs be inspired to an active participation in their country's destiny." They must "remind themselves that the whole political situation depends on how they use their political rights."[25]

While Stein clearly alludes to the Nazi anti-Jewish policy of Aryan purity, she takes a stand in the name of the national body of German women at large. Her objection to the defeat of women's emancipation, as well as her exhortation to women to respond actively to the deteriorating situation, attests to her premise that women have equal standing as concerned patriots and citizens. The involvement of women in the body politic signifies the joint responsibility of men and women to determine the democratic future of their country.

In view of Stein's position as a feminist activist who considers women's social equality as a fundamental right, Weil's silence as a socialist who is well aware of the unequal position of female workers in relation to their male counterparts is quite perplexing. It is important to note that, unlike Stein, who asserted equal rights for both Jews and women, Weil maintained complete silence with regard to each of these groups. As we observed regarding her silence about the fate of the persecuted Jews, her lack of response toward women is all the more conspicuous in view of her readiness to sacrifice herself for the afflicted.

As Nevin notes, Weil remained totally unresponsive regarding the oppression of women laborers, although she noted their exploitation during her work experience in a factory. Weil was aware of the terrible treatment proletarian women received, yet she persistently maintained the stance of a detached observer. When she describes the poverty and inhuman conditions of women factory workers, she does not protest their exploitation, which, she notes, is worse than that of the male workers. And when she observes the misery of the women in the Portuguese village, where she had a mystical insight into the essence of Christianity, she realizes their condition of slavery but prefers to focus on the mystical qualities of suffering rather than denounce it as blatant social injustice.[26]

Weil's uncritical position on female victimization is quite surprising in view of her passionate involvement in revolutionary, social causes and her constant struggle for the afflicted who cannot speak for themselves. For instance, she was remembered to have berated a fellow student, "How can you laugh when there are children suffering in China?"[27] By contrast, there are no recollections of Weil protesting the inhuman conditions and brutal treatment of her women factory co-workers.

Weil must have been aware of feminist movements and the struggle for women's emancipation. She was the contemporary of Simone de Beauvoir, the founding mother of modern feminism, with whom she met at least once. Yet Weil never spoke about women's rights and never singled out women as an oppressed group that needed particular attention. In fact, as de Beauvoir recalls, during their meeting Weil kept moralizing, demanding "the Revolution which would feed the world."[28]

A devout and fearless fighter for the causes of the workers, the peasants—all the oppressed people in history and even, during her short stay in New York, for the blacks in Harlem—Weil nevertheless kept completely aloof from the problems of women's oppression and exploitation.

The discrepancy between Weil's endorsement of Luxemburg and her socialist platform, and her dissociation from the masses of women workers, highlights Weil's derogatory attitude toward women in general. Only a woman like Luxemburg, who had endured the vicissitudes of life with "virile Stoicism," gained Weil's admiration and praise. In other words, a woman willing and able to forgo her femininity and the emotional needs peculiar to her gender can attain the degrees of sainthood and genius that, as a rule, are the domain of men. Indeed, Weil's interpretations of her beloved fairy tales and Greek tragedies are invariably characterized by motifs of purity and steadfast determination to persevere through all adversity.

The sister in "The Fairy Tale of the Six Swans in Grimm" spends six years in silence sewing six shirts out of white anemones for her brothers, who had been transformed into swans by a witch. Weil's comment on the story was that "to make six shirts from anemones and to keep silent: this is our only way of acquiring power. . . . All anemones are almost impossible to sew into shirts, and this difficulty prevents any other action from altering the purity of this six-year silence. The sole strength in the world is purity."[29] The theme of sisterly devotion that saves the brothers, of the sister's innocent triumph over evil, and of her total attention recur in Weil's comments on other fairy tales, such as "The Almond Tree," in which the stepmother kills the brother, and the sister contrives to please her father, kill her stepmother, and revive her brother.[30]

The emphasis on the ideal of chastity marked in the brother-sister relationship also emerges in Weil's comments on Electra and Antigone, the Greek tragic heroines whom Weil emulated. Electra, Weil notes, represents the "culmination [of affliction] when abandonment becomes complete through the death of one friendly and protecting being [her brother, Orestes]. Then recovery of him, and salvation."[31]

Antigone, who displays the same characteristics of self-sacrifice, sisterly love, and willingness to suffer affliction for justice is included in Weil's list of images of Christ.[32] In a letter, Weil identifies with "the beautiful lines spoken by Sophocles'

Antigone: 'I was born to share, not hate, but love.' "[33] It is significant that she refers to herself as "Antigone as usual" when writing about her brief imprisonment upon her arrival in London in 1942.[34]

The literary female characters Weil admired demonstrate virtues that she saw as particularly male. Let us recall that, for Weil, male holiness is inseparable from sexual abstinence. The sisters in the stories opt for chastity, purity, and determination to sacrifice themselves for the brotherly other. These images of truly worthwhile women, those capable of attaining "manly" holiness, are in accord with Weil's perception of her own femininity. We have discussed Weil's renunciation of the body and physical needs in terms of her desire to erase her ethnic identity. Her derogatory perception of female sexuality illuminates Weil's ascetic treatment of her body as an attempt to eradicate her femininity as well. Her negation of the body communicates a twofold denial of gender and ethnicity.

The roots of Weil's denial of her femininity may, to an extent, be attributed to her upbringing and her relationship with her brother. Her friend and biographer, Simone Pétrement, reports that Mme. Weil insisted on raising Simone as a boy. Her parents called her "Simon," and when writing to them Weil spoke about herself in the masculine gender. Pétrement recalls that Weil claimed it was a great misfortune to have been born a woman.[35]

Weil dressed in monklike clothes and remained celibate.[36] We also note that Weil's identification with chaste sisterly figures who save their brothers reverberates with the problematic of Weil's sibling rivalry with her brother, whose mathematical genius, she notes in "Spiritual Autobiography," brought her to the brink of despair.

These psychoanalytical conjectures are substantiated by Weil's own account of her choice of sexual abstinence. In "Spiritual Autobiography" she recounts how "the idea of purity . . . took possession of me at the age of sixteen . . . when I was contemplating a mountain landscape and little by little it was imposed on me in an irresistible manner."[37] The mystical reason for her decision to remain sexually "pure" is further amplified by a sociopsychological explanation that connects the determination to defy her female gender to her self-denial as a Jew.

In one of her letters to the ministry of education, Weil offers a revealing explanation of her celibacy. She recounts her employer's complimentary remark that her work in the vineyard was good enough for her to marry a farmer and then commented: "He doesn't know . . . that simply because of my name I have an original defect that it would be inhuman for me to transmit to children."[38]

The statement explains Weil's strategy to attain complete assimilation by keeping "chaste" and childless. Her womanhood had to be denied in order to deny Jewish identity altogether. Acknowledged through marriage and childbearing, her femininity would reaffirm her Jewish origins in her Jewish name, which she considers a "defect," to her children. Seen in the light of Weil's self-denial, the negation of her Jewishness and femininity are ineluctably connected.

The Destiny of Jewish Women

Having established that women have inferior qualities, Weil demonstrated a total aversion to her being counted among their ranks. Her self-denial as a woman and her admiration for the characters of "virile," saintly sisters indicate the destiny that Weil ascribed to only very few exceptional women, such as Luxemburg, Antigone, and herself. She thereby endeavored to create a self-image that would dissociate her from identity—and specifically from both her ethnic identity and her gender identity.

Before the war, Weil's vigorous support of trade unions, both as ideologue and factory worker, identified her as a political activist and an indefatigable advocate and defender of the universally oppressed. Weil aspired to create a self-image of an idealist totally dedicated to humanity and humanism and therefore practiced absolute abstinence from any attachments of a personal nature. This image of a totally devoted revolutionary allowed her to minimize the distinctions of ethnicity and gender. The self-image of an altruistic worker for humankind implied total self-abnegation in terms of her life as a woman and as a Jew.

At the time of the war, Weil's desire to erase her feminine inferiority is clearly expressed in her plan. We shall recall that Weil wished to head a squad of women nurses to die on the battlefields of Europe while tending to wounded soldiers. Weil's specifications about the type of women to be chosen for the mission reflect her low esteem of womankind: only a woman who can overcome the weaknesses of feminine nature will be able to participate in the nurses' mission. Indeed, Weil admitted that women who would measure up to the task are not easily available. They must be brave, "possess a certain amount of that cool and virile resolution," and at the same time demonstrate "the tenderness required for comforting pain and agony."[39]

We shall also recall Weil's offer to die in a Resistance mission behind the front lines. We have discussed the rationale for these missions as the desire for a spectacular act of martyrdom that will erase her identity as a Jew. Her self-denial as a woman illuminates yet another aspect of her desire for self-sacrifice. The magnitude of her heroism will not only relieve her of the stigma of being a Jewish outcast, but also highlight her aptitude for holiness and thus obliterate her inferiority as a woman. Offering herself as a scapegoat, Weil promises to become more manly than a man. "A woman," she claims, "is as suitable for this type of mission as a man, even more so provided she has a sufficient amount of resolution, sang-froid, and spirit of sacrifice . . . [to] accept any degree of risk."[40]

In his study *Simone Weil: A Modern Pilgrimage*, Robert Coles ends his discussion of Weil's unrealized martyrdom with a spectacular image: "She saw herself perhaps shot by the Nazis as her parachute approached the earth—the gravity . . . at last banished, her soul rising through grace, leaving the white handkerchief of war far behind."[41]

Coles's image of Weil seems to tune in the memory she wanted to impress on the world. The world will remember how in an act of supreme sacrifice her soul arose, while her body, liberated and purified from the gravity of her "base defects" of Jewishness and femininity, rerooted itself in the soil of France.

It is important to note that the linkage between misogyny and anti-Judaism in Weil is by no means unprecedented. In fact, it reflects an assimilation of prevalent discriminatory attitudes that linked women and Jews. As Joanne Cutting-Gray notes in her analysis of Arendt's biography of the Berlin Jewish salonière, Rahel Vernhagen, the reaction to liberalism in the Enlightenment turned against both Jews and women. Cutting-Gray notes that, as the two increasingly emancipated social classes, Jews and women, were opposed by the "new nationalistic, ethnically pure German groups, . . . antifeminism took the *same form* as anti-Semitism."[42]

Sander Gilman points to the negative attributes ascribed to women and Jews in his discussion of the work of Otto Weininger, who combined his self-hatred of a Jew with his misogyny in his 1903 philosophical study, *Sex and Character*. Weininger drew parallels between the most common antiwomen and anti-Semitic arguments: both use faulty logic, are prone to mental illness, and lie compulsively.[43]

Weil's pronouncements about the Jews and women sound very much like Weininger's postulations that "Jews and women have 'no genius,' " that "what passes for genius in the Jew—and the woman—is but 'exaggerated egotism' " and that, like femaleness, Jewishness "is condemned to be 'uncreative.' "[44] Although Weil never explicitly connects the inferiority of Jews and women, Weininger's aspersions reflect her disparaging views of these two unprivileged groups.

To prove herself worthy, women, in Weil's understanding, and especially Jewish women, must manifest qualities that Weil considered typically manly. Only then will they be able to attain the holiness of self-sacrifice for the redemption of their country and the world. Such certainly was not the position of Stein, who, unlike Weil, proudly acknowledged her Jewish origins. Also, contrary to Weil, who saw woman's finest accomplishment in a "virile" act of self-destruction, Stein saw woman as a redeemer of the world due to her inherent feminine qualities.

We have noted Stein's insistence on women's responsibility of political involvement. But women's political activity is only secondary to women's principal moral obligation to the world. Women have the potential, Stein claims, to provide "a blessed counter-balance precisely here where everyone is in danger of becoming mechanized and losing his humanity."[45] The question that arises is: Why are women, in Stein's perspective, more suitable than men to become moral reformers? And how, in Stein's view, are they going to restore humanism to humanity?

In diametrical opposition to Weil, Stein claims that women's greatest contribution to society lies in cultivation of their distinctness from men. While she is in favor of the emancipatory gains of the suffrage movement, she strongly objects to undifferentiating equality of men and women. Absolute indiscriminateness between men and women signifies obliteration of distinctions between the genders and therefore amounts to complete disregard of the needs, roles, and capabilities of women.

Such a notion of equality, according to Stein, actually demands that women enter society "*as men.*"[46] Instead of liberating women, the concept of equality subjugates them to the male vision of society. A woman who "has entered one of the traditionally masculine professions . . . sees herself forced into conditions of life and work alien to her nature."[47]

Stein's perception of the detrimental effects of gender effacement anticipates current deliberations over gender equality. Her notion of woman's defeat when feminine particularity is erased recurs in the argumentation of today's thinkers, such as Ivan Illich, who claims that "in the games where you play for genderless stakes . . . both genders are stripped and, neutered, the man ends on top."[48] Gender, Illich argues, is like the vernacular: "One is born and bred into gender. . . . Gender implies a complementarity within the world that is fundamental."[49]

Stein thus presages the current feminist insistence on innate feminine characteristics when she dispraises those who offer women "the bait of radical equalization with men" and thus abuse women through "callous disregard of woman's nature and destiny."[50] What, then, in women's nature does Stein see as distinct from man's nature? And what is the destiny the feminine nature designates to women?

Stein's view of womanhood focuses on women's "intrinsic feminine value," whose redemptive potential she considers to be far superior to that of man. Women's capacity to grow and develop surpasses men's inherent capabilities. "Man," claims Stein, "appears more *objective,*" but his objectivity subjects him to his discipline; *"woman's attitude is personal,"* and therefore she is more likely to attain the freedom of *"a complete human being."* Women's natural predisposition toward the personal is ethically more valuable, because "the human person is more precious than all objective values."[51]

In contrast to Weil, who sees women's reproductive capacity reductive to genius and holiness, Stein sees woman's ethics irreducibly grounded in her "mission as a mother." The value of motherhood "enables her to understand and foster organic development, the special, individual destiny of every living being."[52] The notion of woman's particular distinction as a mother reechoes in Illich's claim that the "special space that sets the home apart from nest and garage is engendered *only* by women, because it is they who bear living bodies."[53]

We note, however, that for Stein the notion of motherhood is that of women's natural proclivity to motherly nurturing and to empathy, rather than the physical ability to bear children. That is why the empathic sensitivity of woman is by no means limited to her own children; her inherent "awareness of the needs of the living being benefits not only her posterity but all creatures as well."[54]

Women's intrinsic feminine value of empathy determines their destiny as educators of humankind. In terms of vocational proclivities, therefore, women naturally tend toward the teaching profession. As she did in the case of motherhood, Stein redefines the normative approach to woman's professional role in society. Teaching is a truly feminine vocation, not as a secondary social task traditionally delegated to women, but as a means to accomplish women's difficult assignment to reeducate humanity.

That is why teaching does not necessarily take place in the classroom. The notion of education underscores every form of professional discourse, and so, whatever her professional orientation and choice, woman must educate and teach how to "counterbalance against another deterioration of *masculine objectivity.*"[55] Whether a teacher, or a physician, or a social worker, or a scientist, woman, Stein claims, will "assert her singularity anew in such areas of knowledge by the way she instructs"[56]—that is, through her professional activity she will convey the value of empathic subjectivity.

The roots of Stein's proud assertion of woman's destiny as a reformer of humanity can be traced to her own upbringing. Unlike Weil, who was raised in a family that considered her femininity an unwanted weakness, Stein was raised in a family of strong, capable, intelligent women. "When advice was needed on important matters," she writes in her autobiography, "one went to my grandmother: not only her husband and children and brothers and sisters, but many friends as well."[57] On becoming a widow, her mother made the decision "to cope by herself without accepting support from any one."[58] Indeed, Frau Stein managed her late husband's lumber business so successfully that, as mentioned before, Stein remembers that men considered her "the most capable merchant in the whole trade in town."[59]

As a reaffirmation of ties with her Jewish past, Stein's autobiography also establishes her belonging to strong, matriarchal tradition. Her choice of the women writers and *mater familias* Glückel of Hameln and Pauline Wengeroff as her autobiographical role models once again reaffirms both her loyalty to her Jewish origins and her high regard for woman's intelligence and creativity. Stein's self-identification as a Jew, a woman, and a daughter implies a degree of self-acceptance that stands in total opposition to Weil's self-denial as a Jew, a woman, and, as well, a daughter.

Ironically, Weil's desire to attain freedom from her ethnicity and gender through destruction of the body actually played into the Nazi design to turn Jewish individuals into a mass of indistinguishable objects of annihilation. Instead of setting herself free, she found herself locked into a system of social politics of power marked by the twofold marginality of a Jew and a woman. She embarked on daring but futile strategies in order to unlock the system and pervade the center. Weil's introjection of the world's prejudice and bias against Jews and women turned her into the victim of the system that she resisted all her life. Weil's silence as a Jew and a woman thus constitutes a significant subtext to her life and work, which allows a better understanding of the complexity of this self-tortured, enigmatic figure.

In contrast to Weil, Stein's cultural and emotional affiliation with Jewishness and with Jewish women placed emphasis on ethnic and gender identity, an attitude that countervailed the intent of the perpetrators to depersonalize the victim.

13

TOWARD INTELLECTUAL
AND EMOTIONAL MATURITY

[The woman] craves for an unhampered development of her personality
just as much as she does to help another toward the same goal.

—Edith Stein

In contrast to Weil's derogatory view of women's intellectual, ethical, and artistic capabilities, Stein's notion of the singular qualities of women assigned to her the prominent position of an educator of humanity. Unlike Weil, who apart from the atypical sisterly figures she admired considered women to be imprisoned in their biological destiny of reproduction, Stein's perception released women from the context of the immediate, nuclear family. "A high vocation," she claims, "is designated in feminine singularity—that is, to bring true humanity in oneself and in others to development."[1]

This succinct description of feminine vocation allots a woman a twofold obligation: obligation toward herself and toward others. Before women can help others actualize their moral potential, they must fulfill their own potential. To become an educator of humanity, Stein argues, "necessitates that [woman] possess true humanity herself."[2] While Stein acknowledged the natural capabilities of women, she did not assume that those capabilities became fully developed without a rigorous process of self-education.

Stein aptly identifies the areas in which women need to improve. The post-Fall subjection to sexual promiscuity blocked "the *correct personal attitude*" toward others, resulting in excessive needs to "secure her own personal importance" and to "penetrate into personal lives." On the one hand, woman's immoderate interest in herself is manifest in "blind feminine love," which unrealistically glorifies everything about herself and her life. On the other hand, women's extreme interest in others manifests itself in the urge to appropriate the other, or, as Stein puts it, in "a passion to confiscate people." These weaknesses of narcissism and of the will to control reveal desperate neediness for the other, a tendency that brings forth the loss of distinct personality. The typically feminine need to be reaffirmed by others precludes a woman's self-actualization as a whole person and thus hinders her destiny as a redeemer of humanity.[3]

The stunted "correct personal attitude" engenders the aberration of possessiveness in loving relationships. The need to be loved causes women to strive to possess the object of love in order to gain a sense of self-importance, an attitude that causes distorted and superficial perceptions of themselves and of humanity.

The flaw of possessiveness preoccupied all four women. Each acknowledged a need to extricate herself from the instinctual inclination to appropriate the object of love. All four subscribed to the notion that the will to power hinders the proper, or "correct," attitude toward the other. And all four sought ways to transform possessive love into unqualified devotion and generosity free of the pursuit of egotistic satisfaction.

Weil promulgates that true love is chaste love, chaste not only because the physical aspect of possession is absent, but also because "illusion" or "imaginary future" is absent. True love, she claims, must focus on the "real" and the "naked." We soil the naked reality of love by infusing it with desire and enjoyment.[4]

The need "to possess is to soil," because it communicates will to power. Therefore, according to Weil, "to love purely is to consent to distance, it is to adore the distance between ourselves and that which we love." It is "necessary to be dead"— devoid of any desire to possess— in order to be able to love things from a distance or to love the distance that prevents one from becoming possessive. That is why, Weil argues, "the love we devote to the dead is perfectly pure." Such love is directed toward "a life that is finished" and therefore cannot incite the desire to possess.[5]

In her personal life, Weil actualized her notion of pure love by vanquishing all desires connected to the body. In both the metaphorical and the literal sense—

recall her theology of de-creation—Weil mortified her flesh and her soul to extricate all illusions and enjoyment.

Stein, in contrast to Weil, wanted to achieve liberation from possessiveness in the reality of living, interpersonal, and constructive relationships, so she outlined the process that would enable a woman to unblock the "correct attitude" toward herself and the world. The ability to become "objective" constitutes the first step toward "a definite freedom of self," which is "a basis for self-control." Once the objective outlook is attained, a woman can proceed "to the proper personal one, which is also the attitude that is most highly objective."

The personal outlook is "the realization of the true humanity," Stein says, because its true objectivity allows us to see "the predispositions towards [the ideal image of humanity] as well as departures from it within ourselves and others." In other words, an unbiased acknowledgment of my perceptions of others, and of my consciousness of being reflected in the perceptions of others, constitutes the self-set educational goal of the future educator of humanity.[6]

A woman's self-education toward intersubjectivity is aimed at bringing out her whole personality—that is, actualizing her potential. Wholeness implies the development of emotions, which, according to Stein, "occupy the center of [woman's] being." The emotional center, however, does not direct itself, but rather "needs the control of reason and the direction of the will." Therefore, a woman's emotional wholeness cannot be attained without the "cooperation of intellect and will," because, Stein says, "where discipline of mind and will is lacking, emotional life becomes a compulsion without secure direction."[7]

Stein's notion of the "discipline of the mind" in women's self-development as a redeeming influence on humanity is important on several levels. In terms of its perception of the wholeness of woman's personality, she succeeds in presenting women as thinking, rational beings, while acknowledging the significance of their emotional life for the world.

It is important to note that Stein is talking not about repression of emotions and feelings—which, as Freud would have it, was needed for civilization to survive—but rather about the "un-repression" of intrinsic emotions and feelings that had been displaced, or "blocked," by the egotistical proclivity of the post-Edenic world. For Stein, the mind is not Freud's repressive mechanism to subdue the self-centered, pleasure-seeking, aggressive instincts. Neither is it a destructive mechanism, which, according to Weil, should eliminate "every desire for enjoyment [as] it belongs to the future and the world of illusion."[8] As Stein sees it, the mind can restore a woman's singular "threefold attitude towards the world—to know it, to enjoy it, to form it creatively."[9] The "discipline of the mind," or self-education, is, according to Stein, a liberating system that can bring out the good in humanity even, or perhaps especially, at times of the rule of evil.

Freud's concurrent view of humanity highlights the particularity of Stein's outlook. In *Civilization and Its Discontents* (1929–30), Freud expresses doubt that the thin layer of civilized behavior imposed on basic human instincts can withhold the increasing threat of violence. Noting that human beings have gained so much technological knowledge that "they would have no difficulty in exterminating one another to the last man," Freud says: "The fateful question for the human species seems to me to be whether and to what extent their cultural development will succeed in mastering the disturbance of their communal life by the human instinct of aggression and self-destruction."[10] Freud's pessimistic outlook points out that a civilized society and the overpowering instinct of aggression are incompatible. Therefore, according to Freud, the process of civilization is predicated on endless struggle with "the mental constitution of human beings."[11]

It is interesting to note Weil's similarly negative representation of the self-destructive construct of civilization. In her essay "Analysis of Oppression," she offers a dark picture of humanity imprisoned forever in its inherent desire for power. "The race for power enslaves everybody, strong and weak alike," and she says, "every oppressive society is cemented by this religion of power."[12] The progress of civilization enslaves humankind in an endless struggle for power. Weil concludes with a gloomy picture of the world in which "man was born a slave, and . . . servitude is his natural condition."[13]

In contrast to Freud and Weil, Stein sees in the mental constitution of the individual an intrinsic value of empathy, which if and when developed through an adequate educational system will bring forth an ethically abiding society. It is true that Freud's prophecy about the breakdown of civilization was tragically fulfilled. Both Freud and Stein became the victims of the horrific outburst of violence and aggression of the Nazi regime. Nevertheless, it is important to keep in mind that even today, in the post-Holocaust world, our view of education is predicated on the assumption of certain fundamental ethical and empathic values that need to be developed. Rather than implementing a repressive educational system, the ethical emphasis on education in the enlightened world aims at bringing out the intrinsic empathic and intellectual potential in human beings.

In terms of our discussion, the principle of the discipline of the mind, as presented in Stein's feminist work, guides both Frank and Hillesum in their efforts to actualize their destiny as women. It is, of course, tragically ironic that the self-education intended to bring forth the moral reform of the world was taking place in a world doomed to destruction. In Frank's and especially Hillesum's development, we witness a poignant struggle to actualize their full potential as women in order to bear with dignity the reality of degradation, terrible victimization, and unavoidable death.

At the time she was lecturing on women and their social destiny, Stein sensed the approaching danger, but she could not foresee the reality of Westerbork, where Hillesum would be fulfilling her destiny as an empathic helper of condemned Jews. Neither could she foresee the reality of the hiding place in which, under the constant threat of discovery and deportation, Frank would attempt to shape her own destiny as a woman. Nonetheless, Frank's maturation process shows a remarkable degree of affinity with Stein's perception of woman's inner development as the redeemer of the world.

Frank wanted to actualize her intellectual potential as a writer and as an individual contributing to the world, and she did not perceive her gender as an obstacle to her success. In order to fulfill her potential, she knew she would have to assert herself against her mother. As early as November 1942, Frank decided: "I have to be my own mother. . . . I must become good through my own efforts, without examples and without good advice; then later on I shall be all the stronger."[14] Even in April 1944, Frank still maintained her determination to educate herself and accomplish her goals, despite her mother's negative model: "I face life with more courage than Mummy; my feeling for justice is immovable, and truer than hers. . . . I shall attain more than Mummy ever has done."[15]

As she asserts her independence, Frank draws on the strength of her womanhood and a sense of her destiny. "Let me be myself and then I am satisfied. I know that I'm a woman, a woman with inward strength and plenty of courage. If God lets me live, . . . I shall work in the world and for mankind."[16] Frank sees her future as indelibly connected to her femininity, which will help her actualize her goal to contribute to humanity. In terms of her present, her strength will help her develop the faculties of "courage and cheerfulness,"[17] which will protect her against fear and despair. Indeed, we hear Stein's view of emotions governed by reason reverberate in Frank's declaration "My work, my hope, my love, my courage make me go on and help me cope."[18]

Frank's resourcefulness and determination to keep her ideals, her self-command, and her independence as a woman are tested in her relationships with Peter. Her critical self-examination of her infatuation with Peter, especially in the circumstances of the Annex, shows that she has extraordinarily mature insight and self-command.

In the first stages of her relationship with Peter, Frank realizes with a hint of self-disapproval that she is "no longer independent of Peter."[19] Her infatuation with Peter, however, does not preclude a lucid evaluation of his character. She sees through his weaknesses and opines that he has "not enough will power, too little courage and strength." At the same time, she is conscious of being egotistical and possessive, as she admits to herself: "You would not be able to marry him, but yet, it would be hard to let him go."[20] Finally, Frank asserts her emotional independence of Peter, as she realizes that "he could not be a friend for my understanding" and that he cannot help her maintain her courage and ideals in the situation of the world's total moral collapse.[21] She does "let him go," and her refusal to compromise her integrity in the circumstances of impending discovery by the Gestapo, deportation, and death constitutes a most poignant example of self-assertion as resistance.

The struggle between the desire to hold on to the other and the need to affirm herself as a strong, principled individual marks Frank's maturation. That the imperative to remain faithful to her ideals and principles wins out proves that Frank is no longer a girl, but an adult woman who sees her moral, intellectual, and emotional potential as elements that determine her destiny.

The question of women's dependency on love relationships is also the focal point in Hillesum's consideration of the meaning of femininity. Hillesum realizes that woman's "wanting to be desired by man . . . is only a primitive instinct." It is, as she puts it, "a handicap, a woman's handicap."[22] Is this "handicap" of sexual subjugation and possessiveness, Hillesum wonders, "an ancient tradition from which [woman] must liberate herself?" or is it "so much part of her very essence that she would be doing violence to herself if she bestowed her love on all mankind instead of on a single man?"[23]

This question places Hillesum between the poles of Stein's belief in women's potential as empathic redeemers of the world, and Weil's notion of women's inherent dependency on their sexuality, which determines her inferiority. Such confessions as "Right now I feel that all I want is to fling myself into his arms, and just be a woman, or perhaps even less, just a piece of cherished flesh"[24] mark Hillesum's affinity with Weil's derogatory consideration of woman's inability to attain holiness. On the other hand, Hillesum's emerging notion of the "essential emancipation" as liberation from "centuries-old traditions" of sexual dependency that will signify the rebirth of women as "full human beings"[25] indicates an increasing affiliation with Stein's outlook.

Hillesum does not leave the question of the "essential emancipation" in the sphere of theoretical considerations. The battle to transform the obsessive need for sexual conquest to obsessive love for suffering humanity marks her progress toward actualizing her potential as a woman. From the beginning, she sets her goal, claiming: "The urge—fiction or fantasy, whatever you want to call it—to possess one man for life. It's something I must eradicate."[26]

Her inner struggle leads her to the realization of "a sudden sense of complete emancipation from him [Spier, her lover], of continuing all by myself."[27] Eventually, her inner liberation leads her to understand that she "now [has] a right to a 'destiny.' It is no longer a romantic dream or the thirst for adventure, or for love. . . . It is a terrible, sacred, inner seriousness, difficult and at the same time inevitable."[28]

What is this sacred destiny that replaces Hillesum's desire for the man she loved so deeply? At the end of her diary, Hillesum answers this question with a realization: "I have too much love to give it all to just one person. The idea that one can love one person and one person only one's whole life long strikes me as quite childish. . . . Will people ever learn that love brings so much more happiness and reward than sex?"[29]

Happiness is the ability to give of oneself to the suffering other, but this ability does not point toward a consciously incurred martyrdom in the sense that Weil envisaged herself dying on the battlefield. Rather, the need to practice the altruistic properties of love, which supersede the limitations of sexual relationships, is reminiscent of Stein's notion of woman as an empathic redeemer of the world.

In her service in Westerbork, Hillesum proved that she had been emancipated from the confining mentality that women are sexual objects. But under the circumstances of the deportation camp, her self-assertion in the face of the "centuries-long traditions" of women's subjugation and dependency gains an even deeper significance. As an indicator of her inner emancipation, Hillesum's voluntary service in Westerbork becomes the expression of her resistance of the rule of terror set on reducing her to an indistinguishable particle in the gray, uniform mass of suffering Jews.

CONCLUSION:
LEGACIES OF RESISTANCE

The knot of subjectivity consists in going to the other without concerning oneself with his movement towards me.

—Emmanuel Levinas

The feminist aspect in the thought and work of Edith Stein, Simone Weil, Anne Frank, and Etty Hillesum reemphasizes the humanistic world view that informed their resistance. While Stein, Frank, and Hillesum strove to actualize their destiny as women, Weil strove to actualize her destiny despite being a woman. For none of the women, however, did the wish to fulfill her destiny get in the way of her adherence to the concept of *Bildung*— that is, self-education and self-edification. On the contrary, even in its denial the feminist component of their responses to the world underlined each woman's sense of responsibility for ethical and spiritual self-development. The processes of self-development evolved, without exception, in relation to a deep concern about the welfare of humanity.

The women's standpoints with regard to their persecution, their religious beliefs, their destiny, and their art were infused with empathic concern about the world in crisis, and this concern manifested itself at three levels.

As individuals, they demonstrated solidarity, sympathy, and identification with the suffering victims of the war (Weil identified with the suffering French people; the other women's sense of solidarity, as "catastrophe Jews," was with the persecuted Jews). As post-Emancipation, assimilated Jews, all four were deeply distressed about the disintegration of the warring world's humanistic, enlightened image. And as adherents to the humanistic ideal, they were preoccupied with envisioning and planning for the postwar world—which they knew they would not live to see.

The intense preoccupation of these four women with the contemporary and future moral image of humanity constituted the core of their defiance of terror. Their concern for the world therefore stood in complete opposition to the Nazi design to deprive them, like all other Jews of Europe, of their humanity before extermination.

The women expressed solidarity with the victims of the Nazi oppression, even though each knew that, as a Jew, she herself was destined to death. In the "illogical logic" of resisting the "irresistible logic of destruction," in the words of Fackenheim, the women continued to care. Their creativity counteracted any despondency, because in their consciousness it replaced them in the world. To open oneself to the world signified a stance of accountability. But the four women were not addressing a responsive world. Their insistence on caring for humanity, which had stopped caring about them, represented, especially in Weil and Hillesum, relationships of receptivity rather than reciprocity. In all four cases the insistence on caring points to a defiant humanistic position.

At the outset of this study we asked: What forces helped them to maintain their humanity at the time of humanity's apocalyptic disintegration? The question implies the traumatic legacy of the Holocaust, which confronts us with a related question: What force will maintain our humaneness in a world that is imbued with consciousness of the evil of Holocaust? The quest for ethic in a world that witnessed an apocalyptic surge of human evil posits the problem of faith in a godless world.

Writing after the Holocaust, Emil Fackenheim struggled with the issue of acting in a world that had lost its humanity. How can we rediscover meaning in a world that had become meaningless? The Midrash, a story that in the Jewish rabbinic tradition interprets the wisdom of God and the order of God's world, had been silenced. The world the Midrash was meant to reflect had turned into a grotesque, horrifying travesty of the order of creation. The shattering of the world order requires a "Mad Midrash," capable of dwelling on that which is no longer to be seen. According to Fackenheim, the "Mad Midrash" is "the Word spoken in the anti-world which ought not to be but is. The existence it [the Mad Midrash] points to acts to restore a world which ought to be but is not, committed to the faith that what ought to be must and will be, and this is madness."[1]

In her own way, each of the four women anticipated Fackenheim's paradoxical directive. Each of them wrote her own "Mad Midrash," clinging to the absurd notion that they could conduct what Hannah Arendt called a "humanizing discourse with a world" in the reality of the Final Solution.

Yet the writings and actions of these four women convey more than a desire to carry on a humanizing discourse with the world at large. They also express a selfless and seemingly incongruous solidarity with the sufferers. It does not appear too far-fetched to discern here a foreshadowing of Emmanuel Levinas,[2] whose thought could provide a theoretical framework for interpreting their altruism.

The realization of the individual's altruistic connections with others is not new. For instance, Plato argued that "the desire for wholeness through union with others [is] a force almost stronger than necessity."[3] Relatedness to others is essential to human existence, but Levinas's consideration of human relatedness in the wake of the Holocaust is pertinent.

Referring to the Holocaust, Levinas poses a poignant question: "Can we speak of morality after the failure of morality?"[4] In response, Levinas defines moral relationships as the prehistorical, preintellectual, absolutely fundamental being *for* the other. In contrast to being *with* the other, being *for* the other indicates an irrevocable sense of moral accountability that places the interest of the other above one's self-interest. Levinas postulates: "The uniqueness of the responsible ego is possible only in being obsessed by another."[5] Being "obsessed" with the other's well-being determines one's own humanity, because, as Levinas argues, "no one can save himself without the Others."[6]

From this point of view, therefore, the resistance that focused on the other defied the Nazi politics of dehumanization through horror. "In horror," Levinas tells us, "a subject is stripped of his subjectivity, of his power to have private existence. The subject is depersonalized."[7] The empathic stance that each woman strove to maintain until the last possible moment counteracted the horror and therefore resisted depersonalization.

The final moments of Stein, Frank, and Hillesum in the unspeakable reality of the concentration camp will never be known, but their insistence on struggling against fear and despair through devotion to the world in crisis attests to their "being for the other." Stein's identification with the suffering Jews, Weil's wish to die caring for soldiers on the battlefield, Frank's feeling of betrayal for not being able to help homeless Jews, Hillesum's voluntary work at Westerbork—these examples seem both to anticipate and to affirm Levinas's thinking on the meaning of responsibility.

"In the responsibility which we have for one another," Levinas maintains, "I have always one response more to give."[8] I am the "hostage" of the other, says Levinas, and this condition commands me "to give to the Other by taking the bread out of my own mouth, and making a gift of my own skin."[9] "It is my power to support the suffering of the others. It is the moment when I recognize this power and my universal responsibility."[10]

On the one hand, Levinas claims, "the other is in me and in the midst of my very identification."[11] On the other hand, "the very relationship with the other is the relationship with the future."[12] My contact with the other extends me beyond myself. My being for the other is not a function of compassion, but rather a function of absolute necessity, as the other is a part of my inner self but also a part that extends my "I" beyond the limits of my self.

These seemingly impossible moral demands become actual in Hillesum's growing sense of responsibility not only for those for whom she cares in Westerbork but also for those who had left on transports to Auschwitz. "I shall never be able to sit quietly at a desk. I want to travel all over the world and see with my own eyes and hear with my own ears how they fared, all those we sent on their way. . . . If I could only be there to give some of those packed thousands just one sip of water."[13] While she admits that "Dante's Inferno is comic opera by comparison" with the camps,[14] Hillesum insists that she wants "to be there right in the thick of what people call 'horror' and still be able to say: life is beautiful."[15]

We notice that hope does not manifest itself in an endorsement of ideals that no longer make sense. On the contrary, Hillesum is aware of the unspeakable reality of horror. In order to maintain her humanity, she therefore constructs a "Mad Midrash" that asserts both horror and beauty in the concentration camp. What makes this absurd notion possible is the hope infused by an overwhelming sense of love for humanity and solidarity with the afflicted.

In her study of Levinas, Catherine Chalier speaks of Hillesum's conduct of solidarity with the afflicted as an illustration of Levinas's ethics. Hillesum's attitude toward the other, Chalier claims, provides evidence that "a truly good act springing from this incomprehensible disinterestedness . . . can restore hope and support the whole world even during the darkest time."[16]

While undoubtedly correct about Hillesum's boundless solidarity with the suffering, Chalier's notion of Hillesum's restoring hope and support to the whole world at the time of the Holocaust evokes the risk of trivializing the horror by abstracting it. Chalier's hopeful claim seems to disregard the hopelessness of the situation of all the imprisoned Jews at Westerbork, including Hillesum. Expressing formulaic, facile optimism about the global effect of Hillesum's deed "in the darkest time" does more than just diminish the heroism of her resistance.

Such interpretations shift attention from the Holocaust world itself to its post-Holocaust optimistic re-vision, which minimizes the horror by transcribing it in terms of humanistic hopefulness. This unwarranted attitude indicates the desire to evade the horror experienced by the Holocaust victim by opting for sentimentalized sanctification.

Such a hagiographical approach emerges not only in the case of Hillesum, who was also described by Jacob Boas as "saintly in her selflessness," bringing others "a ray of warmth and kindliness."[17] It is true of the other three women as well. Referring to the theatrical and cinematic adaptations of Frank's diary, Hannah Arendt points to the phenomenon of evasion when she argues that "the world-wide success of *The Diary of Anne Frank*" testified to the general tendency to "[forget] the 'negative' aspect of the past and [reduce] horror to sentimentality."[18] The tendencies to hagiography are conspicuous in the treatment of Weil as well. Her self-inflicted starvation established her as a saintly altruist and drew attention to the prophetic vision of her philosophical writings. Stein was beatified by the pope and thereby is officially entitled to be a subject of veneration by Catholics. The Church interpreted her death as a symbolic act of Christian martyrdom.[19]

Their proponents present these women as paragons of selflessness, moral fortitude, and endurance; their opponents dismiss the symbolic quality of their acts and works.[20] This study's intent is to represent the four women neither as saints nor as emblems of ideological controversies, but rather as individuals who opposed the terror by insisting on their own humanity. The intensity of their despair, as well as the equally intense desire to fend off the increasing despondency, is evident. The openness of their communication, and their vacillations between concern and despair, hopelessness and hope, in the intellectual act of writing, highlight the absurd faith that the world that "ought to be, must and will be." Invariably, even if controversially, these women's writings point to the extraordinary extent of obligation toward the world and toward identification with the other.

The women's preoccupation with the world defied the Final Solution, not because they were saints but because they were human. Through solidarity with the pain of the world, they were able to achieve a sense of liberation from the fear of the apocalyptic ending. To salvage morality in a world that is devoid of morality requires establishing the future in the present. The future, as these four women saw, was present in the overriding concern about humanity and humanism, present in their acts of writing.

"Action," Hannah Arendt claims, "is never possible in isolation; to be isolated is to be deprived of the capacity to act. . . . Action . . . always establishes relationships and therefore has an inherent tendency to force open all limitations and cut across all boundaries."[21] In their acts of writing, the four women defied tyrannical limitations, cut across the boundaries of the decree, denied isolation, and established a relationship that speaks the language of humanism in resistance to terror. Their apparently absurd defiance, manifest in deeds as well as in intellectual acts of writing, raises the issue of the significance of moral concern in a world that had reached complete moral disintegration.

Should we see their intellectual engagement and spiritual sensitivity as psychologically protective barriers against the horror? As a heroic but tragically futile repulsion of the perpetrators? As vestiges of faith in humanistic, enlightened ideals that had proved empty of meaning? Or should we perceive these responses as serious attempts to restore meaning to humanism? As foresights of postwar social, theological, and ethical concerns? As legacies relevant to postwar Weltanschauung?

Stein's views of empathy and its applications, as they emerge in her feminist thought, open this concluding discussion of the pertinence of the four women's orientations in the postwar feminist, theological, and ethical thought. Her view of women's destiny as educators of humanity resonates in the feminist orientation today, especially in the school of "cultural feminism." As represented also in Frank's and Hillesum's feminist directions, the particular ability to care that Stein attributed to women has been, to a remarkable degree, endorsed by such contemporary feminist thinkers as Nancy Chodorow, Sara Ruddick, Carol Gilligan, and Nel Noddings.

Stein's premise of the mother-daughter bond as the factor that shapes women's proclivity to connectedness reverberates in Nancy Chodorow's psychoanalytical work. In Stein, the mother-daughter relationship, based on "caring love," creates "vital solidarity between mother and daughter, . . . a spiritual-intellectual tie scarcely to be severed."[22]

In her *Reproduction of Mothering*, Chodorow shows how the mother who brings into the relationship with her daughter "her own internalized early relationship with her mother" provides a model that emphasizes connectedness, continuity, and recognition of the other.[23] Furthermore, Chodorow asserts that identification with the mother accounts for the "sentiment of empathy" that emerges in the daughter's "primary definition of self."[24]

But it is not only the personal, psychological observation of the generational tie that connects Stein to contemporary feminist thought. Stein's consideration of the universal value of motherhood presages Sara Ruddick's social concept of "maternal thinking." Recall that in Stein's view woman's empathic understanding extends to humanity at large. "Maternal thinking," Ruddick concurs, is inherently feminine "because we are all daughters." It is "a unity of reflection, judgment, and emotion" that transcends a mother's interest in her own children and makes the interest of all children her own.[25]

Stein's notion of women's empathic proclivity, which allows women to construct intersubjective relationships, prefigures Carol Gilligan's observation of female "orientation toward relationships and interdependence" as the basis of the female ethical self.[26] Gilligan's emphasis on the position of women in relation to the world reinforces the theoretical psychological view of the feminine gender, which claims that "the basic feminine sense of self is connected to the world" and that "feminine personality comes to include a fundamental definition of self in relationship."[27]

These correspondences—also implied in Frank's self-assertion as a woman who wants to work for humankind, and in Hillesum's desire to develop her capacity for love of humanity—demonstrate the foresight of prewar feminist thought in terms of feminine proclivity to relatedness. However, it is inaccurate and perhaps even unwise to categorize the proclivity to social-relatedness as a feminine value. Suffice it to recall E. M. Forster's epigraph to *Howards End:* "Only connect," to realize that, while labeled "feminine," or even "feminist," the notion of empathic relationships as elemental to social intercourse applies to humanity at large, regardless of gender.

To typify social behavior that highlights relatedness as gender-specific would verge on an unwarranted generalization. Perhaps it is possible to argue that the feminist emphasis on relatedness in the wake of World War II indicates a significant shift in cultural perception from the Kantian notion of the absolute "perfect duties" to the "imperfect duties" of responsibility, caring, and compassion. That is, in view of the collapse of all moral values and injunctions, the so-called "feminine" value of relatedness gains importance over the so-called "masculine" principle of justice, which, according to Kant, "enjoy[s] absolute priority over imperfect duties."[28]

It is impossible to develop this hypothesis more fully here, but we can argue that the four women's positions of resistance certainly presage those postwar feminist orientations, as well as the theological and ethical orientations, which highlight the individual's "imperfect duties" of responsibility and caring toward God, the world, and the other.

At the same time, certain differences are noteworthy. For instance, Nel Noddings's phenomenology of caring, which highlights the reciprocal and the receptive modes of caring, helps us understand the responses of the four women to the unresponsive world are relevant to the post-Holocaust world.

Noddings argues that relatedness emerges from one's self-understanding as "one-caring" as well as one "cared-for."[29] The ethical self, as she defines it, "is an active relation between my actual self and a vision of my ideal self as one-caring and cared-for."[30] But although reciprocity is assumed, Noddings emphasizes that "the ethical self can emerge only from caring for others" and that caring is possible because of the value of empathic receptivity whereby "I receive the other into myself, and see and feel with the other."[31]

The symmetry of Noddings's notion of "one-caring and cared-for" calls attention to the asymmetry of the relationships the four women had to the world. In the reality of the Holocaust and its "logic of destruction," the notions of caring-for and being cared-for had become meaningless. I have explored the transformation of the value of reciprocity into the value of receptivity in this study.

Another interesting comparison may be drawn with the thought of theologian Paul Tillich. The women in this study insisted on disregarding that which it was impossible to disregard—a direct threat of annihilation—for the sake of the discredited values and beliefs of humanism. Tillich would undoubtedly have consented to call this attitude the "courage to be."

Like Fackenheim's concept of the "Mad Midrash," Tillich's notion of the "courage to be" points to the absurd yet absolutely vital undertaking of sustaining an ethically meaningful existence in a meaningless world. The hope lies in striving to restore ethics and faith despite the consciousness that ethics and faith had been obliterated. *"The courage to be,"* Tillich emphasizes, *"is rooted in the God who appears when God has disappeared in the anxiety of doubt."*[32]

The God of justice and providence is no longer with us. In order to be able to exist humanely in a godless world, we must replace the disappeared God with a sense of his existence. For both Tillich and Fackenheim, the existence of God lies no longer in his commanding presence but in the human courage to think and act as if God and his divine order existed—that is, to maintain the values without the support of the Divine.

In the situation of the Holocaust, the "courage to be" of the four women manifested itself in the "midrashic madness" of remaining in social space and historical time while knowing that such space and time no longer existed. Their "courage to be" affirmed the world as it should be rather than as the "other planet" it had become. Their courage to reflect on the present and the future and to document the unfolding catastrophe placed the women in history at the time when the history of Jews, and consequently the history of civilization, was approaching an apocalyptic ending.

This stubborn faith in the world as it ought to be implies neither ethical naiveté nor ideological shortsightedness. To preserve the "courage to be," the women needed to reaffirm God, even if God had disappeared from the horizon of the historical present. Without denying that God might have a place in the historical future—indeed, the hopes they expressed for the future indicate that they believed the horror they were experiencing was not to have the last word in history—it was not the God of history to whom they turned. That God could no longer inspire confidence and inner peace. Their quest for communion with God proceeded along more self-reflective and ethical routes. We have noted Stein's desire to take up the Cross for her people, Weil's obsession with reaching God through de-creation, Frank's search for a comforting God through the intermediary of nature, and Hillesum's acknowledgment of the weak God in need of her protection.

Hillesum's "weak God" theology may be compared to Jürgen Moltmann's "theology of divine vulnerability." Moltmann claims that in the event of the Cross God is not absolute or active or victorious. Neither is the Cross of Christ without powerful postfigurations. On the contrary, the Holocaust is the most dramatic interpretation of the Cross because it proves that, through the Cross, God participated in the suffering of the victims. "God himself," Moltmann says, "[was] in Auschwitz, suffering with the martyred and the murdered."[33]

Paul Van Buren also struggles with the role of the Christian God in the Holocaust. Unlike Moltmann, Van Buren sees God not as with the sufferers but as suffering the transgressions his Christian believers were committing: "God steps back to leave us free to work His will, if we will, and suffers with us in all our failures." Human beings, Van Buren claims, inflict suffering and agony on God when they abuse the freedom of will he bestowed on them. "[We Christians]," he argues, "lacked the audacity to see God precisely in the suffering and the failure of the cross."[34]

A prominent Jewish theologian, Irving Greenberg, offers a Jewish perspective that bars God from determining the future. His position highlights the four women's persisting hope that God would reappear in the future despite God's present disappearance from history. He directs his attention, first of all, to the problematic of the Covenant. The event of the Holocaust undermined the viability of the Covenant for the Jewish people and, by implication, for Christians and Muslims as well. God can no longer claim his people as the people of the Covenant. He can no longer be a commanding God. Now the Covenant is "voluntary," whereby the Jewish people have become "a senior partner in action." Greenberg claims that in the Holocaust God abdicated the role of absolute ruler. Now he is telling "the humans," "You stop the Holocaust. . . . You act to ensure that it will never again occur. I will be with you totally in whatever happens, but you must do it."[35]

In effect, Greenberg denies God an active role in future human history. According to thinkers like Greenberg, the responsibility for the world's welfare can therefore no longer remain in the sphere of the Divine. In the post-Holocaust world, the responsibility for humanity becomes the exclusive domain of humankind.

The four women of this study, on the other hand, understood themselves and expressed themselves in another way. Their solidarity with God, even and particularly in his weakness, was absolute—to the point, in Weil's case, of striving for self-annihilation. Their empathy reached beyond the sufferers around them to God himself. They (with perhaps the exception of Frank) saw God in the sufferer. Their devotion to the suffering was understood to be devotion to God. At the same time, the emerging image of God as a suffering God, and the sense of obligation to protect him, communicates the complexity of their humanism.

A human obligation of solidarity with the world, self, and God under most terrifying circumstances is perhaps best expressed in Hillesum's remonstration "God is not accountable to us. . . . We are accountable to Him! I have already died a thousand deaths in a thousand concentration camps";[36] or in Weil's confession: "The suffering all over the world obsesses me and overwhelms me to the point of annihilating my faculties and the only way I can revive them and release myself from the obsession is by getting for myself a large share of danger and hardship";[37] or in Stein's declaration that "the destiny of this [Jewish] people was my own"; or in Frank's anguish at the realization that others were suffering while she was safe. These examples leave us with the legacy of resistance that persists in the reaffirmation of one's humanity as a spark of the Divine.

NOTES

Introduction

1. Etty Hillesum, *Letters from Westerbork,* trans. Arnold J. Pomerans (New York: Pantheon Books, 1986), 146.

2. Emil L. Fackenheim, *To Mend the World: Foundations of Future Jewish Thought* (New York: Schocken Books, 1982), 248.

3. Pelagia Lewinska, quoted in ibid., 217.

4. Testimony 58, Helen K., in Fortunoff Video Archive for Holocaust Testimonies, Yale University. Quoted in Shoshana Felman and Dori Laub, *Testimony: Crises of Witnessing in Literature, Psychoanalysis, and History* (New York: Routledge, 1992), 44.

5. Mendel Mann, quoted in Sidra Ezrahi, *By Words Alone: The Holocaust in Literature* (Chicago: University of Chicago Press, 1980), 21.

6. Geoffrey Hartman, "The Book of Destruction," in *Probing the Limits of Representation: Nazism and the "Final Solution,"* ed. Saul Friedlander (Cambridge: Harvard University Press, 1992), 324.

7. Felman and Laub, *Testimony,* 81, 84 (italics in the original).

8. See Alvin H. Rosenfeld, *A Double Dying: Reflections on Holocaust Literature* (Bloomington: Indiana University Press, 1980), 42–46.

9. Ibid., 42.

10. Viktor Frankl, *Man in Search of Meaning,* trans. Ilse Lasch (1946; reprint, New York: Washington Square Press, 1984), 176, 133.

11. Rosenfeld, *A Double Dying,* 43.

12. James Young, *Writing and Rewriting the Holocaust: Narratives and the Consequences of Interpretation* (Bloomington: Indiana University Press, 1988), 26.

Chapter 1

1. Hannah Arendt, *Men in Dark Times* (New York: Harcourt, Brace & World, 1968), 22.

2. Quoted in Waltraut J. Stein, "Reflections on Edith Stein's Secret," *Spiritual Life* 34 (Fall 1988), 131.

3. Simone Weil, *Waiting for God,* trans. Emma Craufurd (New York: G. P. Putnam's Sons, 1951), 99.

4. Etty Hillesum, *Etty: A Diary, 1941–1943,* trans. Arnold J. Pomerans (London: Jonathan Cape, 1983), 130–31. (Hereafter: Hillesum, *Diary.*)

5. Anne Frank, *The Diary of Anne Frank: The Critical Edition,* ed. David Barnouw and Gerrold van der Stroom, trans. Arnold J. Pomerans and B. M. Mooyaart-Doubleday (New York: Doubleday, 1989), 694. (Hereafter: Frank, *Diary.*)

6. Anne Frank, *Tales from the House Behind: Fables, Personal Reminiscences, and Short Stories*, trans. H. H. B. Mosberg and Michel Mok (Kingswood: The World's Work, 1960), 130. (Hereafter: Frank, *Tales*.)

7. Albert Camus, *The Plague,* trans. Stuart Gilbert (New York: Random House, 1972), 174.

8. George Mosse, *Germany Beyond Judaism* (Bloomington: Indiana University Press, 1985), 2.

9. Zygmunt Bauman, *Modernity and Ambivalence* (Ithaca: Cornell University Press, 1991), 108.

10. See, for instance, Lawrence Baron, "The Dynamics of Decency: Dutch Rescuers of the Jews During the Holocaust," in *The Nazi Holocaust,* ed. Michael R. Marrus, vol. 5 (Westport, Conn.: Mecklermedia, 1989).

11. Paula Hyman, *From Dreyfus to Vichy: The Remaking of French Jewry, 1906–1939* (New York: Columbia University Press, 1979), 8–9.

12. Donald L. Niewyk, *The Jews in Weimar Germany* (Baton Rouge: Louisiana State University Press, 1980), 9.

13. Jacob B. Agus, *Jewish Identity in an Age of Ideologies* (New York: Frederick Ungar Publishing Company, 1978), 84.

14. Bauman, *Modernity and Ambivalence,* 112.

15. Arendt, *Men in Dark Times,* 30, 31.

16. Mosse, *German Jews Beyond Judaism,* 11.

Chapter 2

1. Frank, *Diary,* 690.
2. Hillesum, *Diary,* 46.
3. Weil, "Spiritual Autobiography," *Waiting for God,* 64.
4. Ibid., 66.
5. Edith Stein, *Edith Stein: Life in a Jewish Family, 1891–1916,* trans. Josephine Koeppel (Washington, D.C.: ICS Publications, 1986), 348. (Hereafter: Stein, *Life in a Jewish Family.*)
6. Ibid., 397.
7. Edith Stein, *On the Problem of Empathy,* 3rd ed., trans. Waltraut Stein (Washington, D.C.: ICS Publications, 1989), 109–11ff.
8. Frank, *Diary,* 438.
9. Ibid., 517–18.
10. Ibid., 518.
11. Stein, *Life in a Jewish Family,* 73–79.
12. Frank, *Diary,* 690.
13. Hillesum, *Diary,* 110–11.
14. Weil, *Waiting for God,* 60.
15. Simone Weil, *Seventy Letters,* trans. Richard Rees (London: Oxford University Press, 1965), 144.
16. Mosse, *German Jews Beyond Judaism,* 6.
17. Ibid., 4.
18. Ibid., 48.
19. Zygmunt Bauman, *Modernity and the Holocaust* (Ithaca: Cornell University Press, 1989), 179.
20. Frankl, *Man in Search of Meaning,* 87.

Chapter 3

1. Quoted in Michael D. Barber, *Guardian of Dialogue: Max Scheler's Phenomenology, Sociology of Knowledge, and Philosophy of Love* (Lewisburg, Pa.: Bucknell University Press, 1993), 124.

2. Quoted in Ron Perrin, *Max Scheler's Concept of the Person: An Ethics of Humanism* (New York: St. Martin's Press, 1991), 87–89, 99.

3. Barber, *Guardian of Dialogue*, 49, 116.

4. Stein, *On the Problem of Empathy*, 6.

5. Ibid., 43–44.

6. Ibid., 38.

7. Ibid., 62–63.

8. Ibid., 89.

9. Ibid., 82.

10. Ibid., 83.

11. Frank, *Diary*, 683.

12. Arendt, *Men in Dark Times*, 30.

13. Scheler, quoted in Barber, *Guardian of Dialogue*, 119.

14. Scheler, quoted in ibid., 158.

15. Simone Weil, "Human Personality," in *The Simone Weil Reader*, ed. George A. Panichas (New York: David McKay Company, 1977), 315. (Hereafter: *Simone Weil Reader*.)

16. Ibid., 332.

17. Ibid., 333.

18. Simone Weil, *First and Last Notebooks*, trans. Richard Rees (London: Oxford University Press, 1970), 210.

19. Weil, "Human Personality," in *Simone Weil Reader*, 318.

20. Anne Frank, "Give," in *Tales*, 127–29ff.

21. The first phrase is almost a direct quotation from Luke 6:38 and an indication of the influence of Christian thought on Frank's ethical orientation. I thank John Hobbins for drawing my attention to this connection. Frank, "Give," in *Tales*, 130.

22. Ibid., 129, 130.

23. Ibid., 128.

24. Ibid., 127–28.

25. Frank, *Diary*, 332.

26. Hillesum, *Diary*, 150.

27. Etty Hillesum, *Letters from Westerbork*, trans. Arnold J. Pomerans (New York: Pantheon Books, 1986), 77. (Hereafter: Hillesum, *Letters*.)

28. Simone Weil, *Gravity and Grace*, trans. Arthur Wills (New York: G. P. Putnam's Sons, 1952), 134–36 and passim.

29. Hillesum, *Letters*, 112.

30. Frankl, *Man in Search of Meaning*, 88.

31. Ibid., 136.

32. Hillesum, *Letters*, 63.

33. Hillesum, *Diary*, 115.

34. Hillesum analyzes her feelings of possessiveness toward her former lover, Max, and struggles to overcome her dependency on her last lover, the psychochirologist Julius Spier.

35. *Simone Weil Reader*, 318.

36. Hillesum, *Diary*, 48. See also Weil, *Gravity and Grace*, 180, 181.

37. Hillesum, *Diary*, 106.

38. Ibid., 144.

39. Ibid., 192.

40. Ibid., 51.

41. Hillesum, *Diary*, 142.

42. Ibid., 191.

43. Ibid., 187.

44. Ibid., 176.

45. Weil, *Seventy Letters*, 145.

46. Thomas R. Nevin, *Simone Weil: Portrait of a Self-Exiled Jew* (Chapel Hill: University of North Carolina Press, 1991), 1.

47. Weil, *Seventy Letters*, 148.

48. Ibid., 149.

49. Ibid., 150.

50. Robert Coles, *Simone Weil: A Modern Pilgrimage* (Reading, Mass.: Addison-Wesley Publishing Company, 1987), 15. See also Dorothy Tuck McFarland, *Simone Weil* (New York: Frederick Ungar Publishing Company, 1983), 143–44; John Hellman, *Simone Weil: An Introduction to Her Thought* (Waterloo, Ont.: Wilfred Laurier University Press, 1982), 80–82; and Sian Miles, ed., *Simone Weil: Anthology* (London: Virago Press, 1986), 38–39.

51. Weil, *Seventy Letters*, 151.

52. Ibid., 149.

53. Ibid., 151.

54. Ibid., 147.

55. Ibid., 174–75.

56. Weil, "Spiritual Autobiography," 63.

57. Weil, *Seventy Letters*, 178–79.

Chapter 4

1. Quoted in Hilda C. Graeff, *The Scholar and the Cross: The Life and Work of Edith Stein* (London: Longmans, 1955), 32.

2. Weil, *Waiting for God*, 69.

3. Ibid., 83.

4. Hillesum, *Diary*, 195, 196.

5. See Frank's stories "Fear" and "Cady's Life" in *Tales*.

6. Quoted in Agus, *Jewish Identity*, 237, 260.

7. Ibid., 332.

8. Rosenzweig seriously contemplated conversion to Christianity. He is quoted as saying with reference to the New Testament: "Here is everything, here is the truth. There is only one way, Jesus" (Nahum Glatzer, *Franz Rosenzweig: His Life and Thought* [New York: Schocken Books, 1953], 25).

9. Richard A. Cohen, *Elevations: The Height of the Good in Rosenzweig and Levinas* (Chicago: University of Chicago Press, 1994), 17.

10. Franz Rosenzweig, *The Star of Redemption*, trans. William W. Hallo (Notre Dame, Ind.: University of Notre Dame Press, 1985), 348.

11. Cohen, *Elevations*, 20.

12. Maritain converted from Protestantism to Catholicism.

13. *Jacques Maritain and the Jews*, ed. Robert Royal (Notre Dame, Ind.: American Maritain Association, 1994), 86.

14. Jacques Maritain, *A Christian Looks at the Jewish Question* (New York: Longmans, Green, 1939), 41–42.

15. James V. Schall, "The Mystery of the Mystery of Israel," in *Jacques Maritain and the Jews*, 65.

16. Hegel, quoted in Lionel Gossman, "Philhellenism and Antisemitism: Matthew Arnold and His German Models," *Comparative Literature* 46 (Winter 1994), 8.

17. Ibid., 9.

18. Quoted in Emil L. Fackenheim, *God's Presence in History: Jewish Affirmations and Philosophical Reflections* (New York: New York University Press, 1970), 55–56.

19. Ibid., 56.

Chapter 5

1. See Sister Teresia de Spiritu Sancto, *Edith Stein*, trans. Cecily Hastings and Donald Nicholl (London: Sheed & Ward, 1952), 117ff.

2. John M. Osterreicher, *The Walls Are Crumbling: Seven Jewish Philosophers Discover Christ* (London: Hollis & Carter, 1952), 311.

3. Ibid., 324.

4. Ibid., 323.

5. Waultraud Herbstrith, *Edith Stein: A Biography*, trans. Bernard Bonowitz (San Francisco: Harper & Row, 1983), 95.

6. Osterreicher, *The Walls Are Crumbling*, 103.

7. Simone Weil, *The Notebooks of Simone Weil*, trans. Arthur Wills (London: Routledge & Kegan Paul, 1956), 575–76.

8. Michael R. Marrus and Robert O. Paxton (*Vichy France and the Jews* [New York: Basic Books, 1981], 348) attest that the roundups of the French Jews in July–August 1942 were "impossible to conceal" and that "as early as 1 July 1942, the BBC had broadcast accounts in French of the massacre of 700,000 Polish Jews."

9. Weil, quoted in Nevin, *Simone Weil: Portrait*, 243.

10. Quoted in Simone Pétrement, *Simone Weil: A Life*, trans. Raymond Rosenthal (New York: Pantheon Books, 1976), 509, and discussed in Nevin, *Simone Weil: Portrait*, 244–47.

11. *Simone Weil Reader*, 80.

12. Weil, *Waiting for God*, 62.

13. Quoted in Teresia de Spiritu Sancto, *Edith Stein*, 218.

14. Ibid., 118, 119.

15. See, for instance, Graef, *The Scholar and the Cross*, 142, and Teresia de Spiritu Sancto, *Edith Stein*, 211.

16. Weil, *Seventy Letters*, 155.

17. Weil, quoted in Pétrement, *Simone Weil: A Life*, 481.

18. Anna Freud, quoted in Coles, *Simone Weil: A Modern Pilgrimage*, 58.

19. Hillesum, *Letters*, 28. The footnote says: "One of the nuns described is Edith Stein with whom Etty has often been compared."

20. Weil, *Simone Weil Reader*, 318–19.

21. Weil, *Waiting for God*, 54.

22. Weil, *First and Last Notebooks*, 298, 295.

23. Weil, *Waiting for God*, 79.

24. Weil, *Seventy Letters*, 155.

25. Ibid., 159.

26. Simone Weil, *Gateway to God*, ed. and trans. David Raper (London: Fontana Books, 1974), 109.

27. See Norman Perrin and Dennis C. Duling, *The New Testament: An Introduction* (San Diego, Calif.: Harcourt Brace Jovanovich, 1974), 343, 348.

28. Simone Weil, *Letter to a Priest*, trans. A. F. Wills (London: Routledge & Kegan Paul, 1953), 85.

29. Ibid., 85.

30. Ibid., 84.

31. Weil, *Gateway to God,* 146.

32. Giambattista Vico, *The New Science of Giambattista Vico,* trans. Thomas Goddard Bergin and Max Harold Fisch (Ithaca: Cornell University Press, 1968), 111, 35.

33. Weil, *Gateway to God,* 73.

34. Ibid.

35. Quoted in *Simone Weil: Philosophe, historienne et mystique,* ed. Gilbert Kahn (Paris: Aubier Montaigne, 1978), 54, 159 (the translations from the French are mine).

36. J. Viard, in ibid., 157.

37. Conor Cruise O'Brien, "Patriotism and *The Need for Roots:* The Antipolitics of Simone Weil," in *Simone Weil: Interpretations of a Life,* ed. George Abbott White (Amherst: University of Massachusetts Press, 1981), 103.

38. Robert Coles, in ibid., 31.

39. J. M. Cameron, in ibid., 45.

40. Betty McLane-Iles, *Uprooting and Integration in the Writings of Simone Weil* (New York: Peter Lang, 1987), 148–49.

41. Wladimir Rabi, "La conception weilienne de la Création: Rencontre avec la Kabbale juive," in Kahn, *Simone Weil: Philosophe, historienne et mystique,* 154.

42. Emmanuel Levinas, "Simone Weil Against the Bible," in *Difficult Freedom: Essays on Judaism,* trans. Sean Hand (Baltimore: Johns Hopkins University Press, 1990), 133.

43. Levinas, quoted in Kahn, *Simone Weil: Philosophe, historienne et mystique,* 141.

44. Nevin, *Simone Weil: Portrait,* 389.

45. George Steiner, "Sainte Simone: The Jewish Bases of Simone Weil's *Via Negativa* to the Philosophic Peaks," *Times Literary Supplement,* June 4, 1993, 3.

46. See Carole Fink, *Marc Bloch: A Life in History* (New York: Cambridge University Press, 1989), 295.

47. Quoted in ibid., 256.

48. Quoted in Agus, *Jewish Identity,* 237–38.

49. Steiner, "Sainte Simone," 3.

50. Paul Giniewski, *Simone Weil ou la haine de soi* (Paris: International Editeurs, 1978), 336 (the translation from the French is mine).

51. *Simone Weil: Anthology,* ed. Sian Miles, 105.

52. Quoted in Hellman, *Simone Weil: An Introduction,* 1, 17.

53. T. S. Eliot in his Preface to Simone Weil, *The Need for Roots: Prelude to a Declaration of Duties Toward Mankind,* trans. Arthur Wills (New York: G. P. Putnam's Sons, 1952), vi.

54. For instance, Simone Pétrement, Weil's childhood friend, published a monumental biography of Simone Weil; her spiritual advisers, Father Perrin and Gustave Thibon, commemorated her in *Simone Weil as We Knew Her,* trans. Emma Craufurd (London: Routledge & Kegan Paul, 1953); Maurice Schumann, who helped Weil get to London from New York, recounted her final days in *La Mort née de leur propre vie: Péguy, Simone Weil, Gandhi* (Paris: Fayard, 1974).

55. For instance, Richard Rees, translator, editor, and analyst of Weil's work, sees her saintliness as "a more perfect maturity and a finer adjustment than the normal" (*Simone Weil: A Sketch for a Portrait* [Carbondale: Southern Illinois University Press, 1966], 9). John Hellman (*Simone Weil: An Introduction,* 103) claims: "Weil's importance lies in her unique religious perceptions, that remarkable sense of God which set her off from the rest of her generation." J. P. Little (*Simone Weil: Waiting on Truth* [New York: St. Martin's Press, 1988], 3, 152) suggests: "In Simone Weil's lucid prose can be found all that she was concerned to say, mindful of the 'deposit of pure gold' that she had to transmit, and more and more desperate at finding so few to receive it." Weil's "deposit of gold," Little observes, was eventually received by many prominent men and women of letters. In George Abbott White's collection of essays,

Simone Weil: Interpretations of a Life, 3, Weil is placed alongside George Orwell, T. E. Lawrence, Dorothy Day, Ignazio Silone, and others.

56. Jean Améry, *At the Mind's Limits: Contemplations by a Survivor on Auschwitz and Its Realities,* trans. Sidney Rosenfeld and Stella P. Rosenfeld (Bloomington: Indiana University Press, 1980), 94.

57. Ibid., 98 (emphasis added).

58. Ibid., 94.

59. Weil, *Waiting for God,* 54–55.

Chapter 6

1. Waultraut J. Stein, "Edith Stein, Twenty-Five Years Later," *Spiritual Life* 13 (Winter 1967), 250–51.

2. Cohen, *Elevations,* 23.

3. Teresia de Spiritu Sanctu, *Edith Stein,* 129.

4. Stein, quoted in ibid., 122.

5. Graef, *The Scholar and the Cross,* 218–19.

6. Stein, *Life in a Jewish Family,* 23.

7. Ibid., 24.

8. Ibid.

9. Ibid.

10. Wolfgang Iser, *The Implied Reader: Patterns of Communication in Prose Fiction from Bunyan to Beckett* (Baltimore: Johns Hopkins University Press, 1974), 290–94.

11. Stein, *Life in a Jewish Family,* 24.

12. Erik Erikson, quoted in James Olney, "Some Versions of Memory / Some Versions of *Bios:* The Ontology of Autobiography," in *Autobiography: Essays Theoretical and Critical,* ed. James Olney (Princeton: Princeton University Press, 1980), 244.

13. Stein, *Life in a Jewish Family,* 23.

14. Ibid., 24.

15. Hannah Arendt, *The Jew as Pariah: Jewish Identity and Politics in the Modern Age* (New York: Grove Press, 1978), 76–77.

16. Georges Gusdorf, "Conditions and Limits of Autobiography," in *Autobiography,* ed. James Olney, 43.

17. Stein, *Life in a Jewish Family,* 24.

18. Gusdorf, "Conditions and Limits of Autobiography," 37–38.

19. Herbstrith, *Edith Stein: A Biography,* 66.

20. Stein, *Life in a Jewish Family,* 25.

21. Ibid., 61.

22. Ibid., 411.

23. Sidonie Smith, *A Poetics of Women's Autobiography: Marginality and the Fictions of Self-Representation* (Bloomington: Indiana University Press, 1987), 19.

24. Stein, quoted in Graeff, *The Scholar and the Cross,* 50.

25. Ibid., 52.

26. Ibid., 50.

27. Stein, *On the Problem of Empathy,* 112.

28. William Earle, *The Autobiographical Consciousness* (Chicago: Quadrangle Books, 1972), 159.

29. Weil, quoted in Pétrement, *Simone Weil: A Life,* 201–2.

30. *Simone Weil Reader*, 252.

31. The essay was published in the collection *Oppression et liberté* in 1955, and its translated version, by A. Wills and J. Petrie, appears as *Oppression and Liberty* (New York: Routledge & Kegan Paul, 1958). Dorothy Tuck McFarland (*Simone Weil*, 47) describes the essay as "a measured, profound, and often extraordinarily beautiful meditation on the nature of modern industrial civilization."

32. "The *Iliad* or the Poem of Force" appears in Sian Miles's *Anthology*, 182–215; "The Great Beast" can be found in *Simone Weil: Selected Essays, 1934–1943*, selected and trans. Richard Rees (London: Oxford University Press, 1962), 89–144.

33. White, *Simone Weil: Interpretations*, 3.

34. Gabriella Fiori, *Simone Weil: An Intellectual Biography*, trans. Joseph R. Berrigan (Athens: University of Georgia Press, 1989), 8.

35. Weil, "Human Personality," in *Simone Weil Reader*, 333.

36. Ibid., 318.

37. Weil, *First and Last Notebooks*, trans. Richard Rees (London: Oxford University Press, 1970), 132.

38. Ibid., 263.

39. Ibid., 218.

40. J. P. Little, "Simone Weil's Concept of Decreation," in *Simone Weil's Philosophy of Culture: Readings Toward a Divine Humanity*, ed. Richard H. Bell (Cambridge: Cambridge University Press, 1993), 49.

41. H. L. Finch, "Simone Weil: Harbinger of a New Renaissance," in *Simone Weil's Philosophy of Culture*, 303.

42. Wladimir Rabi, in *Simone Weil: Philosophe*, 141–53.

43. Martin Buber, "The Silent Question: On Henri Bergson and Simone Weil," in *The Writings of Martin Buber*, ed. Will Herberg (New York: New American Library, 1956), 312.

44. Ibid.

45. John H. Nota, *Max Scheler: The Man and His Work*, trans. Theodore Plantinga and John H. Nota (Chicago: Franciscan Herald Press, 1983), 62, 67.

46. Paul Tillich, *Love, Power, and Justice: Ontological Analyses and Ethical Applications* (London: Oxford University Press, 1967), 22.

47. Ibid., 24–25.

48. Weil, *First and Last Notebooks*, 309.

49. Weil, *Gravity and Grace*, 165.

50. Weil, *Waiting for God*, 89.

51. Weil, *First and Last Notebooks*, 333 (italics in the original).

52. Ibid., 217.

53. Ibid., 333.

54. Little, "Simone Weil's Concept of Decreation," 37.

55. Weil, *First and Last Notebooks*, 404.

56. Weil, *Gravity and Grace*, 180, 181.

57. Weil, *First and Last Notebooks*, 244.

58. Weil, *The Need for Roots*, 174.

59. Ibid., 170–71.

60. Weil, *Waiting for God*, 118–19.

Chapter 7

1. Lawrence Langer, *Admitting the Holocaust: Collected Essays* (New York: Oxford University Press, 1995), 70.

2. Sander L. Gilman, *Jewish Self-Hatred: Anti-Semitism and the Hidden Language of the Jews* (Baltimore: Johns Hopkins University Press, 1986), 349–50.

3. Young, *Writing and Rewriting the Holocaust,* 28.

4. Frank, *Diary,* 600.

5. Hillesum, *Diary,* 35.

6. Ibid., 129.

7. Hilesum, *Letters,* 31.

8. Hartman, "Book of Destruction," 324.

9. Hillesum, *Diary,* 147.

10. Ibid., 18–19.

11. Ibid., 80.

12. Ibid., 113, 118, 127.

13. Ibid., 130.

14. Hillesum, *Letters,* 56.

15. Frank, *Diary,* 331.

16. Ibid., 372.

17. Ibid., 272, 273.

18. Ibid., 317.

19. Ibid., 351.

20. Ibid., 328.

21. Hillesum, *Diary,* 122.

22. Frank, *Diary,* 393.

23. John Berryman, "The Development of Anne Frank," in *The Freedom of the Poet* (New York: Farrar, Straus & Giroux, 1976), 97.

24. Hillesum, *Diary,* 136.

25. Frank, *Diary,* 694.

26. Hillesum, *Diary,* 141.

27. Frank, *Diary,* 416.

28. Frank Kermode, *The Sense of an Ending* (New York: Oxford University Press, 1967), 6, 8, 30.

29. Ibid., 38–39.

30. Ibid., 8.

31. Frank, *Diary,* 375.

32. Hillesum, *Letters,* 126.

33. Frank, *Diary,* 416.

34. Ibid., 411.

35. Ibid., 660, 662.

36. Hillesum, *Letters,* 27.

37. Frank, *Diary,* 411.

38. Hillesum, *Letters,* 100.

39. Frank, *Diary,* 498.

40. Hillesum, *Diary,* 149.

41. "Save" signals twofold meaning in this context. It indicates salvation, but also "health" through its relation to the noun *salus* in Latin. In the second meaning, "save" indicates mental health, which amounted to salvation under the circumstances. I am indebted to John Hobbins for this comment.

42. Frank, *Diary,* 586.

43. Hillesum, *Diary,* 194.

44. Lawrence Langer reminds us, "Auschwitz is often described . . . as an 'antiworld,' a separate planet, though in fact the camp was in Poland in Europe on planet earth" (*Admitting the Holocaust,* 5).

45. Frank, *Diary,* 526.

46. Frank, *Tales*, 47–48.

47. Ibid., 49.

48. John T. Pawlikowski, "The Shoah: Continuing Theological Challenge for Christianity," in *Contemporary Religious Responses to the Shoah*, ed. Steven L. Jacobs (Lanham, Md.: University Press of America, 1993), 149–50.

49. Hillesum, *Diary*, 113.

50. Ibid., 169.

51. Ibid., 151–52.

52. Ibid., 155.

53. Hillesum, *Letters*, 36.

Chapter 8

1. For a detailed explanation of perspective in autobiography, see Philippe Lejeune, *On Autobiography* (Minneapolis: University of Minnesota Press, 1989), 4–5.

2. William L. Howarth, "Some Principles of Autobiography," in *Autobiography: Essays Theoretical and Critical*, ed. James Olney, 85.

3. Hannah Arendt, *The Human Condition* (Chicago: University of Chicago Press, 1969), 176.

Chapter 9

1. Barret J. Mandel, "Full of Life Now," in *Autobiography: Essays*, ed. Olney, 67–68.

2. As Stein documents (*Life in a Jewish Family*, 24), the memoirs of Glückel von Hameln (1646–1724) were published in Berlin in 1920. Pauline Wengeroff's (1833–1916) *Memoirs of a Grandmother: Pictures Out of the Cultural History of Russia* was published in Berlin in 1913.

3. Weil, "Spiritual Autobiography," in *Waiting for God*, 70.

4. Ibid., 79.

5. Ibid., 72.

6. A few passages later, Weil makes the following statement about the validity of her dissenting position regarding the Church: "I regard it as legitimate on my part to be a member of the Church by right but not in fact. But it is not only legitimate. So long as God does not give me the certainty that he is ordering me to do anything else, I think it is my duty" (75).

7. Olney, "Some Versions of Memory," 240.

8. Herbstrith, *Edith Stein: A Biography*, 24.

9. Stein, *Life in a Jewish Family*, 462.

Chapter 10

1. Quoted in Rosenfeld, *A Double Dying*, 14. Other post-Holocaust philosophers, writers, and thinkers deny the possibility of the art of the Holocaust that Rosenfeld mentions (see ibid., 13–14). For the problem of representing the Holocaust in art, see Lawrence L. Langer's "In the Beginning Was the Silence," in *The Holocaust and the Literary Imagination* (New Haven: Yale University Press, 1975).

2. Quoted in Langer, *Admitting the Holocaust*, 54.

3. Ibid.

4. Hillesum, *Letters*, 146.

5. Paul Ricoeur, *Time and Narrative,* trans. Kathleen McLaughlin and David Pellauer, 3 vols. (Chicago: University of Chicago Press, 1984), 2:28.

6. Hillesum, *Letters,* 88.

7. Frank, *Diary,* 578–79.

8. See Lawrence Rosenwald, *Emerson and the Art of the Diary* (New York: Oxford University Press, 1988), 5.

9. Hillesum, *Diary,* 151.

10. Aristotle, "Poetics," in *Criticism: The Major Texts,* ed. Walter Jackson Bate (New York: Harcourt, Brace & Company, 1952), 20.

11. Ibid., 24–25.

12. Ibid., 27.

13. Ibid., 36.

14. Hillesum, *Diary,* 140.

15. Frank, *Diary,* 541.

16. Ibid., 588.

17. Hillesum, *Diary,* 186.

18. Frank, *Diary,* 595.

19. Hillesum, *Diary,* 182.

20. Paul Tillich, *Love, Power, and Justice: Ontological Analyses and Ethical Applications* (New York: Oxford University Press, 1967), 77.

21. Saul Friedlander, "Introduction," in *Probing the Limits of Representation,* 10.

22. Rosenwald, *Emerson and the Art of the Diary,* 6.

23. Henri Bergson, *Creative Evolution* (London: Macmillan & Company, 1911), 359–60.

24. Rosenwald, *Emerson and the Art of the Diary,* 22.

25. Steven E. Kagle, *American Diary Literature, 1620–1799* (Boston: Twayne Publishers, 1979), 17.

26. Frank, *Diary,* 521.

27. Hillesum, *Diary,* 91.

28. Rosenwald, *Emerson and the Art of the Diary,* 12.

29. Frank, *Diary,* 438.

30. Hillesum, *Diary,* 166.

31. Frank, *Diary,* 61. The rewritten diaries appear as version "b" in the Critical Edition.

32. Frank, *Diary,* 578–79.

33. Ibid., 331.

34. Ibid., 628–29.

35. Ibid., 569.

36. Ibid., 415.

37. Ibid., 623.

38. Ibid., 415.

39. Hillesum, *Letters,* 124.

40. Ibid., 23.

41. Hillesum, *Diary,* 146.

42. Benjamin committed suicide when trying to seek refuge from the Gestapo in Spain.

43. Walter Benjamin, *Illuminations,* trans. Harry Zohn (New York: Schocken Books, 1969), 96.

44. Ibid., 94–97ff.

45. Hillesum, *Diary,* 165.

46. Ibid., 178.

47. Ibid., 177.

48. Ibid., 191.

49. Ibid., 190.

Chapter 11

1. Yasmine Ergas, "Growing Up Banished: A Reading of Anne Frank and Etty Hillesum," in *Behind the Lines: Gender and the Two World Wars,* ed. Margaret Randolph Higonnet et al. (New Haven: Yale University Press, 1987), 85.

Chapter 12

1. See Ellen M. Umansky and Dianne Ashton, eds., *Four Centuries of Jewish Women's Spirituality: A Sourcebook* (Boston: Beacon Press, 1922), 35.

2. See Judith R. Baskin, ed., *Women of the Word: Jewish Women and Jewish Writing* (Detroit: Wayne University Press, 1994), 88 n. 12.

3. See *Encyclopaedia Judaica,* 16 vols. (Jerusalem and New York: Macmillan Company, 1971–72), 16, 450.

4. Lawrence Blum and Victor J. Seidler, *A Truer Liberty: Simone Weil and Marxism* (New York: Routledge, 1989), 9.

5. Quoted in Pétrement, *Simone Weil: A Life,* 184.

6. See Hannah Arendt, "Rosa Luxemburg: 1871–1919," in her *Men in Dark Times* (New York: Harcourt, Brace & World, 1968), 44, 45.

7. Edith Stein, *Essays on Woman,* trans. Freda Mary Oben (Washington, D.C.: ICS Publications, 1987), 59.

8. Ibid., 71.

9. Phyllis Trible, "Eve and Adam: Genesis 2–3, Reread," in *Womanspirit Rising,* ed. Carol P. Christ and Judith Plaskow (San Francisco: Harper & Row, 1979), 75.

10. Ibid., 80–81.

11. Ibid., 81.

12. For detailed correspondences between Stein and today's feminism, see my "Edith Stein: A Reading of Her Feminist Thought," *Studies in Religion* 23, no. 1 (1994), 43–57.

13. Weil, *Notebooks,* 591.

14. Ibid., 578.

15. Ibid., 577.

16. Ibid.

17. Ibid., 421.

18. Ibid., 577.

19. Stein, *Essays on Woman,* 253.

20. Ibid., 197.

21. Ibid., 136.

22. For detailed discussion of the economic, political, and cultural achievements of German women, see Mary Nolan, " 'Housework Made Easy': The Taylorized Housewife in Weimar Germany's Rationalized Economy," *Feminist Studies* 16, no. 3 (1990), 579–606.

23. Stein, *Essays on Woman,* 145.

24. Ibid., 256.

25. Ibid., 140–41ff.

26. See Nevin, *Simone Weil: Portrait,* 18–19.

27. Ibid., 8.

28. Quoted in ibid.

29. Weil quoted in Pétrement, *Simone Weil: A Life,* 36.

30. Weil, *First and Last Notebooks,* 161–62.

31. Ibid., 32.

32. Ibid., 322.
33. Weil, *Seventy Letters,* 91.
34. Ibid., 161.
35. Pétrement, *Simone Weil: A Life,* 27.
36. Ibid., 27–28.
37. Weil, *Waiting for God,* 65.
38. Weil, quoted in Pétrement, *Simone Weil: A Life,* 444.
39. Weil, *Seventy Letters,* 153.
40. Ibid., 154.
41. Coles, *Simone Weil: A Modern Pilgrimage,* 41.
42. Joanne Cutting-Gray, "Hannah Arendt, Feminism, and the Politics of Alterity: 'What Will We Lose If We Win?' " *Hypatia* 8 (Winter 1993), 41 (emphasis in the original).
43. Gilman, *Jewish Self-Hatred,* 245.
44. Sander L. Gilman, *The Jew Body* (New York: Routledge, 1991), 134ff.
45. Stein, *Essays on Woman,* 48.
46. Ibid., 247 (emphasis in the original).
47. Ibid.
48. Ivan Illich, *Gender* (New York: Pantheon Books, 1982), 178.
49. Ibid., 81.
50. Stein, *Essays on Woman,* 145.
51. Ibid., 247, 248 (emphasis in the original).
52. Ibid., 73.
53. Illich, *Gender,* 122.
54. Stein, *Essays on Woman,* 73.
55. Ibid., 258 (emphasis in the original).
56. Ibid., 257.
57. Stein, *Life in a Jewish Family,* 31.
58. Ibid., 42.
59. Ibid., 61.

Chapter 13

1. Stein, *Essays on Woman,* 259.
2. Ibid., 249.
3. Ibid., 250 (emphasis in the original).
4. Weil, *Gravity and Grace,* 115.
5. Ibid.
6. Stein, *Essays on Woman,* 251.
7. Ibid., 96–97.
8. Weil, *Gravity and Grace,* 115.
9. Stein, *Essays on Woman,* 72.
10. Sigmund Freud, *Civilization and Its Discontents,* trans. Joan Riviere (London: Hogarth Press, 1982), 82.
11. Ibid., 80.
12. Weil, "Analysis of Oppression," in *Simone Weil Reader,* 137, 142.
13. Ibid., 152.
14. Frank, *Diary,* 297.
15. Ibid., 601.
16. Ibid.

17. Ibid.
18. Ibid., 603.
19. Ibid., 566.
20. Ibid., 623.
21. Ibid., 693.
22. Hillesum, *Diary,* 27.
23. Ibid.
24. Ibid., 42.
25. Ibid., 27–28.
26. Ibid., 48.
27. Ibid., 53.
28. Ibid., 112.
29. Ibid., 193.

Conclusion

1. Emil L. Fackenheim, *The Jewish Return to History* (New York: Schocken Books, 1978), 269.
2. Incidentally, Zygmunt Bauman sees Levinas as "the greatest moral philosopher of this century" (Bauman, *Mortality, Immortality, and Other Life Strategies* [Stanford, Calif.: Stanford University Press, 1992], 41).
3. Joseph Katz, "Altruism and Sympathy: Their History in Philosophy and Some Implications for Psychology," *Journal of Social Issues* 28, no. 3 (1972), 62–63.
4. Levinas, quoted in Morny Joy, "Levinas: Alterity, the Feminine and Women–A Meditation," *Studies in Religion* 22, no. 4 (1993), 464.
5. Levinas, quoted in *Re-Reading Levinas,* ed. Robert Bernasconi and Simon Critchley (Bloomington: Indiana University Press, 1991), 124.
6. Ibid.
7. Sean Hand, ed., *The Levinas Reader* (Oxford: Basil Blackwell, 1989), 33.
8. Emmanuel Levinas, *Otherwise Than Being; or, Beyond Essence,* trans. Alphonso Linges (The Hague: Martinus Nijhoff, 1981), 84.
9. Bernasconi and Critchley, *Re-Reading Levinas,* 125.
10. Levinas, quoted in ibid., 125–26.
11. Levinas, *The Levinas Reader,* 114.
12. Ibid., 44.
13. Hilesum, *Diary,* 189, 192.
14. Ibid., 155.
15. Ibid., 192.
16. Catherine Chalier, "Ethics and the Feminine," in *Re-Reading Levinas,* 126.
17. Jacob Boas, *Boulevard des Misères: The Story of Transit Camp Westerbork* (Hamden, Conn.: Archon, 1985), 92.
18. Arendt, *Men in Dark Times,* 19.
19. On the controversy surrounding Stein's beatification and her connection with the Carmelite convent in Auschwitz, see Harry James Cargas, *The Unnecessary Problem of Edith Stein* (Lanham, Md.: University Press of America, 1994).
20. For contradictory responses to Stein's, Weil's, and Frank's deaths, compare, for instance, Neville Braybrooke, who claims that "it was Hitler's persecution of the Jews that turned them both [Stein and Weil] into spiritual heroes of the Twentieth Century" (Neville Braybrooke, "Edith Stein and Simone Weil," *Hibbert Journal* 64 [Winter 1956–57], 75–80), and Cecilia McGowan, who rejects the idea of Weil's martyrdom and claims that it was her hubristic determination to die for France and her

frustrated desire to master fate that caused Weil's death. McGowan does not doubt Stein's martyrdom, which "consisted in accepting death; in choosing not to run away, either physically or psychologically" (Cecilia McGowan, "Simone Weil and Edith Stein: Two Great Women of Our Century," *Desert Call* 24 [Summer 1989], 4–6; 24 [Fall 1989], 16–19; 24 [Winter 1989], 16–18). In contrast, Emanuel Tanay, a Holocaust survivor, dismisses all notions of Stein's martyrdom and claims that she was elevated to the rank of martyr only because she did not escape Auschwitz (Emanuel Tanay, "Is There Honor Only After Death for Survivors of the Holocaust?" *Opinion*, February 28, 1988). For the denial of the image of Anne Frank as the quintessential child-martyr, see Bruno Bettelheim, who argued that her death could have been avoided (Bruno Bettleheim, "The Ignored Lesson of Anne Frank," *Surviving, and Other Essays* [New York: Seabury Press, 1982], 251–75). We have already discussed Sander Gilman, who denies Frank's Jewish particularity because she was an assimilated Jew and "does not speak with a Jewish accent" (Gilman, *Jewish Self-Hatred*, 349–50), and James Young, who claims that because of her assimilated world view Frank cannot be perceived as a Jewish victim (Young, *Writing and Rewriting the Holocaust*, 28).

21. Arendt, *The Human Condition*, 188, 190.

22. Stein, *Essays on Woman*, 214.

23. Nancy Chodorow, *The Reproduction of Mothering: Psychoanalysis and the Sociology of Gender* (Berkeley and Los Angeles: University of California Press, 1978), 166–67.

24. Ibid., 167.

25. Sara Ruddick, "Maternal Thinking," in *Philosophy, Children, and the Family,* ed. Albert C. Cafagna, Richard T. Peterson, and Craig A. Staundenbaur (New York: Plenum Press, 1982), 105–6.

26. Carol Gilligan, *In a Different Voice: Psychological Theory and Women's Development* (Cambridge: Harvard University Press, 1982), 22.

27. Chodorow, *The Reproduction of Mothering*, 169.

28. See Gertrud Nunner-Winkler, "Two Moralities? A Critical Discussion of an Ethic of Care and Responsibility Versus an Ethic of Rights and Justice," *In An Ethic of Care: Feminist and Interdisciplinary Perspectives,* ed. Mary Jeanne Larrabee (New York: Routledge, 1993), 144–46.

29. Nel Noddings, *Caring: A Feminine Approach to Ethics and Moral Education* (Berkeley and Los Angeles: University of California Press, 1984), 24.

30. Ibid., 49.

31. Ibid., 14.

32. Paul Tillich, *The Courage to Be* (London: James Nisbet, 1961), 180 (emphasis in the original).

33. Jürgen Moltmann, discussed in John T. Pawlikowski, "The Shoah: Continuing Theological Challenge for Christianity," in *Contemporary Religious Responses to the Shoah,* ed. Steven L. Jacobs, 154.

34. Paul Van Buren, quoted in Michael McGarry, "A Contemporary Religious Response to the Shoah: The Crisis of Prayer," in ibid., 133.

35. Irving Greenberg, discussed in Pawlikowski, "The Shoah," in ibid., 147–48.

36. Hillesum, *A Diary*, 127.

37. Weil, *Seventy Letters*, 156.

BIBLIOGRAPHY

Works by Stein, Weil, Frank, and Hillesum

Edith Stein

Stein, Edith. *Edith Stein: Life in a Jewish Family, 1891–1916.* Trans. Josephine Koeppel. Washington, D.C.: ICS Publications, 1986.

_____. *Essays on Woman.* Trans. Freda Mary Oben. Washington, D.C.: ICS Publications, 1987.

_____. *On the Problem of Empathy.* 3rd ed. Trans. Waltraut Stein. Washington, D.C.: ICS Publications, 1989.

Simone Weil

Weil, Simone. *First and Last Notebooks.* Trans. Richard Rees. London: Oxford University Press, 1970.

_____. *Gateway to God.* Ed. and trans. by David Raper. London: Fontana Books, 1974.

_____. *Gravity and Grace.* Trans. Arthur Wills. New York: G. P. Putnam's Sons, 1952.

_____. *Letter to a Priest.* Trans. A. F. Wills. London: Routledge & Kegan Paul, 1953.

_____. *The Need for Roots: Prelude to a Declaration of Duties Toward Mankind.* Trans. Arthur Wills. New York: G. P. Putnam's Sons, 1952.

_____. *The Notebooks of Simone Weil.* Trans. Arthur Wills. London: Routledge & Kegan Paul, 1956.

_____. *Oppression and Liberty.* Trans. A. Wills and J. Petrie. New York: Routledge & Kegan Paul, 1958.

_____. *Seventy Letters.* Trans. Richard Rees. London: Oxford University Press, 1965.

_____. *Simone Weil: Anthology.* Ed. Sian Miles. London: Virago Press, 1986.

_____. *The Simone Weil Reader.* Ed. George A. Panichas. New York: David McKay Company, 1977.

_____. *Simone Weil: Selected Essays, 1934–1943.* Trans. Richard Rees. London: Oxford University Press, 1962.

_____. *Waiting for God.* Trans. Emma Craufurd. New York: G. P. Putnam's Sons, 1951.

Anne Frank

Frank, Anne. *The Diary of Anne Frank: The Critical Edition.* Ed. David Barnouw and Gerrold van der Stroom. Trans. Arnold J. Pomerans and B. M. Mooyaart-Doubleday. New York: Doubleday, 1989.

_____. *Tales from the House Behind: Fables, Personal Reminiscences, and Short Stories.* Trans. H. H. B. Mosberg and Michel Mok. Kingswood: The World's Work, 1960.

Etty Hillesum

Hillesum, Etty. *Etty: A Diary, 1941–1943.* Trans. Arnold J. Pomerans. London: Jonathan Cape, 1983.

_____. *Letters from Westerbork.* Trans. Arnold J. Pomerans. New York: Pantheon Books, 1986.

Other Sources

Agus, Jacob B. *Jewish Identity in an Age of Ideologies.* New York: Frederick Ungar Publishing Company, 1978.

Améry, Jean. *At the Mind's Limits: Contemplations by a Survivor on Auschwitz and Its Realities.* Trans. Sidney Rosenfeld and Stella P. Rosenfeld. Bloomington: Indiana University Press, 1980.

Arendt, Hannah. *The Human Condition.* Chicago: University of Chicago Press, 1969.

_____. *The Jew as Pariah: Jewish Identity and Politics in the Modern Age.* New York: Grove Press, 1978.

_____. *Men in Dark Times.* 1955. Reprint, New York: Harcourt, Brace & World, 1968.

Aristotle. "Poetics." In *Criticism: The Major Texts,* ed. Walter Jackson Bate, 13–19. New York: Harcourt, Brace & Company, 1952.

Barber, Michael D. *Guardian of Dialogue: Max Scheler's Phenomenology, Sociology of Knowledge, and Philosophy of Love.* Lewisburg, Pa.: Bucknell University Press, 1993.

Baron, Lawrence. "The Dynamics of Decency: Dutch Rescuers of the Jews During the Holocaust." In *The Nazi Holocaust,* ed. Michael R. Marrus. 9 vols., 5:608–25. Westport, Conn.: Mecklermedia, 1989.

Baskin, Judith R., ed. *Women of the Word: Jewish Women and Jewish Writing.* Detroit: Wayne State University Press, 1994.

Bauman, Zygmunt. *Modernity and Ambivalence.* Ithaca: Cornell University Press, 1991.

_____. *Modernity and the Holocaust.* Ithaca: Cornell University Press, 1989.

_____. *Mortality, Immortality, and Other Life Strategies.* Stanford, Calif.: Stanford University Press, 1992.

Benjamin, Walter. *Illuminations.* Trans. Harry Zohn. New York: Schocken Books, 1969.

Bergson, Henri. *Creative Evolution.* London: Macmillan & Company, 1911.

Bernasconi, Robert, and Simon Critchley, eds. *Re-Reading Levinas.* Bloomington: Indiana University Press, 1991.

Berryman, John. "The Development of Anne Frank." In *The Freedom of the Poet*, 91–107. New York: Farrar, Straus & Giroux, 1976.

Bettleheim, Bruno. "The Ignored Lesson of Anne Frank." In *Surviving, and Other Essays*, 251–75. 1979. Reprint, New York: Seabury Press, 1982.

Blum, Lawrence A., and Victor J. Seidler. *A Truer Liberty: Simone Weil and Marxism*. New York: Routledge, 1989.

Boas, Jacob. *Boulevard des Misères: The Story of Transit Camp Westerbork*. Hamden, Conn.: Archon, 1985.

Braybrooke, Neville. "Edith Stein and Simone Weil." *Hibbert Journal* 64 (Winter 1956–57): 75–80.

Brenner, Rachel F. "Edith Stein: A Reading of Her Feminist Thought." *Studies in Religion* 23 (1994): 43–57.

Buber, Martin. "The Silent Question: On Henri Bergson and Simone Weil." In *The Writings of Martin Buber*, ed. Will Herberg, 306–15. New York: New American Library, 1956.

Camus, Albert. *The Plague*. Trans. Stuart Gilbert. New York: Random House, 1972.

Cargas, Harry James. *The Unnecessary Problem of Edith Stein*. Lanham, Md.: University Press of America, 1994.

Chalier, Catherine. "Ethics and the Feminine." In *Re-Reading Levinas*, ed. Robert Bernasconi and Simon Critchley, 119–30. Bloomington: Indiana University Press, 1991.

Chodorow, Nancy. *The Reproduction of Mothering: Psychoanalysis and the Sociology of Gender*. Berkeley and Los Angeles: University of California Press, 1978.

Cohen, Richard A. *Elevations: The Height of the Good in Rosenzweig and Levinas*. Chicago: University of Chicago Press, 1994.

Coles, Robert. *Simone Weil: A Modern Pilgrimage*. Reading, Mass.: Addison-Wesley Publishing Company, 1987.

Cutting-Gray, Joanne. "Hannah Arendt, Feminism, and the Politics of Alterity: 'What Will We Lose If We Win?' " *Hypatia* 8 (Winter 1993): 35–54.

Earle, William. *The Autobiographical Consciousness*. Chicago: Quadrangle Books, 1972.

Eliot, T. S. Preface to Simone Weil, *The Need for Roots: Prelude to a Declaration of Duties Toward Mankind*, v–xii. New York: G. P. Putnam's Sons, 1952.

Ergas, Yasmine. "Growing Up Banished: A Reading of Anne Frank and Etty Hillesum." In *Behind the Lines: Gender and the Two World Wars*, ed. Margaret Randolph Higonnet et al., 84–99. New Haven: Yale University Press, 1987.

Ezrahi, Sidra DeKoven. *By Words Alone: The Holocaust in Literature*. Chicago: University of Chicago Press, 1980.

Fackenheim, Emil L. *God's Presence in History: Jewish Affirmations and Philosophical Reflections*. New York: New York University Press, 1970.

———. *The Jewish Return to History*. New York: Schocken Books, 1978.

———. *To Mend the World: Foundations of Future Jewish Thought*. New York: Schocken Books, 1982.

Felman, Shoshana, and Dori Laub. *Testimony: Crises of Witnessing in Literature, Psychoanalysis, and History*. New York: Routledge, 1992.

Finch, H. L. "Simone Weil: Harbinger of a New Renaissance." In *Simone Weil's Philosophy of Culture: Readings Toward a Divine Humanity*, ed. Richard H. Bell, 295–310. Cambridge: Cambridge University Press, 1993.

Fink, Carole. *Marc Bloch: A Life in History.* New York: Cambridge University Press, 1989.

Fiori, Gabriella. *Simone Weil: An Intellectual Biography.* Trans. Joseph R. Berrigan. Athens, Ga.: University of Georgia Press, 1982.

Frankl, Viktor. *Man in Search of Meaning.* Trans. Ilse Lasch. 1946. Reprint, New York: Washington Square Press, 1984.

Freud, Sigmund. *Civilization and Its Discontents.* Trans. Joan Riviere. 1930. Reprint, London: Hogarth Press, 1982.

Friedlander, Saul. "Introduction." In *Probing the Limits of Representation: Nazism and the "Final Solution,"* ed. Saul Friedlander, 1–22. Cambridge: Harvard University Press, 1992.

Gilman, Sander L. *The Jew Body.* New York: Routledge, 1991.

————. *Jewish Self-Hatred: Anti-Semitism and the Hidden Language of the Jews.* Baltimore: Johns Hopkins University Press, 1986.

Gilligan, Carol. *In a Different Voice: Psychological Theory and Women's Development.* Cambridge: Harvard University Press, 1982.

Giniewski, Paul. *Simone Weil ou la haine de soi.* Paris: International Editeurs, 1978.

Glatzer, Nahum. *Franz Rosenzweig: His Life and Thought.* New York: Schocken Books, 1953.

Gossman, Lionel. "Philhellenism and Antisemitism: Matthew Arnold and His German Models." *Comparative Literature* 46 (Winter 1994): 1–40.

Graeff, Hilda C. *The Scholar and the Cross: The Life and Work of Edith Stein.* London: Longmans, 1955.

Gusdorf, Georges. "Conditions and Limits of Autobiography." In *Autobiography: Essays Theoretical and Critical,* ed. James Olney, 28–48. Princeton: Princeton University Press, 1980.

Hand, Sean, ed. *The Levinas Reader.* Oxford: Basil Blackwell, 1989.

Hartman, Geoffrey. "The Book of Destruction." In *Probing the Limits of Representation: Nazism and the "Final Solution,"* ed. Saul Friedlander, 318–37. Cambridge: Harvard University Press, 1992.

Hellman, John. *Simone Weil: An Introduction to Her Thought.* Waterloo, Ont.: Wilfred Laurier University Press, 1982.

Herbstrith, Waultraud. *Edith Stein: A Biography.* Trans. Bernard Bonowitz. San Francisco: Harper & Row, 1983.

Howarth, William L. "Some Principles of Autobiography." In *Autobiography: Essays Theoretical and Critical,* ed. James Olney, 84–114. Princeton: Princeton University Press, 1980.

Hyman, Paula. *From Dreyfus to Vichy: The Remaking of French Jewry, 1906–1939.* New York: Columbia University Press, 1979.

Illich, Ivan. *Gender.* New York: Pantheon Books, 1982.

Iser, Wolfgang. *The Implied Reader: Patterns of Communication in Prose Fiction from Bunyan to Beckett.* Baltimore: Johns Hopkins University Press, 1974.

Joy, Morny. "Levinas: Alterity, the Feminine, and Women—A Meditation." *Studies in Religion* 22, no. 4 (1993): 463–87.

Kagle, Steven E. *American Diary Literature, 1620–1799.* Boston: Twayne Publishers, 1979.

Kahn, Gilbert, ed. *Simone Weil: Philosophe, historienne et mystique.* Paris: Aubier Montaigne, 1978.

Katz, Joseph. "Altruism and Sympathy: Their History in Philosophy and Some Implications for Psychology." *Journal of Social Issues* 28, no. 3 (1972): 59–69.

Kermode, Frank. *The Sense of an Ending.* New York: Oxford University Press, 1967.

Langer, Lawrence L. *Admitting the Holocaust: Collected Essays.* New York: Oxford University Press, 1995.

_____. "In the Beginning Was the Silence." In *The Holocaust and the Literary Imagination,* 1–31. New Haven: Yale University Press, 1975.

Lejeune, Philippe. *On Autobiography.* Trans. Katherine Leary. Minneapolis: University of Minnesota Press, 1989.

Levinas, Emmanuel. *Otherwise Than Being; or, Beyond Essence.* Trans. Alphonso Linges. The Hague: Martinus Nijhoff, 1981.

_____. "Simone Weil Against the Bible." In *Difficult Freedom: Essays on Judaism,* trans. Sean Hand, 133–42. Baltimore: Johns Hopkins University Press, 1990.

Little, J. P. "Simone Weil's Concept of Decreation." In *Simone Weil's Philosophy of Culture: Readings Toward a Divine Humanity,* ed. Richard H. Bell, 25–52. Cambridge: Cambridge University Press, 1993.

_____. *Simone Weil: Waiting on Truth.* New York: St. Martin's Press, 1988.

Mandel, Barret J. "Full of Life Now." In *Autobiography: Essays Theoretical and Critical,* ed. James Olney, 49–73. Princeton: Princeton University Press, 1980.

Maritain, Jacques. *A Christian Looks at the Jewish Question.* New York: Longmans, Green, 1939.

Marrus, Michael R., and Robert O. Paxton. *Vichy France and the Jews.* New York: Basic Books, 1981.

McFarland, Dorothy Tuck. *Simone Weil.* New York: Frederick Ungar Publishing Company, 1983.

McGarry, Michael. "A Contemporary Religious Response to the Shoah: The Crisis of Prayer." In *Contemporary Christian Religious Responses to the Shoah,* ed. Steven L. Jacobs, 123–39. Lanham, Md.: University Press of America, 1993.

McGowan, Cecilia. "Simone Weil and Edith Stein: Two Great Women of Our Century." *Desert Call* 24 (Summer 1989): 4–6; 24 (Fall 1989): 16–19; 24 (Winter 1989): 16–18.

McLane-Iles, Betty. *Uprooting and Integration in the Writings of Simone Weil.* New York: Peter Lang, 1987.

Mosse, George. *Germany Beyond Judaism.* Bloomington: Indiana University Press, 1985.

Nevin, Thomas R. *Simone Weil: Portrait of a Self-Exiled Jew.* Chapel Hill: University of North Carolina Press, 1991.

Niewyk, Donald L. *The Jews in Weimar Germany.* Baton Rouge: Louisiana State University Press, 1980.

Noddings, Nel. *Caring: A Feminine Approach to Ethics and Moral Education.* Berkeley and Los Angeles: University of California Press, 1984.

Nolan, Mary. " 'Housework Made Easy': The Taylorized Housewife in Weimar Germany's Rationalized Economy," *Feminist Studies* 16, no. 3 (1990): 579–606.

Nota, John H. *Max Scheler: The Man and His Work.* Trans. Theodore Plantinga and John H. Nota. Chicago: Franciscan Herald Press, 1983.

Nunner-Winkler, Gertrud. "Two Moralities? A Critical Discussion of an Ethic of Care and Responsibility Versus an Ethic of Rights and Justice." In *An Ethic of Care: Feminist and Interdisciplinary Perspectives,* ed. Mary Jeanne Larrabee, 143–57. New York: Routledge, 1993.

O'Brien, Conor Cruise. "Patriotism and *The Need for Roots:* The Antipolitics of Simone Weil." In *Simone Weil: Interpretations of a Life,* ed. George Abbott White, 95–111. Amherst: University of Massachusetts Press, 1981.

Olney, James. "Some Versions of Memory / Some Versions of *Bios:* The Ontology of Autobiography." In *Autobiography: Essays Theoretical and Critical,* ed. James Olney, 236–67. Princeton: Princeton University Press, 1980.

Osterreicher, John M. *The Walls Are Crumbling: Seven Jewish Philosophers Discover Christ.* London: Hollis & Carter, 1952.

Pawlikowski, John T. "The Shoah: Continuing Theological Challenge for Christianity." In *Contemporary Religious Responses to the Shoah,* ed. Steven L. Jacobs, 139–67. Lanham, Md.: University Press of America, 1993.

Perrin, Joseph-Marie, and Gustave Thibon. *Simone Weil as We Knew Her.* Trans. Emma Craufurd. London: Routledge & Kegan Paul, 1953.

Perrin, Norman, and Dennis C. Duling. *The New Testament: An Introduction.* San Diego, Calif.: Harcourt Brace Jovanovich, 1974.

Perrin, Ron. *Max Scheler's Concept of the Person: An Ethics of Humanism.* New York: St. Martin's Press, 1991.

Pétrement, Simone. *Simone Weil: A Life.* Trans. Raymond Rosenthal. New York: Pantheon Books, 1976.

Rabi, Wladimir. "La conception weilienne de la Création: Rencontre avec la Kabbale juive." In *Simone Weil: Philosophe, historienne et mystique,* ed. Gilbert Kahn, 141–53. Paris: Aubier Montaigne, 1978.

Rees, Richard. *Simone Weil: A Sketch for a Portrait.* Carbondale: Southern Illinois University Press, 1966.

Ricoeur, Paul. *Time and Narrative.* Trans. Kathleen McLaughlin and David Pellauer. 3 vols. Chicago: University of Chicago Press, 1984.

Rosenfeld, Alvin H. *A Double Dying: Reflections on Holocaust Literature.* Bloomington: Indiana University Press, 1980.

Rosenwald, Lawrence. *Emerson and the Art of the Diary.* New York: Oxford University Press, 1988.

Rosenzweig, Franz. *The Star of Redemption.* Trans. William W. Hallo. Notre Dame, Ind.: University of Notre Dame Press, 1985.

Royal, Robert, ed. *Jacques Maritain and the Jews.* Notre Dame, Ind.: American Maritain Association, 1994.

Ruddick, Sara. "Maternal Thinking." In *Philosophy, Children, and the Family,* ed. Albert C. Cafagna et al., 101–27. New York: Plenum Press, 1982.

Schall, James V. "The Mystery of the Mystery of Israel." In *Jacques Maritain and the Jews,* ed. Robert Royal, 51–72. Notre Dame, Ind.: American Maritain Association, 1994.

Schumann, Maurice. *La Mort née de leur propre vie: Péguy, Simone Weil, Gandhi.* Paris: Fayard, 1974.

Smith, Sidonie. *A Poetics of Women's Autobiography: Marginality and the Fictions of Self-Representation.* Bloomington: Indiana University Press, 1987.

Stein, Waultraut J. "Edith Stein, Twenty-Five Years Later," *Spiritual Life* 13 (1967): 244-51.

_____. "Reflections on Edith Stein's Secret." *Spiritual Life* 34 (Fall 1988): 131-36.

Steiner, George. "Sainte Simone: The Jewish Bases of Simone Weil's *Via Negativa* to the Philosophic Peaks." *Times Literary Supplement,* June 4, 1993, 3-4.

Tanay, Emanuel. "Is There Honor Only After Death for Survivors of the Holocaust?" *Opinion,* February 28, 1988, 2.

Teresia de Spiritu Sancto. *Edith Stein.* Trans. Cecily Hastings and Donald Nicholl. London: Sheed & Ward, 1952.

Tillich, Paul. *The Courage to Be.* London: James Nisbet, 1961.

_____. *Love, Power, and Justice: Ontological Analyses and Ethical Applications.* London: Oxford University Press, 1967.

Trible, Phyllis. "Eve and Adam: Genesis 2-3, Reread." In *Womanspirit Rising,* ed. Carol P. Christ and Judith Plaskow, 74-84. San Francisco: Harper & Row, 1979.

Umansky, Ellen M., and Dianne Ashton, eds. *Four Centuries of Jewish Women's Spirituality: A Sourcebook.* Boston: Beacon Press, 1922.

Vico, Giambattista. *The New Science of Giambattista Vico.* Trans. Thomas Goddard Bergin and Max Harold Fisch. Ithaca, N.Y.: Cornell University Press, 1968.

"Wengeroff, Pauline." *Encyclopaedia Judaica.* 16 vols. Jerusalem and New York: Macmillan, 1971-72.

White, George Abbott, ed. *Simone Weil: Interpretations of a Life.* Amherst: University of Massachusetts Press, 1981.

Young, James. *Writing and Rewriting the Holocaust: Narratives and the Consequences of Interpretation.* Bloomington: Indiana University Press, 1988.

INDEX